connecting
the dots

connecting
the dots

aligning projects
with objectives
in unpredictable times

CATHLEEN BENKO

F. WARREN McFARLAN

HARVARD BUSINESS SCHOOL PRESS
Boston, Massachusetts

Library of Congress Cataloging-in-Publication Data
Benko, Cathy, 1958–
     Connecting the dots : aligning projects with objectives in unpredictable times /
Cathy Benko and F. Warren McFarlan.
       p. cm.
     Includes bibliographical references and index.
     ISBN 1-57851-877-6 (alk. paper)
       1. Strategic planning. 2. Organizational change. 3. Information technology—
Management. 4. Technological innovations—Management. I. McFarlan,
F. Warren (Franklin Warren) II. Title.
     HD30.28 .B4536 2003
     658.4'012—dc21

                                                                    2002015132

The paper used in this publication meets the requirements of the American National
Standard for Permanence of Paper for Publications and Documents in Libraries and
Archives Z39.48-1992.

To Karen.

And to stars and glitter,

and all the joy this phrase represents.

contents

acknowledgments

Gratitude is not only the greatest of virtues,
but the parent of all others.

CICERO (106–143 B.C.), ROMAN STATESMAN AND PHILOSOPHER

As with many major undertakings, this work is the unabashed synthesis of a diverse set of insights and experiences. It was astonishing, at times, how welcoming and candid a host of companies, clients, analysts, and media were in researching and providing feedback for this effort. This timely access and insight is very much appreciated.

Particular acknowledgment to our partners and colleagues who both directly and indirectly influenced this effort is also in order. This work is a far richer result thanks to your individual and collective contributions. Partnership works, and the whole is surely greater than the sum of any individual's knowledge and experience.

Special recognition goes to several individuals. Doug McCracken and George Duebner, what a blessing it is to have your unwavering support. And to Matthew Burkley and Molly Anderson, how humbling it is to work in your presence. Your contributions will be long remembered.

Special thanks also to colleagues Linda Applegate, Richard Nolan, Ann Baxter, and Dan Gruber for their advice and insight. Thanks to Kim Clark, dean of the Harvard Business School, for his support of this project.

Lastly, an extraordinary team delivers extraordinary results. In this spirit, thanks to Maureen Donovan, Lisa Sellers, Chris Bonner, Supina Mapon, Negina Rood, Susan Krauss, Elizabeth Lee, Ryan Hartman, Jeff Cruikshank, and David Landau for your invaluable effort in bringing this project to fruition.

preface

In Japanese mythology, the archipelago rests upon a giant catfish, or namazu. To prevent earthquakes, a carefully balanced stone pins the fish down. If the stone is not balanced, the fish thrashes and an earthquake results. While people try not to think about this precarious balance, their fate hinges on it.[1]

Today, nearly every large organization across the globe is feeling the impact of its internal misalignment. Each company struggles to control its own catfish—its portfolio of projects. As billions of dollars flow into project- and technology-related investments, the ability to manage the portfolio is not keeping pace.

Individually, each project may appear to be adding value to the organization. But when projects are examined together, a different picture emerges. Some may be working at cross-purposes, others may be needlessly duplicating each other, still other projects may be aiming to meet outmoded objectives—but *all* are competing for scarce resources. This unintended disorder in a company's project portfolio consumes valuable time and energy, leaves good money on the table, and fails to provision the organization for the future.

This book aims to help managers harness their portfolios of disparate, proliferating projects into an efficient, coherent whole. Our prescription for achieving this ambitious goal is called *alignment*.

Alignment has several facets that each leads to greater business performance. It's about better matching the portfolio's objectives and the company's strategies to the realities of today's business environment. It's about creating greater value and efficiency by managing the relationships among projects. And finally, it's about building the organizational capacity to respond effectively to *whatever future presents itself*.

In this book, we'll introduce you to the "information frontier," a metaphor for the unpredictable business environment in which we all find ourselves. We'll explain how you can respond to today's uncertainty and how your project portfolio is a vehicle to increase shareholder value and confidence. The project portfolio, we argue, is your frontier currency, and an overlooked instrument for unlocking latent value.

To spend this currency wisely, managers must shift mind-sets and change the way they think about the future. Rather than targeting a specific future destination, organizations are better served by preparing for whatever tomorrow may hold—while still coping with today's realities. And they are also better served by adjusting the project portfolio to enhance the *adaptability* of the organization. In this way, alignment becomes dynamic, rather than static.

As authors, we bring complementary experiences and perspectives to bear on this task. Distinguished Professor F. Warren McFarlan, Senior Associate Dean and Director of Harvard Business School's Asia-Pacific Initiative, has been studying these issues and their antecedents for many years. His earliest research on this topic was first published by the *Harvard Business Review* in 1981.[2]

Cathy Benko, Deloitte Consulting's Global e-Business Leader, has dual responsibilities. As a leader in a large organization, she, too, is confronted with the challenges of meeting today's objectives while preparing for the future. And as a practitioner in a global consultancy, she and her colleagues work with clients grappling with similar challenges every day.

The views and prescriptions in this book grew out of what we are witnessing in the workplace, channeled and confirmed by relevant theory. As we shaped an appropriate response to the challenges managers face today, we also drew upon lessons from history, technology, economics, and society to see how technology adoption impacts businesses.

Though there is strong theory underpinning our ideas, this is not a book of grand concepts. Primarily, we think of this book as a *guidebook*. It offers practical tools that companies can use to realize the promise and benefits of alignment.

Our guidebook offers a mutually-reinforcing blend of conceptual and practical thinking. In chapters 1 through 3, we explore today's business context and outline a framework and approach specifically tailored for today's environment. Chapters 4 through 7 provide in-depth discussion of our alignment prescription through a series of real-life case examples, a detailed composite company illustration, and an industry-level study and application. Although these sections may appeal to different audiences, together they deliver on the methods and promise of alignment. We invite you to immerse yourself in either, or both.

As a general rule, we avoid using the "S-word": strategy. Revising an organization's strategy is a complex and time-consuming undertaking. Although our approach is clearly informed by a company's strategy—and can help *shape* strategy—we purposely avoid dwelling on strategic concerns. Instead, we concentrate on providing a no-excuses, in-the-trenches perspective.

Our aim is to help you *play the hand you've already been dealt.* Many business books extol the virtues of where you ought to be, without adequately dealing with the realities of where you are. We don't start from the clean slate of an unencumbered company. Nor do we offer ideas that ignore a company's realities or operating legacies. The truth is, you need to run your business today for your current customers, shareholders, and employees. Being mindful of this, our focus throughout the book is on *what works.*

This focus makes our approach reasonably straightforward and—we believe—accessible. But "straightforward and accessible" does not mean "easy and obvious." If implementing the fundamentals of our approach were easy and obvious, companies would already be doing it. By and large, they aren't. Our experience with dozens of organizations across a wide range of industries and geographies indicates that while progress is being made in the right direction, a coherent and generally accepted framework for dealing with these issues does not yet exist.

Based on our first-hand observations, the need for alignment is clear and palpable. Organizations are under increasing pressure to perform better and create more value. Alignment helps achieve both goals. It enhances shareholder value and confidence through its ability to better meet corporate objectives, increases efficiency, reduces risk, and provides options to hedge against an uncertain future.

So there's the charge, and the promise. Now, let's roll up our sleeves and *get to work.*

connecting
the dots

1

the big picture

With mere good intentions, hell is proverbially paved.

WILLIAM JAMES (1842–1910), PHILOSOPHER AND PSYCHOLOGIST

Research shows that cyclists expend significantly less energy when properly positioned to draft off of one another.[1] Similarly, geese can travel 70 percent farther when aligned in "V" formation.[2] Businesses, too, achieve similar benefits when they are well-aligned. But increasingly, businesses are suffering from a lack of alignment between their objectives and their investments underway. Evidence suggests that in the United States alone, a staggering 40 percent of information technology (IT) investments fail to deliver their intended return each year.[3]

In the following chapters, we explore how you can better connect what your organization is *doing*—as manifested by its project portfolio—with what it intends to *achieve*—as articulated in its corporate objectives—in a manner that is responsive to today's unpredictable environment. Greater alignment, in effect, helps companies to better "fly in formation," which is what this book is all about.

Alignment is a time-honored challenge. But for several reasons, it is today taking on greater urgency. First, project proliferation is consuming increasing levels of precious resources, without necessarily producing commensurate business results. Second, today's earnings-driven economy demands greater project utility to recapture investor confidence and unlock hidden shareholder value. And finally, the evolving market-place and its increasing unpredictability compounds the challenge of meeting current objectives while also preparing for the future.

We argue that this alignment challenge is the proverbial *elephant roaming the halls of your organization.* Recent estimates indicate that $2.3 trillion is spent on projects each year in the United States, an amount equivalent to one-quarter of the nation's gross domestic product. Extrapolating from U.S. data suggests that annual global project spending is nearly $10 trillion of the world's $40.7 trillion gross product.[4]

For further evidence, look to the world of IT spending. According to estimates, this number has doubled in a relatively short period of time; today's "technology spend" in the United States is approximately *half* of all U.S. capital expenditures.[5]

Not only is this spending staggering by any measure, it is also often uncoordinated, even haphazard. A recent study reveals that more than 80 percent of IT projects are conceived of and funded in a fragmented manner, with little in the way of overall planning. In addition, 90 percent of companies do not employ a portfolio management strategy.[6] The result is close to *$1 trillion* in underperforming investment in the United States alone over the last five years (ouch!).

So the opportunity to save money and boost earnings is clear. The question, then, is not *whether* to seek greater alignment, but *how?*

Both classes of related investments just described—technology spending and investments in projects—can be understood as efforts by companies to prepare themselves for the future. This understanding leads us to the project portfolio.

HOW BIG WAS THE TECHNOLOGY INVESTMENT?

- Between 1997 and 2001, $2.5 trillion was spent on technology in the United States—*nearly double the amount for the previous five years.*[7]

- At the same time, Morgan Stanley reports that U.S. IT capital spending has grown to approximately *50 percent of nominal U.S. business capital spending.*[8]

Why? Because, simply put, a company's project portfolio is where plans are translated into reality. It is the manifestation of what a company is doing and where it is going. It's where investments are made and resources are allocated. It has management's attention. And although it is not often framed in this light, the portfolio is a significant agent of organizational change. In fact, we argue, it's the truest measure of organizational intent.

But the environment is changing with extraordinary speed. Do we really know what the future is going to look like? Do all your projects, some launched several years ago, still make sense? As the environment continues to shift, will they deliver the expected payoff, or will their benefits be compromised by changing circumstances?

If the answer to any of these questions is no, then how can an organization think about investing for the future? Our answers to these questions are based on the following principles:

- Companies are better served by adapting themselves for the future rather than by trying to predict its destination.

- The project portfolio is a company's future currency and an overlooked vehicle for unlocking hidden value while the company adapts for the future.

A Portrait of Today

Throughout this book, we develop the case for these principles. Let's start with a selective portrait of a leading bank—a picture that is all too common and all too true.

The CEO of this bank is an astute leader. Over the last decade, he has led his organization through the most sustained period of growth in its history. He has been on the covers of magazines. He has been a guest on *Wall Street Week.*

Lately, however, he feels increasingly challenged. In both the short and long term, he recognizes the need to respond to greater uncertainty. Near-term economic turbulence and geopolitical unrest combined with recent corporate scandals are forcing him to dive into the details and find new ways to increase shareholder value while restoring investor confidence. In addition, restructuring and consolidation of the financial services industry has been underway for some time, and the acquisitions the bank made in recent years are not quite digested yet. Yes, indigestion drags down earnings.

What concerns the CEO is the sense that something more fundamental is going on. It seems the bank's customers, partners, and suppliers are experiencing similar changes in their industries. As he looks across the landscape, he sees a plethora of new realities. Markets are becoming increasingly commoditized, even as products are becoming more complex. Nontraditional entrants—even local supermarkets—are multiplying in number and impact. With startling quickness, players in the industry are morphing into entirely new entities, and the traditional walls, both internal and external, are crumbling. In a heartbeat, it seems, the bank's most important partners have also become its competitors. Customers are increasingly doing their homework and demanding products and services uniquely tailored to their needs—and they want these solutions delivered in *days,* not weeks or months (or years).

It is clear that the bank's former role—as a prime provider of funds to industry—is fading fast, but the organization's future sources of economic value aren't emerging nearly as quickly. With the future so uncertain, the CEO questions whether the organization's existing set of well-articulated, shorter- and longer-term goals will reposition it successfully for the future.

He also realizes that the traditional walls inside the organization are being stressed. The bank has long been organized by product groups, but the market is demanding hybrid products. The environment is promoting integration and coordination, and the need for a collaborative entity grows by the day. But it feels like the bank isn't keeping pace. With laudable goals and massive and continuing investments, the projects under way don't appear to be linked in coherent ways—in other words, in ways that draw upon common resources and deliver on common objectives.

With analysts challenging him to translate these investments into bottom-line results, the CEO convenes his top managers to put together an effective response. The end result of the meeting? He issues the following e-mail:

> *The relentlessly challenging and uncertain business environment forces*
> *us to confront a twofold challenge: increase shareholder value and re-*

*store investor confidence. These challenges require us to more rigor-
ously focus our time, attention, and resource investments toward the
projects and initiatives that meet these most pressing needs. Our past
efforts at establishing investment priorities illustrate the difficulty
ahead. However, our future success depends on our ability to selec-
tively invest in projects and initiatives that best achieve these business
imperatives.*

The message is clear: *We must rationally realign our project portfolio.*
But to every seasoned manager, the e-mail's implicit message is equally
clear, and far more compelling: *Let the budget games begin!* Immediately,
each pulls out his or her list of pet projects and calls his or her team
together. They start to strategize about the ensuing negotiations and
turf battles. How will they protect those projects that are important, but
hard to sell? What projects can be served up without doing sustained
damage to their individual agendas? How can they survive the ROI
analyses that they'll likely be asked to prepare? With whom can they ally
themselves to better protect favored projects?

And soon enough, the word begins to circulate: *An off-site may be
needed.*

Sound familiar? We chose to focus on a banking example, but we could
have looked at any number of industries. And although we took the
CEO's perspective, we could just as easily have looked at the changing
landscape through almost any manager's eyes. Consider, for example,
the HR executive who wakes up one morning and discovers that the
confidential restructuring plan that she has been working on for
months has been posted on an Internet chat room, effectively shutting
down local operations and destroying the trust built over many years
with the union local.

Or the operations director who has just learned that, unbeknownst
to her, three other initiatives were under way in different parts of the
company, some with goals contradictory to her effort. Now she is being
asked to reconcile the conflicting purposes of the projects and create
one unified vision.

Or the channel manager who lies awake at night because it falls to
him to convince senior management to join an online exchange that is

partly owned by the company's fiercest competitor. The once-clear delineations between customers, competitors, and suppliers are blurring, and the industry is filling up with strange bedfellows.

Or the CIO who knows that the company's expensive and highly touted global customer relationship management system—which depends on global real-time access to customer information—is lagging behind reality roughly half the time. Yes, the information links the company across the globe, but many of the subsystems that feed it run on batch cycles, rendering the investment in the larger system suspect.

Maybe you identify with the situation in which our bank CEO—or the HR executive, operations director, channel manager, or CIO—and his other colleagues find themselves. Maybe, as someone who deals with mounting pressures to increase shareholder value and instill investor confidence while also enhancing your organization's future prospects, you are similarly searching for new kinds of insights, tools, and answers.

Adapting for the Frontier

We use a frontier metaphor throughout this book to describe the business context that is creating the challenges we've outlined. This metaphor also becomes the backdrop for our approach to alignment. Why the frontier metaphor? Because it aptly captures recent experience: a decades-long period of progressive and lasting change, rich with opportunity and fraught with uncertainty.

Frontiers are new terrains in which people roam, settle, and create value. Frontiers fundamentally alter not only what we do, but also how we see the world around us. They run a course between our past and our future. They contain many recognizable parts of the past, even while signaling a dramatic departure from it.

By their nature, frontiers are confusing, volatile, and—above all—*unpredictable*. The adoption of new ideas is a *social*, as well as a business, process. This fact, among others, makes frontiers particularly unsuitable for crystal-ball gazers. Steam engines, for example, were not invented to power factories or railroads, but to pump water out of mines.

The frontier metaphor also opens the door to learning. Based on the patterns of previous frontiers, we can hazard the guess that this particular territory, which we'll call the "information frontier," will go through several boom-and-bust cycles. Unfortunately, however, we can't say exactly how many, when they'll start and stop, or where we are in the larger cycle. In other words, the unpredictability we spoke of at the outset of the chapter is an enduring business reality, and one that alignment addresses. By exploring patterns of previous frontiers, as we do in chapter 2, we can get a vivid sense of the journey before us.

So what is this information frontier? In the 1980s and 1990s, a constellation of forces—economic, technological, social, regulatory, and so on—came together to create a substantially new business context. (The roots of this frontier can arguably be traced back much further, but for now, let's start there.) Unlike most previous frontiers, which focused on *terra firma*—land, minerals, factory layouts—the opportunity of this frontier grows out of a many-sided communications medium. It encompasses enabling connections, information flows, and relationships in a dynamic, networked environment.

Today, business leaders and managers are grappling with a frontier-related challenge: *how to deliver for today while adapting for tomorrow's business context.* First and foremost, of course, organizations must continue to meet their traditional objectives. Revenues need to grow, customers must be served, employees trained and paid, and shareholders' expectations satisfied.

In addition to responding to these challenges, organizations must also prepare for the future. But looking back at what you did yesterday to figure out what to do tomorrow doesn't work particularly well during this period of frontier-related discontinuity. Imagine a retailer planning an expansion strategy in the postwar 1940s and failing to take into account the rapid development of the suburbs. That retailer would have focused its expansions on downtown areas of major mass-transit lines— a place of both relative and absolute decline for the next four decades.

This book is a guidebook for how to get comfortable with frontier living, and how to better meet the challenge of aligning the project portfolio with the company's objectives in uncertain times. We provide a balance of theoretical concepts and practical applications. We also provide an approach and a set of tools that help you leverage existing investments and we do so in a way that you can use when you get into the office *tomorrow.*

Road Map to Alignment

Our prescription for adapting is, in a word, *alignment*. Since alignment is the most important concept in this book, let's introduce it properly. Alignment is the correct positioning of things in relation to each other. What, specifically, are we aligning? We are aligning three drivers of business performance: a company's project portfolio—its future currency—with its objectives; the projects in the portfolio to each other; and the portfolio and company's objectives with the shifting realities of the larger business context.

Start with Intentions

Objectives are also a key underpinning of our approach. Every organization has short- and long-term objectives (qualitative, quantitative, or both; implicit or explicit) that it is striving to achieve. Short-term objectives are generally operational goals, achievable in a year or less. Long-term objectives are often, though not always, more strategic.

But we contend that during this period of frontier-driven discontinuity, in which entirely new ways of doing business are emerging, there is a third type of organizational objective, which involves *developing mind-sets necessary to prosper on the information frontier*. We use the term *traits* to refer to these shifts in mind-set.

Collectively, we refer to these three kinds of objectives—short-term, long-term, and traits—as the organization's *intentions*. We use this word throughout the book in a very specific sense to represent a composite set of objectives. The relationship of these objectives is illustrated in our Intentions Framework, shown in figure 1-1.

We will use this framework to paint a portrait of alignment and help you understand where your own organization is on the alignment spectrum. To a significant degree, the three kinds of objectives that comprise the organization's intentions—the two circles and the triangle in figure 1-1—are complementary and mutually reinforcing. In an ideal world, there would be lots of overlap among these shapes. In the real world, of course, limited resources (e.g., management time, available talent, and capital) and the conflicting needs of different constituencies

Figure 1-1: The Intentions Framework

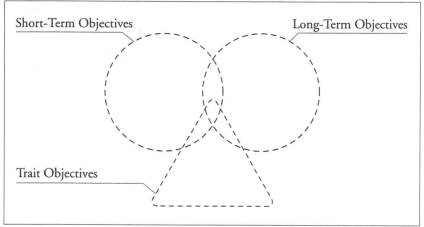

(e.g., customers, employees, and investors) often combine to create tension among these varied objectives.

Dealing with the tension between short- and long-term objectives is a well understood business challenge. But the "traits" we refer to are our own elaboration on the intentions theme. So let's take a moment to describe them before moving forward with our prescription for alignment.

Earlier, we stated that the defining nature of this frontier is a many-sided communications medium and network. This unfolding business context, we argue, is our dominant reality, and it provides insight into how we should conduct ourselves "out there" on the frontier. Companies need to cultivate four traits, which we briefly describe in table 1-1, in response to this forming reality. This table offers a preview of the four traits, which will be introduced in chapter 2.

Focusing on traits as an explicit objective—as part of an organization's intentions—can help organizations adapt to this uncertain terrain. Why? Because *traits promote survival in volatile and changing conditions.* They provide the agility to both respond to and capitalize on changing business contexts. Although our use of the term may sound unfamiliar, most organizations are no stranger to the concepts that stand behind these traits. Many companies are already grappling with

Table 1-1: Traits

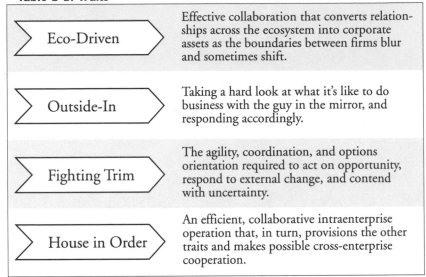

Eco-Driven	Effective collaboration that converts relationships across the ecosystem into corporate assets as the boundaries between firms blur and sometimes shift.
Outside-In	Taking a hard look at what it's like to do business with the guy in the mirror, and responding accordingly.
Fighting Trim	The agility, coordination, and options orientation required to act on opportunity, respond to external change, and contend with uncertainty.
House in Order	An efficient, collaborative intraenterprise operation that, in turn, provisions the other traits and makes possible cross-enterprise cooperation.

the discontinuities and opportunities of the emerging frontier. The traits simply provide a conceptual grid for these transformational efforts.

Again, we'll have more to say about the traits in subsequent chapters, but for the moment, let's tick off a few key highlights:

- *Traits are about mind-set,* rather than tactical maneuvering. Traits are less about capabilities—although they set the stage for capabilities—and more about the kinds of mental models needed to prosper on the information frontier.

- *Traits are mutually reinforcing.* Although we describe them as four distinct attributes, the reality is far less discrete. Together, the four traits help an organization develop a mental stance that is both focused and powerful.

- *Traits provide the power of measurement.* They give rise to measurable elements that can be used to gauge your organization's progress. By focusing on these "mind-sets of the future"—rather than on a fixed future destination—companies can better prepare themselves for uncertainty.

• *Traits help with change, in part by providing constancy.* While a given company's strategies and tactics may change as its business ecosystem evolves, traits provide a consistent frame of reference by which the larger trajectory of the journey can be charted.

At this point, we have introduced the first half of the alignment equation—the intentions of the organization. Now let's take a moment to look at the second half of the equation: the project portfolio.

Your organization has a basketful—or perhaps baskets full—of activities in which it is engaged. Collectively, these comprise your project portfolio. Your portfolio represents your actions and your investments and, as stated earlier, serves as your frontier currency.

Mapping Your Project Portfolio to Intentions

Returning to our framework, let's take a look at how projects and intentions relate. (For simplicity's sake, we will use the term "project" throughout this book to refer to projects, programs, initiatives, and similar efforts.) Each project can be mapped to the intentions of the organization based on its objectives and deliverables. A project that serves only short-term objectives, for example, would fall in the circle representing those objectives. Projects that map to one or more intentions lie within the intersection of the intentions shapes. Projects that don't map to any intention sit outside of the shapes altogether. Figure 1-2 illustrates a sample project portfolio mapped to the intentions of the organization.

Aligning the company's projects to its intentions, to each other, and to the unpredictable environment is a multifaceted endeavor. Let's discuss each of these dimensions in turn.

1. *Aligning the project portfolio to the company's intentions.* When your organization's activities are tightly aligned to its intentions— when its projects deliver on what it is trying to achieve—the portfolio is more coherent and unified, which means less organizational friction at all levels. And when there is less internal friction, people and systems simply perform better.

2. *Aligning projects with other projects.* By coordinating projects more effectively, hidden value is unlocked without significant incremental

Figure 1-2: Projects Mapped to Intentions

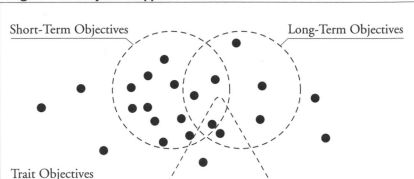

investment. Additional value can be found in several specific areas by better aligning how projects work in relation to each other. First, by looking at where individual projects are headed—meaning both their intended deliverables and outcomes, and how they plan to get there—you can uncover opportunities to streamline and further integrate the portfolio. Looking at projects side by side makes clear where there may be a duplication of effort, or where projects may be working at cross-purposes.

Second, by looking inside the projects and seeing if there are ways to better leverage activities across projects, new opportunities for efficiency and risk reduction can be brought to the surface. Looking at activities ranging from training and process flows to common technologies helps you spot common components. More "swapping of parts" means less reinventing of the wheel, which saves time and money, increases flexibility, and ultimately promotes alignment.

3. *Adapting the project portfolio and the organization for frontier living.* Embracing the traits is an important step in adapting to the changing business context. But this is not sufficient to provision the organization for the volatile and unpredictable journey that lies ahead. Prosperous settlers also need to ensure that their project portfolios reflect the unfolding realities of the frontier. This final aspect of alignment positions the project portfolio for a rapidly changing

environment. It builds options into the portfolio so that it is able to respond to our changing landscape.

By manipulating the scope and timeframe of individual projects, for example, both projects and resources are made more fungible, enabling the company to invest in the next interval. But the company is also able to walk away, if necessary, knowing that a certain amount of value has already been captured.

The Alignment Payoff

Our concept of multifaceted alignment is proactive. In other words, rather than waiting for challenges or changes to arise, the aligned portfolio anticipates and prepares for changes in the environment. Various business scenarios—for example, from fast growth and expansion to economic contraction and belt-tightening—can be considered, and forward-looking contingency plans created for each scenario. As a result, alignment becomes a continuous activity, which is just what's called for on the frontier.

Simply stated, a better-aligned and adaptive organization is not only more focused as it heads in its chosen direction, but it is also more flexible and efficient. Its risks have been spread more broadly, its resources better allocated, its attention more focused on the projects most likely to drive the business forward, and its options more deliberate and better understood. These are means to several critical ends, including:

- *Increased shareholder value and confidence.* The organization better understands the financial and operational drivers that have the biggest impact on the enterprise, thus improving alignment by reducing costs, improving asset allocation, and decreasing operational friction. This, in turn, increases investor confidence in management's ability to deliver on its objectives.

- *Enhanced return on investments (ROI).* Alignment improves ROI in several ways: by decreasing duplication and divergent projects, mitigating portfolio risk, reshaping outlier efforts, and reusing project components. The result is that resources are reliably allocated for the greater good, and the dollars invested deliver greater value.

- *Good habits.* Through active incorporation of the traits into its thinking and behaviors, the organization makes itself more adaptive and better equipped to deal with unpredictability. The organization also develops the good habits of continuing to adapt while maintaining alignment.

Tactics and Tools

In keeping with a guidebook orientation, we offer a pragmatic approach and a set of tools, informed by an in-the-trenches perspective with two key emphases:

1. *Play the hand you're dealt.* You can't change past decisions, so take action from where you are today, and develop a series of practical and manageable steps that will capture hidden organizational value.

2. *Turn up the dial.* We have designed our approach to be scalable across several dimensions, with a benefit at almost any level of effort. You make the call: The more you put in—measured in terms of time and commitment, rather than hard dollars—the greater the benefit you're likely to realize.

Now let's focus on the specifics of our approach for achieving greater alignment. This approach "connects the dots" between your company's project portfolio, its intentions, and the realities of frontier living. It encourages you to get familiar with several tools, listed in table 1-2, that will help you tie your portfolio more tightly to your revenue model, find synergies, eliminate redundancies, discover hidden risk factors, and promote behaviors and options as the best defense against uncertainty.

This table is provided as a preview to later discussions. We introduce the first of these tools, Trait Meters, in chapter 3. Trait Meters are designed to help organizations better understand and set objectives for trait development. The meters are useful tools for figuring out the position of an industry as well as a company's position relative to the development of traits. These meters also help the organization formulate specific trait objectives, inform the shape of short-term and long-term objectives, and provide a touchstone for scoping projects.

Table 1-2: Suite of Alignment Tools

Tool	Description
Trait Meters	Assesses, plans, and measures trait development
Intentions	Assesses alignment of portfolio to intentions
Sides	Removes bias and finds synergies by sorting projects into main business activities
Right Brain	Identifies change capacity issues
Common Threads	Finds common, reusable components
Project Chunking	Structures projects into bite-size pieces that deliver incremental, stand-alone value
What-if Planning	Develops contingencies for varying scenarios

We then move to three additional diagnostic tools designed to assess the current level of alignment and provide insights into potential alignment opportunities. Through the use of these tools—Intentions, Sides, and Right Brain—your organization can gain a clearer understanding of where its portfolio stands today and what it wants to achieve. In addition, ways to better align and build traits become more obvious. We explore these diagnostic tools in chapter 4 and then show them in action in chapter 5.

While these diagnostic tools highlight opportunities to better align the portfolio, a second set of tools—Common Threads, Project Chunking, and What-if Planning—focuses on building flexibility into the portfolio. These options-oriented tools "look under the hood" of the portfolio to find ways to better leverage individual efforts so that they can be more responsive to a rapidly changing environment. These tools also look at the portfolio as a whole, and evaluate how it can proactively change as the company's intentions evolve.

In general, having options lets you off the hook of having to *guess right* all the time in making long-term, bet-the-company kinds of investments. These options-oriented tools—can help you place smaller bets and make decisions in shorter time increments therefore incurring less risk. We discuss this set of tools first in chapter 4 and then explore their applications in depth in chapter 6.

When journeying across a frontier, resources are scarce. Our end goal for you, as we have said before, is *not* necessarily to add, change, or subtract a lot of different projects. We are not encouraging you to get out the red pen and axe scads of projects, nor are we advocating that you turn over the keys to the treasury to fund a raft of new ones.

Instead, we are inviting you to use these tools to better allocate your scarce resources—to create an increased degree of alignment that is consistent with frontier realities. Since alignment is a multifaceted endeavor, there is no one "right answer" or one "perfect tool." *Each company's context is specific.*

Therefore, you'll need to determine what works best for you, in your specific circumstances. Accordingly, we have structured our tools to be both modular and scalable. The tools are designed to address different challenges or opportunities an organization may want to pursue to increase business performance. You decide which tools to use and the depth of their application. Again, our goal is to provision you for your frontier journey.

An Alignment Warm-Up

Most organizations worry about striking an appropriate balance between their short-term and long-term objectives. But surprisingly few organizations put their project portfolios through this screen: *On balance, does your project portfolio reflect and serve your organizational objectives?*

We'll end this chapter with what we'll call an "alignment warm-up." Working with our Intentions Framework, we want to help you develop a preliminary sense of how well aligned *your* organization is today. This modest exercise won't fully hold your organization up to the full mirror of alignment, but it will give you insight into one facet of alignment: that is, the alignment of your project portfolio with the intentions of the organization.

Don't worry about precision or the underlying mathematics as you go through the exercise. (Or, as we like to put it, *check your slide rule at the door.*) This exercise is supposed to be informative and fun, and help prepare you for the lessons in the rest of this book. So get out a sheet of paper to use as your worksheet, and let's begin.

Step One

The first step to understanding whether you're aligned is to determine your company's short-term and long-term objectives. As a continuing contributor to your particular enterprise, you are probably familiar with these objectives. It's often interesting to check the consistency of the company's objectives by comparing documents such as the annual report, planning documents, vision statements, and even notes from the annual retreat. To get started, the objectives do not need to be detailed, in fact, they can often be inferred from the competitive context.

A major tenet of this book, as noted earlier, is that you need to work from wherever you are, with whatever information you already possess. In this spirit, here and elsewhere, you will be asked for information that you can either find or infer. So, it's time to find or infer those objectives. No excuses.

Once you've pulled together a list of key organizational objectives, think about the relative weight your organization places on short-term (operational) versus long-term (strategic) objectives. Equal? Unequal?

Now, on your worksheet, represent these two sets of objectives as two circles that either overlap a little, a lot, or not at all. (Refer back to figure 1-1 for an idea of what we're looking for.) If you think your organization puts more emphasis and focus on either objective, that's

Figure 1-3: Short- and Long-Term Objectives

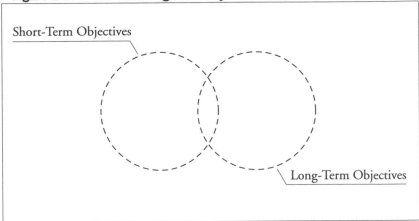

Short-Term Objectives

Long-Term Objectives

fine. Make that circle bigger. If there's more overlap between your two circles than in our earlier drawing, that's OK too; draw them that way. Again, don't worry about any level of precision in your circle-drawing; we're simply talking about orders-of-magnitude impressions.

Depending on your organizational specifics, your circles might look something like the ones in figure 1-3.

Do your organization's two circles overlap almost completely, not at all, or somewhere in the middle? It's probably safe to assume that your organization tries to define and pursue goals in a way that creates at least *some* overlap between these two circles.

Step Two

Next, draw a triangle somewhere in the vicinity of your two circles and label that triangle "traits." (Recall our discussion of traits earlier in this chapter.) Because trait objectives are not traditional objectives, we use a different shape, a triangle, to depict them. Draw a triangle where you think it might fall in relation to your two circles, and label it "trait objectives." (For the moment, simply estimate what your organization's trait objectives may be, and treat the four traits as a single basketful of good intentions.) If you think there's no chance of overlap with the two

Figure 1-4: Example of Organizational Intentions

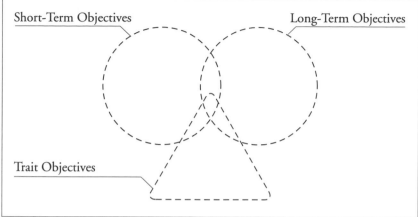

circles, then draw a freestanding triangle. But if you think there's at least *some* overlap—that traits are somehow connected with either your short- or long-term objectives, or both—then indicate that overlap in your drawing. Now your picture may look something like figure 1-4.

Step Three

Up to this point, we've been focusing on your organization's intentions. As noted above, however, intentions are only half the picture. Your organizational intent is also captured, implicitly, in what you're doing to realize these intentions—in other words, your *actions*. And, as argued earlier, the truest measure of organizational intent is the portfolio of projects you're currently pursuing.

How can you figure out whether the *activities* of your organization fit with its intentions? The best way is to identify a representative sample of company projects that are currently funded and under way, assign objectives (short-term, long-term, or traits) to them, and plot them on your diagram.

The next step is to draw up a quick list of the top five or ten projects in your organization. The choice of projects can be based on budget size, expected impact, level of risk, or a simple sample from your view of the organization. We don't prescribe which ones to plot; we leave that to you. Again, this exercise is not about precision; you can always go back and do it again with more and different projects, once you have the mechanics down.

Next, plot each project on your diagram. To do so, you'll have to sort them into one of three categories:

- *Outlier.* A project that does not map to any of the intentions. These are going to land entirely outside the three shapes.

- *Single intention.* A project that meets one objective. Plot this project inside the corresponding shape (i.e., inside a circle, but not in the zone of intersection with the other circle or the triangle).

- *Multiple intentions.* A project that contributes to two or more objectives. Plot it in the appropriate area of intersection.

How much does a project have to contribute to an objective to map to it? Use your best judgment. Generally, a project should make a *reasonable* contribution to an intention to plot in one of the shapes. Also, let's keep this simple by placing your dot within the appropriate shape without concern of exactly *where* inside the shape (to the far left, far right, top, or bottom) the dot should fall. In other words, just placing the dot somewhere inside, outside, or in the intersection of several shapes is good enough.

Now plot each project, putting a dot on your diagram to represent each outlier, single-intention, and multiple-intention project. We've done this exercise with people across various levels, functions, and industries, and the maps they draw vary widely. But the results generally look something like the ones in figure 1-5 or 1-6.

So, How Did You Do?

If you see (1) heavy overlap among your intention shapes, and (2) lots of dots clustering in the overlaps, your portfolio is well aligned in relation to your intentions, and a pat on the back is in order. If you don't see all those overlaps, trust us: You're not alone. In either case, the truth is, we have yet to meet anybody who plots their objectives and activities as in figure 1-7.

Figure 1-5: Alignment of Projects to Intentions—Sample Test Results A

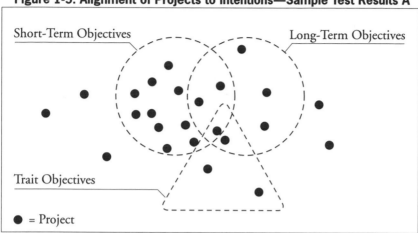

Figure 1-6: Alignment of Projects to Intentions—Sample Test Results B

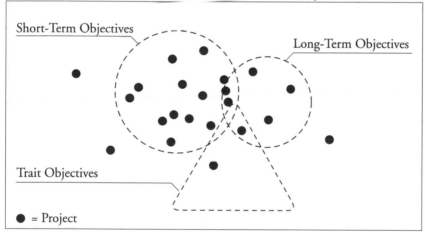

Admittedly, figure 1-7 is aspirational—and it may or may not reflect an ideal state for your organization. But if there's a lot of room between your company's actual (as depicted in your worksheet drawing) and aspirational states, then this gap is latent value waiting to be mined— with little, if any, hard-dollar investment. We believe that it's entirely possible to move in this aspirational direction; it just takes commitment,

Figure 1-7: Aspirational View of Fully Aligned Organization

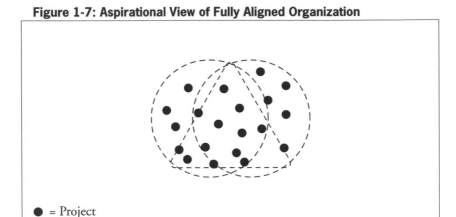

● = Project

some focused time and effort, an appropriate framework, and good managerial judgment.

We also believe that our approach delivers the right combination of (1) a conceptual framework to give you a "direction finder" and (2) practical tools for assessing, implementing, and adapting to a new business context. It can help you to

- capture greater value in the projects you're currently pursuing,

- instill the traits needed to move your organization forward on the frontier,

- build an options-based portfolio to best respond to today's uncertain environment, and

- provide a framework to assess and monitor current and future investments.

DON'T ASSUME . . .

. . . that it is always the project that needs to move toward intentions. Sometimes, an organization's intentions need to better align with projects that are more in tune with the direction of the market.

In Summary

This guidebook is for the majority of organizations doing business out there in the real world—companies that want to find opportunities for greater shareholder value and confidence. Given this real-world focus, we don't start from the clean sheet of an unencumbered new company or offer ideas that ignore the realities of operating legacies. We start from where you are today and seek alignment from that baseline.

We drive this at the portfolio level because the underlying direction of an organization is defined by where it chooses to allocate its currency—resources, financial, and otherwise—*and that place is the project portfolio.*

One contrarian thought: In light of recent frontier troubles, couldn't we simply turn the wagons around and go home? Is this frontier something that we *have* to reckon with?

To these questions, we say "no" and "yes," respectively. First, you can't go home again; you've already changed too much. (Frontiers involve changed mind-sets, right? Imagine life without e-mail.) Second, there's still plenty of opportunity out there to be exploited, and you already have a significant stake. Doesn't it *make sense* to go make sense of that opportunity?

We—your authors and tour guides—are optimists. So we resonate with Winston Churchill's remark: "A pessimist sees the difficulty in every opportunity; an optimist sees the opportunity in every difficulty."[9] We believe that companies have a clear choice as they look to the future. They can conclude that upsets and retrenchments signal the end of this frontier—or perhaps even indicate that the frontier didn't exist in the first place. They can stop trying to build toward their frontier-influenced future. If they do, we believe, their future will be an increasingly difficult place in which to compete, adapt, and thrive.

Or, they can choose to be focused and disciplined about their future. We believe that for those who conscientiously work to embrace its possibilities, the information frontier will reveal amazing opportunities.

2 frontier living

*One thing that distinguishes a frontier is the
precarious nature of the human hold on it.*

KATHLEEN NORRIS (B. 1947), POET

In 1881, Ferdinand de Lesseps started construction on the Panama
Canal. If history was any guide, he and his canal were likely to be a
smashing success. Nearly fifteen years earlier, de Lesseps had been the
mastermind behind the extraordinary Suez Canal project—and, inci-
dentally, a new opera house in Cairo, where an opera to commemorate
the canal's opening and Egypt's modernization (*Aida,* by Verdi) was also
well received. Thousands of investors flocked to his new company, con-
fident of his future success.

Unfortunately, in approaching the new Panama project, de Lesseps
failed to understand that the context in Panama was very different from
that of the Suez Canal. He set out to build the Panama Canal using more
or less the same methods he had at Suez. But the Suez region was a relatively flat desert, whereas the Panama terrain was a wet, mountainous
jungle, traversed by the untamed Changres River and rife with tropical
diseases.

The result was an unmitigated disaster. By 1889, construction had
halted—by which time some twenty-one thousand people had died in
the effort—and the company went bankrupt. The resulting scandal led
to riots in Paris a few years later.

That was not the end of the story, of course. When construction on the Panama Canal resumed in 1902, context was fully considered. Among other changes, the wild Changres was tamed and became an essential part of the lock-based canal design. Malaria and yellow fever were brought under control. The American engineers looked not to the Suez experience, but to the lessons of railroad building, particularly for guidance in ways to move literally millions of tons of earth. Ultimately, the project was brought in under budget, and the first ship, the *Ancon*, went through the canal in August 1914.[1]

The point? Understanding the context of any venture is critical. And we believe that lessons for today's business context can be found in past frontiers. As Mark Twain aptly noted, "History may not repeat itself, but it often rhymes."[2]

The current business context is a convergence of innovative business practices enabled by technologies, new approaches to production and marketing, and historical practices and conditions. While our unpredictable and turbulent environment is unique, it is not without historical precedent. Many of the same forces that generate today's headlines—technology, societal changes, political strife, and economic volatility—could just as easily have been front-page news in the late 1910s or early 1920s, when electrification was beginning to change business productivity in fundamental ways.

This chapter is designed to get you thinking like a settler—to help you and your organization capture value in an unpredictable but opportunity-rich environment. Our prescription for alignment begins with garnering lessons from past frontiers. We then overlay these lessons with the unique characteristics of the information frontier and see how the patterns of the past intersect with those of today. From here, we discern the mind-set shifts needed to best respond to—and take advantage of—frontier living, fully aware of today's unique context, but counseled by history. Informed by this collective perspective, our alignment approach and set of tools are both effective and relevant.

The Frontier Metaphor

The frontier metaphor goes a long way toward explaining today's unpredictable environment. Frontiers are uncharted territories. They require new mind-sets, creativity, and—most important—the ability to envision how the business can exploit the changes that are under way.

Frontiers include four defining features: pervasiveness, changed mind-sets, chain reactions, and irreversibility. Anything short of this fails to make the "frontier threshold," in our book.

"*Space*," intones the captain of the U.S.S. *Enterprise* at the beginning of each episode of *Star Trek*—"the final frontier." Remember, though, that Captains Kirk and Picard are speaking to us from a still-distant future. As of today, space doesn't qualify as a frontier. Yes, it has changed mind-sets. But space exploration remains too expensive to be pervasive. It's simply too exotic and removed from the day-to-day economy to set off chain reactions. (In case you're wondering, Tang and Velcro are spin-offs, not chain reactions.) And for the moment, at least, going to the moon seems like a reversible phenomenon. Humans used to do that, but they don't anymore.

People often confuse a technology with a frontier. In our view a technology, or a family of technologies, can enable the opening and settling of a frontier. But without a constellation of supporting forces and converging trends, a technology can't change mind-sets and become pervasive.

The changes wrought by settlers on frontiers are both pervasive and irreversible. No value judgment involved here—permanence may or may not be a good thing—but we humans rarely turn our backs on frontier-related evolutions. Luddites and others who would turn the clock back to a simpler time simply don't prevail.

To better understand what the frontier metaphor teaches us, let's walk through three historical frontiers. At the end of the tour, we'll cluster our observations around three key lessons: (1) Frontiers are confusing, volatile, and unpredictable; (2) settlers initially walk into the future backward; and (3) there is still gold in those hills.

Hollywood's Favorite Frontier: The American West

We devote the next few pages to the opening of the American West. On the face of it, of course, this is a hopeless assignment. The West is the stage on which millions of pioneers and settlers have played out their dreams over the course of more than three centuries of exploration. But ask people the first thing they think of when they hear the word *frontier*, and most (Americans and non-Americans alike) cite the American West. The West is the archetypal frontier, and therefore is a good jumping-off point for our larger frontier story.

Some date the opening of the Western frontier to the celebrated journey of Lewis and Clark. President Thomas Jefferson commissioned Meriwether Lewis in 1802 to lead a western exploration "for the advancement of geography."[3] But as it turns out, *governments alone can't open frontiers.* Until a whole host of forces converge—economic, social, and technological—governments can't get the settlers out there creating value. For example, despite Jefferson's efforts to open the gates westward, large-scale nonindigenous American migration to the West didn't even begin until about half a century after Lewis and Clark's expedition. As late as 1841, it was still considered newsworthy when a hardy band of thirty-two pioneers made it to California.

In January 1848, an adventurer named James W. Marshall struck gold in the foothills of the Sierras, northeast of the sleepy hamlet of Sacramento. The U.S. federal government—still determined to knit the continent together under one flag—turned up the heat under the frontier pot. In a message to congress at the end of 1848, President James K. Polk made an extraordinary statement. "The accounts of the abundance of gold in that territory," Polk claimed of California, "are of such extraordinary character as would scarcely command belief were they not corroborated by authentic reports of officers in the public service."[4]

This bit of presidential hype, converging as it did with lots of other social and economic pressures, finally was enough; approximately ninety thousand settlers arrived in California in 1849. By 1858, the total number of immigrants had exceeded six hundred thousand. The discovery of gold quickly changed the mind-set of people and got them heading west.

Greed and opportunism showed up on the other side of the counter as well. Many settlers who traveled the California Trail, for example, were woefully unprepared for the scorching deserts of Nevada. A number of sharp-eyed entrepreneurs traveled eastward from California with barrels of water and charged the desperate travelers up to $100 for a glass of water. Flour, sugar, and coffee also got more expensive, the farther west the pioneers ventured.

Lawlessness, too, characterized the new frontier. Frequently, the law consisted of the opinions of whoever got there first, shot the straightest, or had the most powerful friends.

Even success was no guarantee of success. Short-term goals (*how do I get over the next mountain?*) necessarily took precedence over long-term vision (*what will I do with the gold, if I actually find some?*). But as business leaders well know, consistently favoring either the short term or the long term is risky.

Eventually, of course, new links grew between the eastern United States and the western frontier. As transportation and communication networks improved, the hype, exploitation, lawlessness, and physical dangers gradually subsided. In the 1850s, it could take up to six months for travelers to walk across the Great Plains to California and Oregon. When the transcontinental rail route was completed in 1869—more than six decades after Lewis and Clark—travel from New York to California took just ten days. Linked by rail and telegraph, the country now felt smaller and safer and full of new opportunities.

The opportunities for extending one's reach and reaping greater rewards increased significantly. Frontiers generally create opportunity by allowing the *redefinition of a potential market.* For example, Marshall Fields—a pioneer in the creation of the modern department store—was a product of Chicago's exploding population and well-developed transportation infrastructure. And the creation of the supermarket in the 1930s—although originally inspired by retailers' needs to cut costs—was largely fueled by the rise of the automobile.[5]

A final point: Although the opening of the American West involved a physical frontier, it also engendered a *conceptual shift,* which proved critical to the long-term development of the nation and its people.

A Drive through the Automotive Frontier

The first internal combustion engine was built in 1860. In 1876, a German named Nikolous Otto patented the four-stroke gasoline engine, still commonly used today. Ten years later, Karl Benz's first mass-produced automobile pointed the way toward the automotive frontier.

Earlier, we made the point that governments alone don't define or open frontiers. Neither do inventors. Neither Otto nor Benz opened the automotive frontier. That signal event—which moved the car into the mainstream and changed manufacturing and marketing forever—came in 1908, five years after the founding of the Ford Motor Company.

The fundamental shift? Henry Ford found a way to make automobiles affordable to the general populace. He redefined his potential market. Before Ford, cars were more or less handcrafted—the playthings of the wealthy. In 1895, only four cars were registered in the United States. Ford changed the rules and two decades later in 1915, 2.5 million cars were registered.[6] Through mass production, whereby workers assembled interchangeable parts on a moving production line, Ford was able to produce the Model T, an inexpensive but well-constructed vehicle. Introduced in 1908, the Model T sold more than 15 million units over the next two decades and went through only minor changes during that time. The price of the Model T dropped from $850 in 1908 to $360 in 1917. For the first time, even those working the assembly line could afford to own what they were producing.[7]

Ford was not the only pioneer in this highly visible and attractive field, of course. Although he was the first to change in mind-set by thinking of cars as replacements for horses (rather than expensive toys), competition among budding automakers was fierce. Even in the early stages of this frontier, consolidation was rampant. Almost every market—from Germany to Japan to Britain—had its own version of Ransom Olds, Henry Leland, John and Horace Dodge, Henry Ford, and Louis Chevrolet. Many of these pioneers saw their businesses merged and re-merged, ultimately to create new auto superpowers. Today, global consolidation continues to shrink the hundreds of original auto manufacturers down to a select few players.

Frontiers often embrace more than one boom-and-bust cycle, and this was the case with the automobile. In the 1920s, as the auto industry began maturing, the emphasis shifted from low price points and technical specifications to the all-important concept of *image*. Alfred Sloan's multidivision General Motors led the charge by translating Ford's mass production techniques into a new form of "mass customization."

At this time, little actually distinguished one car from another in terms of its technical features. But as consumers gained more disposable income, the marketers stepped to the fore and began to differentiate cars through styling and feature enhancement. In other words, the automotive frontier had entered a new phase. Cars were becoming a commodity. They had become so fully integrated into American life, in fact, that the question was not whether you owned a car but what *kind* of car you had—and increasingly, *how many*.

In a relatively short period of time, the automobile became an indispensable part of American life. It displaced the previous dominant transportation modes—passenger trains, horse-drawn carriages, even walking. It forever changed the world's most fundamental perceptions of quality of life, distance, communication, and efficiency.

At the same time, as noted above, the automobile called forth an enormous infrastructure. Settlers didn't want to get stuck in the mud, run out of gas, or get stranded with flat tires. Settlers demanded highways, parking lots, service stations, dealers, parts suppliers, and so on. Governments responded by paving roads, licensing drivers, and finding new revenue sources. In 1915, the nation spent $302 million annually on roads and highways. By 1925, this number had almost quadrupled to $1.1 billion.[8]

On frontiers, change and settlement often occur in waves. The automotive frontier illustrates this attribute. The first-wave infrastructure opened the door to subsequent waves. The two-lane highway (Route 66, Highway 1) was succeeded by the interstate highway system. This highway infrastructure enabled a new wave of settlement and associated infrastructure development, such as suburbs, motels, shopping malls, and drive-ins. And with each wave of change and settlement, there were associated *mind-set shifts* and lifestyle changes (e.g., home ownership, family road trips, fast food, etc.). All were outgrowths, directly and indirectly, of the automotive frontier.

The Electrification Frontier

Electrification, our third prototypical frontier, also offers interesting parallels to today's business context. Although the principle of induction was demonstrated in 1831 by the English chemist and physicist Michael Faraday, many years passed before people and governments came to understand the full implications of electricity. And still more decades passed before manufacturers figured out how to wring productivity gains out of the use of electricity, before appliance makers found appropriate niches, and before builders designed offices and homes with electricity in mind.

In other words, many years passed before Faraday's demonstration turned into the electrification frontier. Early on, of course, some people had an inkling of its potential. In 1849, the U.S. Commissioner of Patents predicted that a mighty revolution would be sparked by Faraday's discovery. But his words far outran the frontier. It would be another thirty years before Edison invented the first practical incandescent light bulb in 1879 and opened the world's first power station in 1882.

This station—purposefully located near New York City's Wall Street—generated and transmitted "direct current," which could only be delivered effectively within a one-mile radius. Initially, the Edison company provided *free* electricity, as a way of persuading the conservative denizens of Wall Street to leave behind the tried-and-true energy sources of oil and gas, and pay for more power stations. As the electrification frontier captured people's imagination and pocketbooks, in the 1890s small companies began springing up all over the East to provide direct current power to small areas.

But the geographical limits of direct current made it hard to seize the high ground in electrification—in other words, to achieve economies of scale and capture critical mass. This didn't change until George Westinghouse's "alternating current" caught on in the mid-1890s. The distances efficiently served by alternating current allowed the inevitable march toward industry consolidation to begin.

Some industrial facilities embraced electricity early, but initially, few productivity gains resulted. This was mainly because people continued to walk into the future backward, viewing the future through the lens of their past experiences. Factories were still designed and operated as they had been before electrification, when belt-driven systems—which involved a physical transmission of power from running water (or boiler) to belt to machine—reigned supreme. In that earlier era, the power-intensive work in the factory had to be near the power source, which meant that sequential tasks in the production process might wind up at different ends of the factory. Work in progress had to be hauled all over the plant, despite the fact that moving skids and palettes in a vertically oriented factory building was very difficult.[9]

So, although electricity changed the *source* of the power to the factory, it did not actually change the *factory* until the 1920s, when mindsets changed and new plant designs took better advantage of the new and flexible power source. When this happened, the benefits from the electrification frontier started to compound. But again, three-quarters of a century had already passed since great things were predicted for electricity.

Like the auto industry, the electric utility industry went through an astounding degree of consolidation in a relatively short time. By the late 1920s, three New York financial institutions controlled almost half of the nation's electrical output. In fact, one colorful character, Samuel Insull, controlled an electrical empire that delivered power to more than four thousand communities in thirty states.[10]

Lessons from Past Frontiers

Earlier in this chapter, we introduced three key points: frontiers are volatile and unpredictable, settlers initially walk into the future backward, and there is still gold in those hills. Let's see how past frontiers illustrate these lessons.

Frontiers are Confusing, Volatile, and Unpredictable

Frontiers evolve in thick fog. They conceal facts and breed fiction. It's hard to separate the signal from the noise, with so many people benefiting—both scrupulously and unscrupulously—from the hype of new opportunities and the promise of limitless wealth. It's easy to overreact to the inconsequential, and it's equally easy to miss genuine and enduring changes that may be occurring right under one's nose. Thomas Edison, father of the Victrola, thought that recording music was a silly waste of vinyl.

Frontiers are created by people who see opportunities or who want to solve the problems they perceive. This means that technology and innovation are *social constructs* as much as they are leaps of genius by an inventor. When you add in all the other players who take part in a frontier—such as consumers, capitalists, competitors, labor, and government—you get speculation, economic booms and busts, and high levels of confusion. Figuring out the right comparisons, the right strategy, and the proper objectives is nearly impossible. And yet, organizations have to make choices every day and place their bets.

Emerging frontiers are marketers' dreams. In an atmosphere of excitement, promise, and a lack of restraints, people succumb to the siren songs of hype. As people, companies, industries, and nations set out to exploit a frontier, they tend to make overly optimistic assumptions. They invest heavily (boom!). Inevitably, they overinvest (bust!). The bubble pops, and the pioneers and their backers retrench. Very often, however, the value-creation potential of the frontier remains real, and new waves of pioneers are drawn into the fray, often creating their own boom-and-bust cycles.

Finally, frontiers, like inventions, help prove the law of unintended consequences. The Chinese invented gunpowder to make their celebrations more festive, and inadvertently wound up rewriting the rules of war.[11]

Settlers Walk into the Future Backward

People are people, frontier or no frontier. When they attempt to solve a "new" problem, they almost always begin by trying to apply their past experience, existing mental models, and established ways of doing business to the problem. Ferdinand de Lesseps looked at Panama and saw the Suez. The English immigrants to the New World called their new home "New England"; the first locomotives were "iron horses"; the first cars were "horseless carriages"; and the first TV shows were radio shows with pictures.

Settlers begin their journeys on the frontier with a repertoire of traditions, practices, and beliefs. Eventually, new mind-sets are conceived to take advantage of emerging opportunities. (Remember, Henry Ford didn't invent the automobile; he figured out how to turn it into transportation for the masses.) We argue that the more quickly an organization can cultivate the new mind-sets dictated by its business context, the more quickly it can pivot from walking backward into the future to a forward-facing stance. This creates earlier and greater opportunity for the organization, as it stakes its claim on the future.

Moreover, settlers also take their troubles with them. Frontiers are not panaceas. In fact, if you've got troubles back in civilization, the odds are that you will have the same troubles on the frontier. The future is not a clean slate, and legacy issues don't stay behind. When Humphrey Bogart's character in the movie *Casablanca* moved from Paris to Morocco, he took his problems—such as heartaches and difficulties with authority figures—with him. As today's organizations prepare for the future, they start with whatever position they currently hold on the playing field.

Legal and regulatory institutions also walk backward into the future, often with more tenacity than the business community. Sooner or later, though, the sheriff always comes to town. As Michael Faraday is purported to have said about electricity to Britain's Prime Minister, "Sir, I do not know what it is. But of one thing I am certain: Someday you will tax it."[12] While legal and regulatory frameworks are minimal in the early days, allowing pioneers to celebrate their freedoms, over time the structures of private property, fair competition, and the rules of law make their way to the frontier.

There's Still Gold in Them Thar Hills

Frontiers don't close; they just fade into everyday life. Historian Frederick Jackson Turner wrote in the 1890s about the closing of the American West and the psychological implications of the new "crowding" of the North American continent.[13] But more than a century later, the American West is still rich with innovation and opportunity. As the recent census confirms, many people are still migrating to the American West because they see opportunity in those hills.[14] After several booms and busts, there is still value to be captured. The frontier didn't close; it became part of everyday life.

Frontiers usually open with great excitement, as the low-hanging fruit is discovered and the hype begins. Then there's a period of exploitation, which includes periods of both consolidation and stabilization. This phase may be less glamorous, but it brings forth productivity gains that were not achieved during the heady days. Electricity, for example, really began improving employee productivity almost a half century after its discovery. It took decades for automobiles to become ubiquitous. It's at times like these—the voices from past frontiers counsel us—we must remember that there is still gold in the hills.

Our expectations also change, and what was once "leading edge" becomes everyday. Ford's Model T eventually became a commodity, and GM—sensing opportunity—used brands and planned obsolescence to redefine customer expectations. "Customer service" in a bank used to mean you got to see a bank teller; now it means you *don't* have to see a bank teller. Ultimately, the spectacular becomes routine, as companies mine the frontier's value.

This begs two questions. First, are the largest, Gold Rush–like opportunities associated with the information frontier behind us? Perhaps, but not likely. Most companies, even the most advanced ones, have only begun to tap the opportunities and efficiencies of the Internet. And don't bet against our inventors and engineers, who undoubtedly have surprises in store for us.

Second, have the biggest productivity gains likely to be associated with the information frontier been realized? Since we don't have a crystal ball, the answer has to be, *who knows?*

It often takes decades for a frontier to yield significant improvements in business performance. As Alan Greenspan, U.S. Federal Reserve Board Chairman said, "It may be that the truly significant increases in living standards resulting from the introduction of computers and telecommunications equipment still lie ahead. If true, this would not be unusual."[15] One researcher makes the case that computers and other information-frontier technologies can't affect major productivity gains until they achieve a 50 percent penetration rate. This level was only recently reached in the United States, and it hasn't yet been reached anywhere else in the world.[16]

We believe there are still considerable opportunities, and it will be quite a while before we run up against the law of diminishing returns. Yes, there's still "gold in the hills" to be mined.

We'll return to these three themes throughout this work. Like the pieces of a mosaic that form an overall picture, each of these lessons—present in all frontiers—manifests itself differently to create entirely new environments. Although each frontier is unique, the patterns illustrate how frontiers *rhyme with the past.*

The Information Frontier

Today's business environment is very much like prior frontiers. It's volatile and unpredictable. As settlers, most of us are "walking backward" to automate existing processes. For example, early Internet pages were navigated like books, and instead of putting the word "new" in front of everything, for a time we put an "e." We argue that the mind-set has yet to fully change. If past frontiers are any indication, we are just beginning to take advantage of the new opportunities afforded by the information frontier, and we have exciting and prosperous decades ahead.

But this frontier is also unique, in terms of both its particular moment in history and the technological, social, and economic trends that have produced and are defining it. To live comfortably as settlers, we need to understand its *individuality.* Our aim is to distill the underlying trends of the information frontier without getting distracted by the most recent boom or bust of the cycle. First, a restatement of a notion introduced earlier: Today's frontier is *not* a technology, or even a group of technologies. Yes, it is fueled and enabled by technology, but it is not limited to the computer, the Internet, or any other technological advancement.

With this in mind, let's look a little more deeply at the four defining characteristics of the information frontier. The first of these is *organizational transparency.* Transparency refers to the fact that organizations have become easier to see into and out of. On this frontier, extraordinary amounts of information are available on a reasonably democratic basis. In the past, upper-level managers could shape and channel information and distribute it on a "need to know" basis. Today, it is more likely that everyone in and around the organization can get too much data.

Given this attenuation of traditional controls on data flow and dissemination, information has become infinitely more available. When it comes to things like underlying product cost, customer-facing pricing, business relationships, managerial behaviors, and channels, the Internet replaces secrecy with transparency. Transparency shines a harsh spotlight on an organization's weakest links, and companies are compelled

UNIQUE CHARACTERISTICS OF THE
INFORMATION FRONTIER

- Organizational transparency
- Velocity
- Reduced transactional friction
- Role blurring

to fix problems that might otherwise have stayed in the shadows. As David Kirkpatrick, a senior editor for *Fortune,* has commented, "The house of business will be built of glass."[17]

The second characteristic is *velocity.* In the narrow sense, this refers to the speed at which ubiquitous information travels from place to place. But more generally, velocity refers to the telescoping of time. Things happen faster than they did previously—and continue to accelerate. When people talk about living on "Internet time," they are talking about making more and more decisions under the gun, in real time, with greater uncertainty.

The information frontier changes the way we think about time. More things *can* be done in "real time," and therefore *must* be done in real time. It used to be, for example, that purchasing customized computers took a lot of time and a lot of money. Dell and Gateway now deliver them to our doors in a matter of days. Initially, we view this as a valuable differentiating service; but over time, our expectations are permanently adjusted to expect things at ever-faster rates. From procurement to product development to production and delivery, time is being compressed and telescoped.

A third defining feature of the information frontier is *the opportunity for reduced transactional friction.* By this we simply mean that the costs of contracting, communicating, and coordinating required to execute a transaction are being significantly reduced.[18] Information moves more quickly today because the platforms exchanging data have become (1) more robust, (2) more efficient, and (3) more standardized. But stronger and better platforms, used by more and more people, also mean that there can be closer integration among constituents. In other words, the friction inherent in transacting across boundaries can be reduced.

Finally, the information frontier is characterized by *role blurring*. This is a natural outgrowth of, and contributor to, reduced transactional friction. In today's economy, your supplier may also be partner, customer, competitor, owner—or all of the above.

Like previous frontiers, the information frontier has changed the way we think about space and distance. Throughout this book, we will talk about the information frontier as if it were a physical space. This approach strikes us as a more useful mental model than talking about, for example, an "information age." An "age" is something that happens to you, and to which you accommodate yourself. A frontier, by contrast, *calls for action.* We want you to think about, adapt for, and act upon the realities of frontier living.

So think of the information frontier as the business context, or backdrop, to which we offer our response. In subsequent chapters, we bring this perspective to bear on the very practical challenge of better aligning an organization while at the same time adapting it for these uncertain times.

Traits: The Mind-Set for the Information Frontier

On frontiers, as we've seen, settlers initially walk into the future backward until they develop a new mental model—a mind-set that equips them to perceive and respond to frontier-related opportunities. This thinking leads to new behaviors and actions, resulting in a more efficient and productive pattern of settlement.

Traits, introduced in chapter 1 and discussed in greater detail in chapter 3, represent the organizational mind-sets that companies need to prosper on the present frontier. They take full advantage of the frontier's dynamic, networked connections, information flows, and relationships and are derived from the unique characteristics of this frontier— organizational transparency, velocity, reduced transactional friction, and role blurring.

Frontier living requires companies to act, respond, and invest precisely at the greatest moment of uncertainty. Decisions are fraught with risk. In this way, traits help companies respond with greater clarity.

How so? The simple answer is that the right mind-set goes a long way toward helping a settler adapt to whatever the frontier dishes up. An outdated model, mental or otherwise, often drives inappropriate and/or inadequate responses.

Although our definition of traits may sound new, most organizations are no stranger to the concepts behind the term. The good news is that this stuff is *real*, and it works. Companies are now making the kinds of innovations that embody the traits we discuss, reflect the realities of life on the frontier, and create shareholder value. Supply chains and information networks pass information seamlessly. Innovative models of collaboration for selling new business are emerging. Organizations are better integrated internally, with systems that render the business more efficient, responsive, and speedy. To cite just one example: Have you sent a package using the UPS or FedEx Web site recently? These sites do everything but wrap the package for you.

In the following sections, we briefly describe how traits help to achieve alignment. In chapter 3, we further describe these traits and see them in action.

Traits and Alignment

When we talked in chapter 1 about an organization's intentions, we introduced a version of figure 2-1, which we now expand to include each of the four traits.

Again, we encourage you to think of your organization's intentions in three categories: short-term objectives, long-term objectives, and trait objectives. Trait objectives represent the organization's commitment to the mind-sets that will get it in line with the realities of frontier living. We represent traits as a triangle to differentiate this priority from traditional objectives.

Let's be clear. When we say "traits," we mean distinct qualities or attributes. Traits are not project goals or technical requirements, though they contribute to both (e.g., you typically wouldn't launch a project called "Instill Outside-In"). They are not processes or capabilities, though changed mind-sets often result in a new view of which processes and capabilities merit investment. Our notion is to develop traits by leveraging existing activities, rather than by launching new initiatives.

Figure 2-1: Intentions Framework with Traits Added

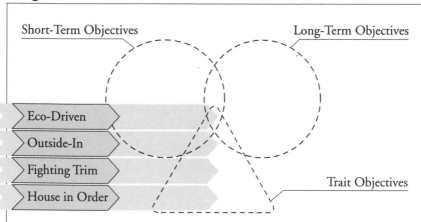

Companies are already grappling with how to respond to the discontinuities and opportunities of the evolving frontier. Defining trait objectives gives form to these challenges. Trait objectives give the organization a concrete way to express, focus, and measure accomplishments in this sometimes elusive realm.

By specifying traits as a third, explicit objective, the organization begins building the characteristics necessary to adapt to and take advantage of the opportunities on the information frontier. It also begins to focus more tangibly and expressly on the *interrelatedness* of the three sets of objectives, so that the impact of decisions can be better understood. At the same time, traits raise organizational awareness. They act as both a reminder and reinforcement of the organizational mind-set shift that we, as settlers, are trying to achieve. They even explain why some of the things you're already doing make sense—and why some may not.

Six Truths about Traits

Consistent with the value proposition that we've articulated for this book—long on context and synthesis; short on grand concepts—we want to make the traits accessible and useful to you, and have them serve as a tool that plugs the organization into today's realities. Traits can be used to create new objectives for the organization as well as to evaluate the design and implementation of your current portfolio of projects. And finally, we want the traits to serve as a fixed point of reference in a constantly changing landscape. Let's frame the discussion by making some general observations about traits.

Traits require care and feeding. Building traits is not something you do over a weekend, in a month, or over the course of a year. Nor is it something you can delegate down the food chain. Traits require cultivation and attention by organizational leaders over a longer period of time—most likely *by you,* if you're reading this book.

Don't think about the incorporation of traits as a radical, one-time event. Most likely, trait development in your organization will begin as a series of small changes—but through commitment and attention over time, the traits will flow throughout the organization.

Traits overlap. Traits are not self-contained, discrete concepts. Ideally, they work together, complementing and reinforcing each other in a myriad of ways. In fact, achieving new mind-sets and enduring behavior changes can't be done with lots of "hard borders" to block them. For simplicity's sake, keep in mind while we call out the traits and explain them one by one, the walls between them are porous indeed.

Traits are context-driven. What they mean to you will depend on the specifics of your environment, corporate culture, industry, competitive positioning, place within the larger landscape, and of course, your good judgment. And while we believe that all four traits apply to all types of organizations, their relative importance and the ways in which they apply vary widely according to individual circumstances.

Traits are not new. As we will demonstrate, leading companies are already committed to adapting to the frontier. We find evidence of these traits—and also of their absence—all around. Your company is likely to have some initiatives under way that at least partially reflect the traits. One of our goals is to bring these efforts into sharp relief.

Traits are a complement, not a substitute. Management-oriented authors often tout their ideas as a substitute for what you are doing today. They suggest (and at times, even demand) that you change your agenda and refocus the organization to take advantage of a "dynamic new platform for change," or whatever new buzzwords apply. In real life, though, you still need to run your business *today* for your customers, shareholders, and employees, and no expert out there knows more about what that means than you do.

Our Intentions Framework acknowledges the need to keep your eye on today, as well as tomorrow. As explained earlier, settlers do not start with a clean slate. Established companies take their legacy—systems, culture, processes—with them as they settle on the frontier. So reality "gets in the way," at least until we find a way to turn this constraint into an advantage.

The triangle eventually goes away. Friedrich Engels, that old Communist, made an interesting assertion about democracy—that it was only necessary as long as there were social classes. (Once people stopped being oppressed by capitalists, Engels wrote, the need for democratic governments would wither away.) We feel the same way about our "traits triangle": Once the frontier fades into everyday life and traits are woven into the very fabric of an organization—absorbed into the organization's short- and long-term objectives—they will become second nature and won't need to be explicitly stated anymore. Until, of course, the next round of discontinuity is served up to us.

An industry-specific example of this transition dating back to the early 1980s is afforded by the U.S. automakers, which then were getting trounced by their Japanese competitors. Belatedly, the Big Three realized that they had to embrace the mind-set (or traits) that governed how the Japanese manufactured cars. This meant abandoning traditional mind-sets (quality can be engineered at the end of the line) and embrace new ones (quality is everyone's responsibility, up and down the line).

These mind-set changes led to the acceptance by U.S. manufacturers of lean manufacturing practices, similar to those of their Asian competitors. (If you fix your process and information flows, you don't need all that expensive and obsolescing inventory lying around.) So for the next decade or so, the U.S. auto industry effectively had a trait objective— attaining the mind-set of lean manufacturing. (Ford's employees, for example, spent a decade reciting the mantra, "Quality is Job 1.") Gradually, those traits were woven into the organizations' thinking. Figuratively speaking, the "triangle" moved up and was absorbed into both their short- and long-term objectives.

A Bird's-Eye View of the Traits

With this background, let's take a quick fly-by of the four traits emphasizing their interrelatedness.

> Eco-Driven   Seeing your relationships as assets, and collaboration as a means to effective competition. This often includes proactive participation in *value networks* with a confluence of players—including suppliers, channel partners, customers, and similar business partners.

> Outside-In   Seeing your organization as others experience it and deliberately informing business processes, structures, and information flows toward these needs. The Outside-In perspective takes a hard look at what it's like to do business with the guy in the mirror.

> Fighting Trim   The willingness and ability to be "knowledgeably nimble" in a constantly shifting landscape, and the resolve to take rapid action in response to new information, uncertainty, and continually changing external factors.

> House in Order   An efficient, streamlined *intra*enterprise operation that, in turn, provisions the other traits and makes possible *cross-*enterprise cooperation. A House in Order organization displays a *change-ready,* rather than a change-weary, mind-set. It provides the behaviors, systems, and tools that allow the organization to listen to its constituents, its markets, its industry, and itself, in an environment where "the art of the possible" keeps changing.

As we have seen, at the end of the nineteenth century and beginning of the twentieth century, managers were faced with the challenges of introducing and capitalizing upon earlier frontiers. The initial incorporation of innovations focused on incremental improvements to existing facilities and processes—in other words, looking for ways to do familiar things better, cheaper, faster, and smarter. Gradually, however, these settlers realized that they could more radically and fundamentally reconfigure their businesses and foment dramatic change.

Revolutions are initially sparked in places like Edison's Menlo Park lab, Ford's garage, or Jefferson's White House. But history tells us that the real benefits of frontiers are realized only when forward-looking settlers *change their mind-sets* about the opportunities: the factory manager who envisions the productivity gains of rearranging the shop floor, or the leader who sees scale opportunity in the mass markets.

Someday, history will decide when the information frontier started, got settled, and faded into everyday life. But the important lesson for the present day lies elsewhere. Seizing this frontier is the job of forward-looking leaders and managers. To mix our frontier metaphors, we're no longer in the waterwheel stage, but psychologically speaking, we're still huddled in our vertically oriented brick factories alongside the mill pond. Undoubtedly, we've got a long way to go and a lot of opportunity to harvest.

With modest investment, mostly in time, plus a lot of discipline and commitment, any organization can achieve better alignment of its future currency (its project portfolio) with what it wants to achieve (its corporate objectives), in a manner responsive to our unpredictable times. In chapter 3, we further explore how to better adapt to frontier living through a more detailed discussion of traits.

3

a primer on traits

I think there is a world market for maybe five computers.

THOMAS WATSON SR., CHAIRMAN OF IBM, 1943

If Thomas Watson, one of the true pioneers of the information frontier, proved unable to predict the future, how can the typical settler hope to do any better?

We believe settlers *can* do better—not by predicting more accurately, but by adapting more deliberately for the future environment. Embracing the traits we've defined is a way of adapting, by developing the mind-sets needed to thrive on the information frontier.

Traits work at numerous levels of an organization, from setting specific trait objectives, to evaluating how an organization is functioning, to influencing the design of individual projects as well as the overall project portfolio. At each level, we can use traits to convert the distinctive aspects of today's business context into tangible changes inside the organization. By applying traits in multiple ways, the organization is more flexible and, therefore, more adaptable—a prerequisite for both achieving and maintaining alignment.

In this chapter, we pick up where we left off in chapter 2 and further explore each trait through case examples, summarizing key points as we go. We'll also introduce our first diagnostic tool, the Trait Meter. This tool gives measurable definition to trait mind-sets, helping companies gauge their relevance and plan and track their development.

As noted earlier, traits overlap and reinforce each other and can't (or shouldn't) be pursued or practiced in isolation. To underscore this point, toward the end of the chapter we offer the case of Li & Fung, which illustrates how individual traits reinforce one other. We'll then return to the Trait Meter tool and walk through how to set trait objectives for your organization. But first, let's describe the elements of the trait meter and how it can be useful.

Introducing Trait Meters

These trait meters translate the principles of each trait into a practical tool that helps companies assess, plan, and track their development of traits within their industry context. Each Trait Meter is portrayed as a spectrum (see figure 3-1). The lower end of the spectrum marks the baseline level needed to gain entry into or participate in a market. The higher end is defined by the leading edge of innovation—either as defined by the behavior of market leaders in a specific industry or by the introduction of innovation across industries and markets.

Specifically, the *baseline* at the far left of the scale describes a "commonplace" company, which defines competitive parity because many companies achieve this level of trait expression. The center (medium) point describes a company breaking away from the pack of baseline companies. And the *leading edge* at the far right describes companies that are generally recognized across industries as "best practice" firms.

It's important to note that neither end of the spectrum is fixed over time. The lower end continually moves upward, spurred on both by competitive pressures and opportunities for doing new things in new ways, or—said another way—for evolving along with the "art of the possible." The high end also evolves, in response to leading-edge innovation.

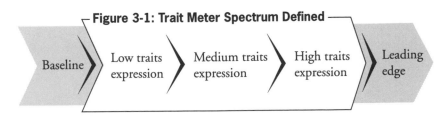

Figure 3-1: Trait Meter Spectrum Defined

Baseline ⟩ Low traits expression ⟩ Medium traits expression ⟩ High traits expression ⟩ Leading edge

So Trait Meters are snapshots of specific moments, and a series of these snapshots will inevitably show change over time.

> Eco-Driven

As transactional and coordination friction declines, the choices about which activities are performed inside and outside the firm begin to shift. Companies are finding it increasingly necessary and advantageous to have others (partners, suppliers, customers, etc.) do for them what they once did for themselves. An Eco-Driven approach more closely connects the company and its partners. This greater connectivity—done right—reduces cycle times and costs, improves flexibility, and facilitates innovation. Eco-Driven companies view their network of relationships as an asset, in line with the shifting basis of competition from a linear, one-way *value chain* to a multidirectional, dynamic *value network*.

The velocity of the environment compels companies to develop partnerships that help them get to market more quickly. As organizations partner, their new relationships reduce friction and create opportunities, but these virtual networks also make the partners more interdependent and mutually transparent.

Furthermore, the blurring of roles creates situations in which your customer may also be your competitor, your competitor may be your "complementor," or your supplier may be your distributor. The realities of this strange new universe are detailed in Adam Brandenburger's and Barry Nalebuff's book, *Co-opetition.* The book cites the example of Intel's $100 million investment in a videophone system to create a new market for Intel's own Pentium Pro chip—a move that actually helped archrival Picturetel by creating a far larger market for *all* videophones.[1] "Attitudes have changed to become comfortable with a duality," Brandenburger explains, "and the duality is that between competition and cooperation."[2]

By making informed decisions on potential collaborators and then developing these relationships, companies spread risk, pool capital, tap into special expertise, share learning, and enter new markets. They become springboards for one another's ideas, creating more innovation together than they could accomplish alone.

WHAT IS A "VIRTUAL NETWORK"?

Networks of actors (producers, suppliers, distributors, etc.) now carry out communications and transactions through the Internet and other electronic media, making geographical boundaries and time zones transparent. Operational and administrative functions—and associated resources—are farmed out, and business activity is conducted through these relationships. The epicenter of the network—the core unit—may only own unique business processes and leverage brands, rather than produce complete products. In effect, vertical integration is replaced by virtual integration.[3]

General Principles of Eco-Driven

As companies work to intelligently view and cultivate their value networks and relationships as key assets, they should give particular consideration to two key principles: (1) focus on core competencies and strategic assets; and (2) foster collaboration.

A focus on core competencies and strategic assets. This is an old lesson, of course, but it has been made more urgent with the onset of the information frontier. With the increased speed and value demanded by today's markets, few companies can both provide core offerings and quickly take advantage of new market trends on their own. As organizations ponder how to make their value networks sources of greater shareholder value, they often find that it's useful to identify both core and non-core activities in addition to the strategic assets they possess. Then, working both alone and in partnership, they develop competitive advantage and marketplace differentiation. This approach sharpens focus within the company and increases a company's agility in responding to changes in the business environment.

One note of caution here: Take care not to outsource your strategic options. If you do, the cost can be high. Think IBM in the early 1980s, when it handed off the PC operating system to Microsoft and the chip business to Intel. Picking and choosing among alternative futures is never a simple task, especially when settling a frontier.

On the other hand, when companies focus it can be enormously rewarding. For example, when a global manufacturer's consumer products division decided to enter the personal electronics marketplace, it recognized from the outset that it needed an OEM supplier even though the partner's core competency would overlap with its own. The main reason was *timing*. It wanted to capitalize on a budding consumer trend and—if drawing only on internal resources—would not be able to design and manufacture the product in time to hit the holiday season. So they sought out a contract manufacturer, and then used their own brand and distribution channels to launch a competitive product on a tight schedule. This collaboration was only one in a series. The operating model of the group is to find partners to better ride consumer trends. "We have modularly designed—rather than hard-coded—our business model," explains the CIO of this company's consumer products division.[4]

Many companies are building better competencies through partnerships. These partnering arrangements are most successful when a company is at subcritical mass in a particular area. DuPont, for example, considers IT to be one of its three core skills. Nevertheless, the chemical giant outsourced three-quarters of its IT positions in the belief that fulfilling these hard-to-develop competencies externally would be a smarter strategy.[5]

The examples illustrated here reflect a related trend toward Business Process Outsourcing (BPO). BPO provides companies with the ability to focus while providing new options for building capabilities, achieving speed to market, or gaining new levels of efficiency. The convergence of outsourcing, contract manufacturing, and consulting, BPO moves entire functions and processes outside the organization, creating new hybrid extended enterprises.

Take Bank of America (BofA) as an example. BofA recently completed the process of moving their entire HR function outside the organization—a partnership worth potentially more than $1 billion. Service to BofA's one hundred fifty thousand associates will now be provided by a strategic partner, allowing its management to both reduce cost and focus attention on what it does best—running a banking institution.[6]

BPO allows an organization to assemble core capabilities through the extension of its value network, a further indication that companies increasingly view competition as occurring between value networks

BUSINESS PROCESS OUTSOURCING (BPO)

> Business Process Outsourcing is becoming big business. Estimates for the total value of BPO range from $200 to $300 billion by 2006.[7]

rather than individual firms. To understand the broader dynamics of how such value network competition can play out, let's consider the case of Hanes versus Fruit of the Loom. In 1996, Hanes was a classic vertically integrated company with a highly diverse product line: men's innerwear, intimates, sportswear, and accessories. Fruit of the Loom, the company's longtime rival, was then a stand-alone firm, but otherwise was very similar to Hanes: vertically integrated with similar product lines and market share. Each company held a 35 percent market share of the boys' and men's innerwear category.[8]

Among its many other effects, the passage of the North American Free Trade Agreement (NAFTA) in 1994 liberalized trade restrictions on processed products such as yarn and fabric—the principal raw materials in the innerwear product category. Lower wage rates in a labor-intensive industry, coupled with the reduction and eventual elimination of tariffs and quotas, soon made it necessary for U.S. companies to transfer the bulk of their apparel production to Mexico. Changes at home, too, were undermining the innerwear industry's traditional practices. Since 1995, there had been more than six hundred horizontal mergers in the retail industry; as a result, the newly consolidated retailers were able to push for better prices, just-in-time (JIT) deliveries, vendor managed inventory (VMI), and electronic data interchange (EDI).[9]

In the face of NAFTA and major global forces, Hanes "de-verticalized," as they called it, selling off thirteen North American manufacturing operations.[10] The goal was to focus on its core strengths of building and managing leadership brands. By 1999, Hanes had divested its operations by outsourcing its yarn and textile operations. The result: The company increased its market share and saved tens of millions of dollars. By contrast, in a vain effort to keep owning and doing it all, Fruit of the Loom fell into bankruptcy.[11]

FIVE FACTS ABOUT COLLABORATION

The following five statements summarize the realities of working together on the information frontier:

1. Collaboration is gaining momentum across most industries.

2. Private networks built on open standards will be the dominant collaborative method that companies use to enable value creation.

3. Companies are leveraging collaborative capabilities to deliver both strategic and operational advantage.

4. Collaborating with customers is just as important as collaborating with suppliers.

5. Successful collaborative implementation is much more than technology.[12]

Foster collaboration. The word *collaboration* is derived from the Latin word *collaborare,* which means "to labor together." It's about a way of working together over time, as opposed to one-time transactions. Until recently, the average company's opportunities to collaborate were limited. The reasons? It was simply too costly and difficult to effectively share decision making, workflows, and information. Beyond that obstacle, lurked the problem of compatible mind-sets. Like Fruit of the Loom, all too many companies are poor at collaboration because they are reticent to share pricing and other key data with partners and, oftentimes, simply have a fear of letting go.

On the information frontier, however, this is changing. Companies of all shapes and sizes are implementing collaborative commerce tools and processes by providing customers, suppliers, and design teams with real-time access to critical data. These companies collaborate on product innovation, share information, and pool intellectual capital on a global basis, which helps them identify conflicts early in the design process, thereby reducing rework, cycle time, required resources, and costs.

As a result, collaboration is not merely a "nice to have" element, but a growing competitive necessity. We wrote earlier about a company's

COLLABORATIVE FACTS

Companies that both leverage their collaborative supply chains and demonstrate a deep understanding of their loyal customers are

- 54 percent more profitable than companies with strong supply chain collaboration but lackluster customer loyalty, and

- 70 percent more profitable than companies that perform below average on both supply chain collaboration and customer loyalty.[13]

value network—the shared asset that sustains, and is sustained by, the Eco-Driven mind-set. Collaboration is the lubricant that keeps the value network engine humming. Collaboration helps companies change the pattern and quality of the connections they have to one another, to their mutual benefit. Dozens of companies have engaged Cleveland-based Hummer Whole Health Management to take over their employee health plans.[14] A company that successfully taps the power of its ecosystem can collaborate with players up, down, and across the value network—and dynamically manage the resulting relationships.

The concept of collaboration, of course, predates recorded history. (Our earliest prehistoric ancestors collaborated by hunting in two groups: Some drove the herd of deer off the cliff while the rest waited at the bottom with clubs and spears.) But as time telescopes, and as the technological component of innovation intensifies, collaboration takes on a new and multidirectional meaning.

One of the most dramatic illustrations in recent years was the collaborative design of the one hundred and thirty thousand unique engineered parts of the Boeing 777. The breadth and complexity of this collaboration—238 teams across 17 time zones—accomplished largely in cyberspace, was unprecedented.[15] According to one account, Boeing designed its 777 by electronically sharing design tools and processes with engineers, customers, maintenance people, project managers, and component suppliers across the globe. No physical model. No paper blueprints. The 777, one observer commented, is a "bunch of parts flying together in close formation."[16]

ECO-DRIVEN COLLABORATION

Eco-Driven collaboration already has a foothold in nine key areas:

- Demand planning
- Channel management
- Product design
- Product innovation
- Relationship management
- Crisis management
- Supply chain planning and scheduling
- Warehousing and fulfillment
- Customer relationships

One result is speed to market. Boeing's customers no longer have to wait three years for a plane. Through its private, collaborative e-marketplace, Boeing aims to deliver a plane in eight to twelve months.[17]

This is collaboration on a grand scale. But even with only modest investments, collaboration now works for a wide range of companies. Let's consider the case of faucet-maker Moen. Turn on a faucet and water comes out. Pretty simple, right? Well, yes and no. A faucet is not a 777, but it nevertheless consists of hundreds of parts, and all kinds of engineers, manufacturers, planners, designers, and suppliers are required to bring those parts together.

In the mid-1990s, there was a surge of demand for faucets that were decorative as well as functional. Suddenly, chrome was out; silver, platinum, and copper were in. Moen realized that its tradition of introducing one new faucet line a year would have to go. Instead, they needed to come up with a way to design multiple new products—and fast. To their credit, Moen's executives resisted the temptation to spend their way out of a bind and change everything all at once. They looked for a more Eco-Driven way to solve their product-introduction problem.

In the past, Moen's designers sent drawings of a new faucet to parts suppliers in fourteen countries, who made one or more of the hundreds of parts that would go into the new faucet. Inevitably, suppliers made changes, sent the drawings back to the designers, and the whole process started all over again. This kind of iterative exchange extended the design process up to sixteen weeks or longer—unacceptably long, in the newly fast-moving faucet marketplace.[18]

So the company looked to the Web. Moen replaced the use of overnight mail, phone calls, and faxes with an online site for communication with suppliers called SupplyNet. Through SupplyNet, Moen's product development teams gained the ability to communicate and collaborate interactively with Moen's worldwide supply chain.[19] This not only sped up communications, but also transformed the product design and manufacturing processes.

Today, Moen posts a 3-D design of a new faucet online, where all suppliers worldwide have access to it. Every supplier can display and update engineering drawings and access documentation related to new product projects earlier in the design phase. Design problems are discovered early, cutting the time to lock in a final design to three days, and ultimately improving both product quality and speed to market. These time savings make it possible for Moen's engineers to work on three times as many projects and introduce from five to fifteen faucet lines a year.[20]

Next, the company attacked the cumbersome process of ordering parts from suppliers by extending SupplyNet. Suppliers can now check the status of Moen's orders online, be alerted to changes, and inform Moen of out-of-stock orders.[21]

Moen has benefited considerably from collaborating on designs with suppliers online and automating its ordering process. Even as Moen provides customers more product choices, its collaboration with suppliers has reduced inventory by 20 to 50 percent. Moreover, getting to market faster has boosted sales by 17 percent since 1998—almost twice the average industry increase of 9 percent over the same period. Moen has jumped from number three in market share to a tie for number one (with archrival Delta Faucet). And this change has come at a relatively low cost. To date, Moen's Web work has cost only $1.5 million, meaning that its Internet initiatives have paid for themselves many times, which equates to increased shareholder value. In an industry traditionally slow to adopt new technologies, this inexpensive embrace of Web-based collaboration has turned the company from industry-average to industry-leading.[22]

Figure 3-2: Eco-Driven Trait Meter

Value network begins to emerge; individual organizational units begin to partner with others

Core value understood and informs priorities; some non-core activities move outside of firm

Periodic, event-based information exchange with value chain partners

Value network strengthens; company proactively manages some relationships and the company's connections to them

Increasing understanding of and focus on core activities; a variety of non-core activities move outside of firm

Begins to collaborate with key partners

Value network is an asset; company proactively manages pattern and quality of relationships and connections among them

Highly focused on core activities

Collaborates seamlessly and extensively across value network

Quick Review

Let's review the general principles of Eco-Driven.

- *Understand your network of relationships as a key asset.* As the information frontier continues to unfold, the velocity, transparency, and role blurring of the environment is moving the basis of competition from the individual company to the value network. Companies must proactively embrace this structural shift.

- *Identify and focus on your strategic assets and core competencies.* As companies look at their value network, they need to understand the role they play in that network and how they contribute to creating value. At the same time, of course, they must worry about retaining and enhancing the qualities that *differentiate* themselves from others in their networks.

- *Foster collaboration within your value network.* The reduction of transaction friction and availability of information are creating new opportunities to collaborate and create value. Both factors are, equally, raising the stakes.

Take a moment to think about where your company is on the Eco-Driven spectrum (see figure 3-2). Later in this chapter, we'll go through a brief exercise designed to develop some trait objectives for your organization.

> Outside-In >

Outside-In is a mind-set that helps organizations form more productive relationships with key constituencies by looking in the mirror—by seeing themselves as their constituencies do. Why is this important? Because compared to the constant acquisition of new customers and other constituencies, engendering loyalty is relatively cheap. A recent study of the financial services industry, for example, showed that it costs *ten times more* to sell an identical product to a new customer than to an existing customer.[23]

Although most companies talk about being "customer focused" and many have been implementing customer-centric activities for some time, Outside-In extends the concept in two important ways. First, the universe of "constituencies" is greater than that of "customers." This is an important distinction, given the role blurring that characterizes the information frontier. J. W. Marriott Jr., the chairman of Marriott International, recently spoke to this point when he likened his employees to his customers: "In the service sector, we know that consumers today are buying not only products, they're buying experiences. And that's what workers are buying when they shop for a job."[24]

This points toward our second observation about this trait. Outside-In is not about building *processes* that are constituency-centric; rather, it is about building *experiences*. Experiences are the result of a series of positive interactions with a company that build loyalty over time.

Ultimately, Outside-In improves experiences and strengthens the bottom line. Take the example of Hallmark Cards, which is using a 24/7 online community called "Idea Exchange" to gain more insight into its customers. To that site, the company invited 150 carefully selected consumers—about half of whom were Hallmark shoppers, and half of whom were not—to gather virtually and share ideas like recipes or decorating tips, discuss issues of interest to members, and even make friends. Hallmark also posted pictures of product concepts, card designs, and advertisements soliciting feedback.[25]

The results? For one thing, *quick turnaround*. Hallmark heard back from consumers on a specific topic within forty-eight hours.[26] Also, the company discovered an unexpected side benefit to giving customers a voice in the company's product decisions. The online community is spending five times more than before on Hallmark products.[27]

This particular online community is small, of course, and Hallmark still uses other types of market surveys to determine broad trends. But by observing these kinds of online chats—rather than relying exclusively on formal surveys—the company learned to *look at the world as its customers do,* gaining the kind of insight into their lives and latent needs that really aids the product development process. "We're trying to establish a dialogue with the marketplace. . . . We have an unprecedented view into their lives," said Thomas Brailsford, Hallmark's manager of knowledge leadership. Since the original site launched, Hallmark has added two more communities—one for Hispanics and one for grandparents.[28]

Why is this ongoing dialogue important? The obvious answer is that it improves new-product development. But looking more broadly—looking Outside-In—it also builds relationships. Because of the transparency of the frontier, customers today can easily examine their alternatives and "switch horses" the instant a better value proposition comes along.

Companies that embrace Outside-In create barriers to switching by building long-term relationships, especially with their most-valued constituencies. The more you can demonstrate your value to your constituencies—the thicker the webs of transaction and information

WHAT IS A CONSTITUENCY?

Based on the Outside-In perspective, "constituencies" are broadly defined and include:

- Customers
- Employees
- Investors
- Suppliers
- Business partners
- Alumni
- Community
- Regulators
- Industry analysts
- Other stakeholders

links—the higher the exit hurdle. This prevents margin erosion due to competitive sales pricing pressures and reduces the cost of future sales.

The constituency value most businesses deliver today is "table stakes"—the price they have to pay simply to be in the game. And those stakes are continually rising. As James Miller, director of Internet strategy for the American Cancer Society, puts it, "Customer expectations continually evolve, and you have to meet those expectations."[29] The information frontier is pushing companies to discard their legacy inside-out processes and practices, and embrace Outside-In as part of their organizational agendas.

To achieve Outside-In, *think interaction, not transaction.* This is how your constituents think. To the customer, for example, a bank deposit is not a transaction that has an input and an output, is processed within a prescribed time frame, or fits into multiple sets of aggregate statistics. Instead, it's *a personal interaction.* The customer remembers things like how easy it was to find parking, how long the line was, whether there was money available through the ATM over a holiday weekend, and how quickly the deposit showed up in her checking account.

If a company doesn't understand the customer's view of an interaction, it can't spend its money on enhancements that have the most value to that customer. A simple example from Duke Energy illustrates this point. In building a new Web site, Duke Energy reached out to its customers and found that they simply didn't value many of the proposed features the company planned to develop. As one Duke Energy executive explained it, "I had some fantastic things I wanted to put on [the site], but the customers said, 'That's great, but *this* is what I need today.'"[30]

When Outside-In is "baked into" the corporate culture, business processes and policies *open up,* rather than close off, the organization. Companies with an Outside-In perspective create appropriate training, financial incentives, nonfinancial recognition, and evaluation metrics to promote a constituency-centric culture. They implement measures whereby they demonstrate their commitment to the constituency experience. This perspective also equips the company to take full advantage of Eco-Driven trends. Customers become valued collaborators who can help open up the company to new directions.

FedEx, mentioned earlier, provides a great illustration—particularly because some of the best arguments in favor of Outside-In, in that company, come from the FedEx IT department. (Too many companies develop a customer focus exclusively in their sales, marketing, and service functions, rather than through the entire company. It's an understandable misstep, but still, a lost opportunity.) At FedEx, CIO Robert B. Carter explains, the IT team "feels empowered to drive solutions through to the customer, but the initiator of change is our customer."[31] Senior technical advisor Alex Vergos in IT agrees: "I get all kinds of encouragement to think more creatively, to do more for the customer. The company doesn't push me from behind; they pull me from the front."[32]

The focus of a project isn't the only thing that changes when you start thinking from an Outside-In perspective. The way that projects are managed also changes. For example, in a traditional project implementation approach, the CIO's domain is technology implementation. Well, consider this dialog among Staples executives, as related by John Mahoney, executive vice president and chief administrative officer:

> We're putting kiosks in our stores to help our store associates sell expanded products and services. The CIO is responsible for that project, and when we talked about the technology, the CEO asked, "Are the kiosks going to face the customer?" The CIO replied, "Well, uh, boy . . . that's Operation's answer." The CEO said, "No, it's not. Your job is not to put technology in the store. Your job is to drive a new program for the business."[33]

Over time, interactions lead constituents to form cumulative attitudes toward your company. Customers may interact with a company through a variety of channels, such as Web sites, storefronts, and call centers. They also tend to interact with multiple functional areas, such as sales, customer service, and accounts payable. Many businesses treat these processes as discrete, but in the customer's mind such interactions are inevitably interconnected. Too often, companies present more than one face to the customer, making it appear that the left hand does not know what the right is doing and damaging the overall experience.

Put more simply, a constituent's attitude toward your company comes from his or her *history with your entire company*—not just his or her interactions with the call center or Web site, and not just yesterday. Smart companies understand that *constituents have long memories.*

An Outside-In company structures its activities through the eyes of its constituencies. This means that the company is proactive about *building the entire constituency relationship holistically,* rather than merely responding to opportunities on an isolated or ad hoc basis. Constituency needs drive the central attitudes, processes, and approaches of the company.

Consider the example of Sears. The company has designed both its store and online operations to make life easier for the customer. At Sears.com, for example, customers can do side-by-side product comparisons before clicking to buy tools or appliances. Many visitors use the site to gather information before heading to the Sears store at their local mall. "We hear story after story about customers who go to the Web site, research what they want, print it out, and bring it to the sales associate," says Dennis Honan, vice president and general manager of Chicago-based Sears.com. Web site customers can also apply for a Sears credit card, get instant approval online, and apply it to the electronic transaction in progress—or to any later purchase, online or off. Says Honan, "Our mission is to make it easy for our customers to do business with us, regardless of how they do it."[34]

Many airline Web sites (for example, Britishairways.com) have adopted a similar strategy. The sites generate high traffic levels, in part because they are great information sources. And although relatively few visits convert directly into sold tickets, many users of the site plan their trips online and then book flights by calling the airline directly, working through their travel agent, or transacting with other Web sites. Again, the goal is to make it easy to do business with the sponsoring airline, no matter how customers choose to pursue the transaction.

Quick Review

Let's review the general principles of Outside-In:

- *Look at the face in the mirror.* Companies begin the process of facing Outside-In by looking at how constituencies experience the organization. This, in turn, influences how the company operates.

- *Migrate from transaction to interaction.* Think of exchanges with constituencies as interactions in extended relationships, rather than

Figure 3-3: Outside-In Trait Meter

Reactive: reacts to constituent feedback	*Proactive:* asks for input and acts on it	*Engaged:* two-way, continuous dialogue
Transaction focus	*Interaction focus*	*Experience focus* across channels, business processes, and organizational boundaries
Variable experience across channels, business processes, and organizational boundaries such as departments, divisions, or ecosystem partners	*More uniform experience* across channels, business processes, and organizational boundaries such as departments, divisions, or ecosystem partners	*Relationships are assets*

as simply transactions, and build organizational "memory" to enhance future encounters and increase switching costs.

- *Build interactions into experiences that engender loyalty.* Over time, companies progress even further to actively managing constituency experiences, which strongly influences extended relationships and loyalty. Loyal constituencies help increase revenue cost effectively through cross- and up-selling and through referrals of new customers, minimizing the costly process of customer acquisition.

Once again, take a moment and begin to think about where you are on the Trait Meter, which this time highlights the Outside-In spectrum (figure 3-3).

> Fighting Trim

Fighting Trim provides a more agile mind-set—the best offense in the face of the enduring unpredictability of frontier life—and helps organizations *sense and respond at market speed.*[35] As a simple example, team members at Ritz-Carlton hotels collect information on customer preferences on slips of paper as they interact with customers. This information is then entered into a database, and the customer's experience is subsequently customized to reflect those preferences. The company not only senses by gathering the data, but it also responds by using that data to anticipate a customer's future needs.

It wasn't all that long ago that the primary challenge for many companies was collecting and gathering the information needed to make informed decisions. Today, companies are awash in data (although not necessarily well-sorted information). So the ongoing challenge is threefold. The first step is getting reliable data into a format that is useful and can drive decisions. Then, the company must identify and quickly assess the relevance of "new information." And finally, in responding, the company must be selective—responding to the signal, rather than the noise—and act relative to its intentions.

Many companies assume that the point is mainly to "speed things up." If they could only find the right turbocharger and stick it on a laggard department, that would do the trick. Unfortunately, speed is only part of the equation. To succeed on the frontier, companies need to also be more *responsive* to the marketplace in general, and to their constituencies specifically. Responses can range from changes in how a company operates (systems, processes, asset base, culture, modes of interaction with business partners) to product offerings to changes in business models or strategy.

Part of the Fighting Trim mind-set is an *options orientation*. This outlook enables effective sense-and-respond systems. Take the Texas-based grocer Butt Grocery (HEB), for example. When online grocery businesses started to take off, HEB had doubts about the validity of this new business model. But new entrants were generating a lot of buzz along with exorbitant valuations. HEB decided that it might need a response, and so, as an option, it developed the capabilities needed for an online grocery service.[36]

Interestingly, although HEB built the system, they didn't implement it. As its competitors launched online services, the company waited to see if the market would accept the new business model. When the most prominent rival, WebVan, declared bankruptcy, HEB had its answer, at least for the time being. The new business model wasn't yet viable, and HEB didn't feel compelled to go ahead and launch the offering, although that option remains open for the future. What is most significant here isn't that HEB created a new capability, but that it demonstrated a willingness to invest in preparing (without necessarily implementing) a response to a potentially game-changing industry shift. This is Fighting Trim in action.[37]

Of course, companies have always had to sense and respond in order to succeed in their particular environments, but this activity is shifting from *occasional* to *continuous*. As information passes with less and less friction among actors and organizations, time is compressing. Trends, innovations, and service expectations continue to move in faster and faster cycles. In the past, for example, retail stores used to have four seasons. Today, European clothing retailer Zara can generate a new line in as little as two weeks.[38] This is an extreme case, but even in Old Economy manufacturing firms, product-design cycles are being dramatically accelerated, as the Moen case illustrates.

Even though—or perhaps because—data is everywhere, organizations still need to mount systematic efforts to translate raw data into actionable information. As we said earlier, Fighting Trim is not about trying to respond to all changes in the environment. Instead, it is about deliberately acting on selected opportunities at the right time, increasingly by exercising options developed earlier.

And this leads us to a key point about Fighting Trim. For most companies, the greater challenge inherent in Fighting Trim lies not in *sensing,* but in *acting in response.* It lies in embracing the bias toward action and driving it deep into the culture. Many companies spend heavily on technologies and data analysts to improve sensing, but often those companies are unwilling or unable to act on the information they glean. "Data rich" does not automatically translate into "information-based." Too many companies focus on assessing which trigger to pull, and then fail to pull it.

Let's make this point by looking at a clear exception: Seven-Eleven Japan. The Japanese branch of the convenience store Seven-Eleven has proved an astonishing success. Several years ago, Seven-Eleven Japan decided to create a system that would improve the efficiency and speed with which orders, ideas, and feedback could be exchanged—in a sense, the latest evolution of the art of the possible. Today, all Seven-Eleven Japan stores are equipped with satellite dishes. This allows the company to constantly monitor customer needs, improve quality control, and predict daily trends. Impressively, the company is able to collect sales data from all of its 8,500 stores three times a day. And more important, it *analyzes and acts on that information in roughly twenty minutes.*[39]

The organization understands which data to pay the most attention to, enabling it to separate the signal from the noise. For example, it turns out that customer preferences for lunch items such as boxed lunches, rice balls, and sandwiches closely correlate with day-to-day changes in the weather. This is important, because these items account for almost 50 percent of daily store sales. So, Seven-Eleven factors weather patterns (among many other variables) into its stocking analysis.[40] By knowing what products customers want on the shelf, and when they're likely to want them, Seven-Eleven also delivers a more Outside-In experience. Remember: Traits are useful in part because they reinforce one another.

Once the data is turned into information, Seven-Eleven acts nimbly. Daily orders are electronically processed by 10 A.M. in fewer than seven minutes, and the company is able to closely monitor its deliveries, which occur the same day.[41] Seven-Eleven Japan also turns its inventory forty-eight times a year (compared with twelve times on average for Seven-Elevens in North America), in part by helping its vendors and manufacturers control their own inventories—an illustration of an Eco-Driven attitude.[42] They change over 70 percent of stock items each year, a remarkable example of Fighting Trim further enhancing Outside-In.[43] The results? In 2001, Seven-Eleven surprised the world by becoming the biggest retailer in Japan, wresting the title away from supermarket giant Daiei.[44]

As we've stated, the Fighting Trim company gets good information and *acts* on that information. Experimentation and the easy embrace of new ideas is a big piece of Fighting Trim. One of our favorite examples of this duality comes from copy giant Kinko's. We like this example in part because it is low tech (or more accurately, *no* tech). It grows out of corporate culture and managerial mind-set, rather than multimillion-dollar investments in new technology. Here's the story:

Kinko's is based in California and has some 800 locations in seven countries. An observant copy-machine operator noticed a change in customer pattern in the month of December where customers were spending more time shopping for gifts than they spent making copies or preparing presentations. The operator then had a brainstorm. His idea was to use the store's color copy technology and its laminating and binding equipment to produce gift calendars using the customer's own photographs. This worker printed a sign and tested his idea. It became an instant hit. Customers walked in with twelve of their own favorite photographs and walked out with unique, personalized holiday gifts. The operator relayed his idea in a simple phone message to Kinko's founder and chairperson, Paul Orfalea, who rushed it to the company's executive management and store manager network via the voice mail system. Total elapsed time—one week. Today, custom calendars are moneymakers worldwide.[45]

Quick Review

Rapid, willing action in response to compelling new information—that's Fighting Trim. Now, let's review its general principles:

- *Separate the signal from the noise.* Seven-Eleven clearly understood the key drivers of the business and then built a system that gives it the information needed to make decisions. The result is the ability to act quickly, without getting caught up in a sea of data.

- *Sense and respond to the market.* The case of HEB demonstrates a willingness to "buy an option" as an interim response to the market, while the Seven-Eleven Japan case illustrates an optimized value network that is flexible and responsive to the data that it collects. In both cases, the organizations have the ability to move at the speed of the market—and in the case of Seven-Eleven, the weather!

- *Be willing and able to act.* All too often, companies invest mighty sums in building the capability to gather data and translate it into a usable form, but internal process problems (often approval-process problems) prevent action. The Kinko's case is a clear counterexample. This is a culture that encourages an operator to dream up and test an innovative idea, and it is also a culture within which innovation can gain scale.

Take a moment to think about where you are on the Fighting Trim spectrum (see figure 3-4).

Figure 3-4: Fighting Trim Trait Meter

Intermittent sense and respond to change in business environment	*Frequent sense and respond* to change in business environment	*Continuous sense and respond* to change in business environment
Data rich	Information-based business process	Information-based mind-set toward action
Diffused: static can obscure focus; can't say no to a good idea; everything's a priority	Prioritizes well but at times has too many irons in the fire	*Selective and discriminating:* separates signal from noise
Decision-making and implementation cycles *often move more slowly than desired*	Decision-making and implementation cycles are *inconsistent,* sometimes occurring at market pace, sometimes lagging	Decision-making and implementation cycles *match market pace*
	Readily changes technology and/or process when merited	Readily changes strategy, business model, organizational structure when merited
	Frequently aligns portfolio to some or all of the organization's intentions	*Continuously* aligns project portfolio to the organization's intentions

> House in Order

In this age of organizational transparency and information ubiquity, velocity, reduced friction, and role blurring, organizations are only as strong as their weakest links, and the frontier has an unkind way of exposing those weak links. Furthermore, the frontier raises the bar for everybody, making House in Order the ever-increasing "price of admission"—the cost of getting and staying in the game.

As we've seen, value creation today is driven less by hard assets and more by the efficient sharing and collaboration between the disparate parts of the value network. House in Order serves as a gentle reminder that sharing and collaborating start at home. The House in Order company is ready for both the opportunity and the challenge of the information frontier. It can focus outwardly because it effectively manages and collaborates inwardly, minimizing the distractions of issues *inside* the four walls of the organization. Federal Express and now AOL Time Warner are succinctly capturing the essence of House in Order with the mantra, "operate independently but compete collectively."[46] House in

Order instigates an efficient, connected, collaborative *intraenterprise* operation that makes possible speedy, productive, *cross-enterprise* activities and relationships.

So what's "new" here? Haven't companies always been striving to get their House in Order? Yes, but traditional boundaries—created by organizations, processes, technology, culture, and the proliferation of project-related investments—fragment the organization over time and reduce value creation (especially in an Eco-Driven environment). As companies close the gaps and knit together the fragments to create a higher level of House in Order, they unlock value from the organization and create new ways to produce additional value.

At first glance, House in Order might seem the logical choice for the "first" trait—that is, the one to worry about initially. Yes, it *is* foundational. Without it, companies will find it difficult to participate effectively in an Eco-Driven environment or to employ the tenets of an Outside-In perspective. So why don't we introduce it first? For one thing, looking only at House in Order would focus the company inside the four walls of the organization, not a wise choice for frontier settlers. And more important, more than any other trait, *the House in Order perspective is informed by the other traits.*

How does House in Order enable the other traits? Change is occurring faster than ever. Competitors are morphing, boundaries are shifting, and technology is evolving. The House in Order mind-set helps the organization seize opportunities by reinforcing the commitment to building agile units—be they teams, departments, process participants, or functions— that can "lift and shift" to meet the needs of the market. It is closely linked to traditional notions of efficiency—doing it better, cheaper, faster, and smarter. But doing it better, cheaper, faster, and smarter merely optimizes the speed and cost dimensions, without adequately capturing the spirit of internal fitness embodied in House in Order.

One example of "lift and shift" involves Fidelity Investment's conversion of their internal systems to XML (Extensible Markup Language). Simply put, Fidelity—the world's largest mutual fund and online brokerage firm—decided to embrace XML technologies to integrate its internal systems that store and manage client information. According to *Internet Week,* Fidelity's program is the most comprehensive use of XML ever implemented.[47] By standardizing this flexible way of sharing data across disparate systems, the company has decreased transaction-processing time and increased the speed to market of its new products and services. Although Fidelity's initiative so far has focused primarily on *intra*company standards, the project has deliberately been implemented in such a way that it can readily be extended to *inter*company relationships and communications.[48] Using our language, the Fidelity initiative uses House in Order to bolster Eco-Driven.

The effort puts Fidelity at the forefront of the financial services industry in the use of XML, and represents a significant competitive advantage for Fidelity in both the near- and mid-term. The benefits for Fidelity include:

- Faster processing of customer online transactions.

- Faster delivery of new intra- and intercompany applications. For example, a new 401(k) service for the Palm handheld was launched in half the time it would have taken otherwise.

- The potential to eliminate over 85 percent of the software and hardware devoted to middle-tier processing.[49]

A word of reassurance for those companies without Fidelity's reach or resources: Fidelity's effort, like Fidelity itself, is enormous. But House in Order doesn't always require a massive scale; in fact, smaller efforts in the same direction can also have real impact.

For example, Southern General Financial Group is making its investment in legacy systems more productive. By adopting a new presentation layer technology, Southern General Financial Group provides real-time access to data in its legacy systems via the Web and cell phones, among other devices. The result is a win-win, with cost efficiency gains

HOUSE IN ORDER AT FIDELITY

"What they've done will take the mainstream five years to do and the conservative companies ten years."

—*Roy Schulte, Gartner Group analyst,
on Fidelity's XML implementation*

of $1 million, acceleration of the pace of its business operations, and better servicing of both its agent and end-customer constituencies.[50]

While these are the immediate benefits, embracing House in Order also prepares you for opportunities that haven't yet been imagined. In the Southern General Financial Group example, the ability to deliver data anytime, anywhere, and on any device lays the foundation for that company to reconceptualize how it may operate in the future—thereby extending the art of the possible.

As noted earlier, most companies above a certain level of complexity eventually succumb to "silo thinking," in which functional areas, departments, or even divisions think and act as isolated units. The House in Order mind-set breaks down silo thinking. It encourages a "for the common good" attitude and is encouraged by "cross-silo" collaboration. Internal integration—sometimes in a literal sense, sometimes figuratively—is a foundation that the other traits build upon. It's an essential ingredient, for example, in meeting the Outside-In elements of presenting a single face and a coordinated experience to all constituencies.

At this point, we'll stress that we are pragmatists first. There are likely very good reasons why you are organized as you are, and we don't suggest that you literally turn your organizational structure upside down to present a single customer view. In later chapters, though, we *do* suggest ways to look across your project portfolio to facilitate cross-silo interactions, thus promoting House in Order, among other traits.

New technologies like knowledge management are making possible much greater internal collaboration than was achievable in the past. But companies that excel in internal collaboration also know that technology alone provides only part of the answer. It can equip a company with capabilities that it never had before, but it can't create the focus and purpose for the collaboration. House in Order—and the other traits—can.

Let's consider the case of Textron and how it is using e-business to improve its operations— and, we argue, move beyond their siloed culture into a culture of internal collaboration.

Textron, a $12 billion diversified manufacturer, employs more than fifty thousand people working in five fairly traditional divisions. Each of these divisions—aviation (think Cessna, Bell Helicopter), industrial (E-Z Go Golf Carts), automotive, fastening systems, and finance—has been profitable. These divisions operate autonomously in a classic holding company/conglomerate mind-set: *Buy good companies, sell bad ones, and don't worry much about synergy among companies or divisions.*[51]

As competition intensifies, however, Textron's chairman, Lewis B. Campbell, worries that the Internet is changing the rules of the game and that small companies will outdo Textron in speed to market and customer care. In its pursuit of Fighting Trim, the company is utilizing e-business to become more efficient and innovative. To gain efficiency, the company plans to share things like technology and human resource services across divisions; to become more innovative, Textron is working to stimulate the development of creative ideas through cross-silo collaboration. Given its conglomerate structure, divisions are quite independent, but as Textron illustrates, companies can still benefit from greater "for the common good" sharing and pooling of information.[52]

Naturally, they are looking to technology for help. But Textron's management also understands that the technology must be linked to broader cultural change. Ken Bohlen, Textron's chief innovation officer, speaks of the Internet as an "enabler of innovation. Yes, [I want] the company to take advantage of the Internet, but [I] also want its people to act like the Internet, constantly exchanging information and ideas."[53] We assert that this goal is trait-embracing behavior.

Let's be clear. House in Order is *not* about technology. On the other hand, when it comes to translating the House in Order mind-set into concrete actions, the technological infrastructure of a company plays a role. Much as the requirements of a building's foundation are driven by its design, a company's infrastructure requirements are also influenced by trait requirements. A powerful technology infrastructure—which normally comprises things like standards, common user interfaces, ubiquitous thin clients, systems integration, and high-bandwidth networking—facilitates cross-enterprise communication and information exchange, thus promoting cooperation and collaboration.

Consider a second example, this one from Harrah's, a major operator of casinos, hotels, and resort properties in several U.S. cities. When the company decided it wanted to get closer to the customer by offering an enterprise-wide "loyalty card," it discovered that it couldn't easily make the transition. The company had successful casino-based loyalty cards, but these stand-alone cards wouldn't work across properties because there was no way to share information among properties. (Inside the company, information from each property was a closely kept secret.) The regional managers felt that if they shared the information, other properties would steal their customers. As CEO Phil Satre explains, "This developed during the course of the early 1990s expansion and is still common among Harrah's competitors today. Regional Harrah's managers, with turf to guard, were possessive of their markets, customers, and data, and had little but their own operation's bottom line on their minds."[54]

The behavior change was painful. The property managers had to get to a mind-set in which they *willingly* shared their information. In short, they had to learn to collaborate and work for the common good. Richard Mirman, senior vice president of marketing, further elaborates: "Regional property managers were worried that promoting certain destinations to customers in those regions would draw business away from their properties." But, he says, Harrah's executives challenged that premise, and instead promoted the value of increasing cross-market visits. They eventually "sold" the regional properties on this new strategy and the information sharing that it would necessitate. They argued, successfully, that all resorts in the larger company would benefit from enhancing the experience of guests *across* the Harrah's empire—and they had satisfaction surveys to back up those assertions.[55]

In the spirit of House in Order (and traits in general), the company overcame the cultural and technical challenges of creating a common customer-loyalty program—setting itself apart from the rest of the industry. And the payoff has been well worth the effort. Within two years of the launch of its loyalty card program, Harrah's more than doubled its profits. Moreover, during these two years, it outdistanced its competitors in profit growth and grew its market share as well.[56]

These benefits alone were spectacular, but the House in Order effort also created new opportunity for the company. Following the September 11 terrorist attacks in the United States, occupancy at Harrah's flagship hotel in Las Vegas dropped by 25 percent. But using its new e-mail and Web site capabilities to offer personalized promotions to select customers almost instantaneously, the company was able to restore occupancy to close to 100 percent by September 30.[57] Additionally, Harrah's has been able to build on its customer database by integrating it with yield management, and as of mid-2002, has grown its profit per occupied room by 20 percent.[58]

In this example, Harrah's better integration of its systems netted it a faster response to an unforeseen event, improving its Fighting Trim. At the same time, it provided a customized response to its customers, enabling it to be more Outside-In.

We recently met with the CIO of a large manufacturer. He showed us how he uses a 2 × 2 grid to assess potential projects. The vertical axis, he explained, indicated how important a particular project was to the organization; the horizontal axis showed an assessment of the organization's ability to deliver the project. In figure 3-5, we've added our own labels to the four quadrants.[59]

He explained that projects in the Rethink quadrant were easy to evaluate, as were the projects in the Easy Wins and Nurture and Support quadrants. But it was the Problem Child quadrant, he told us, that was troublesome. He gave an example concerning data standards. Normalizing data across more than a thousand databases was a huge undertaking, and the CIO said that there wasn't broad sponsorship for such an effort. One reason was that standards, in and of themselves, were gener-

Figure 3-5: Project Assessment Matrix

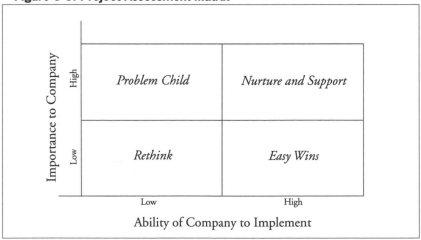

ally viewed as an "infrastructure" project, not directly involved in the value creation process.

We argued that by considering the organization's trait objective, the organization was more likely to find the necessary sponsorship. Why? Because in the context of traits, the broader value of data standards—a cornerstone for enabling House in Order and operationalizing future strategies—becomes more apparent and more tangible.

Projects that enhance organizational efficiency without promoting larger intraenterprise collaboration and communication are laudable in their own right, but they are missing a crucial House in Order component. Remember, one implication of the relationship between traits is that infrastructure should be designed for the company's value network, and not just for the known or anticipated internal needs of the company.

Quick Review

Let's review the general principles of House in Order:

- *Find and correct your weakest links.* As the frontier emerges, the company's walls become windows, exposing your weakest links. House in Order companies address these issues.

- *Think "lift and shift."* Given the volatility and unpredictability of the information frontier, companies increasingly must be prepared to flexibly, and often virtually, reconfigure components of their companies. A House in Order mind-set delivers this state of readiness.

- *To collaborate outside the walls, start inside the walls.* Traditionally, scale, organizational accountability and controls, and good old human nature decreased collaboration among departments, functions, and divisions. Today, embracing House in Order requires organizations to evaluate ways to collaborate for the common good. A House in Order mind-set creates a change-ready environment and enables the other traits. As a result, House in Order moves from being an operational to a more strategic activity.

Now take a moment to think about where you are on the House in Order spectrum (figure 3-6).

Figure 3-6: House in Order Trait Meter

Coordinated: intermittently transcends silos	*Cooperative:* regularly transcends silos	*Collaborative:* organization operates for the common good, seamlessly transcending silos
Adaptable, sometimes accommodating change, but faces organizational resistance as well as process and technology constraints	*Flexible,* but at times hampered by organizational resistance and process and technology considerations	*Plug and play* organization, process and technology fluidly applied
Traits generally do not inform company's approach to House in Order	*Traits inform* company's approach to House in Order	*Traits embedded* in how company thinks about its business

The Interconnectedness of Traits: The Case of Li & Fung

As mentioned earlier, *traits overlap.* Although the specifics of your business context may lead you to put a higher priority on one trait than on another, you can't really pursue any single trait in isolation. So let's take a moment to focus on key connections among the traits by looking at a company that is prospering on the information frontier: Li & Fung, a Hong Kong–based global consumer products sourcing firm. We believe that Li & Fung's successful "frontier living" is due, in part, to a company culture that is infused with the traits and committed to responding to constituency needs and changing realities.

The story of modern-day Li & Fung is especially compelling in light of its antique roots. Far from being an Internet baby, Li & Fung is approaching its hundred-year anniversary. Founded in 1906 in Guangzhou, China, the company initially functioned as a bilingual trader, brokering deals between Chinese manufacturers and English-speaking buyers. Li & Fung moved to British-ruled Hong Kong just after World War II, when the takeover of China by the Communist Party was imminent.[60]

By 2002, Li & Fung had become a $5 billion entity with a worldwide staff of five thousand people, linking four thousand independent textile and toy factories around the world with major retail customers. Today, the company acts as a middleman between Asian manufacturers and retail clothing operations such as Levi Strauss, Abercrombie & Fitch, and The Limited.[61]

Over the decades, Li & Fung's focus has evolved from simple trading to what might be called "process orchestration." Perhaps reflecting its many years of serving as a translator and intermediary between Chinese, English, and U.S. companies, Li & Fung has an instinctive feel for relationships, and this serves the company well as it adapts to the value network model described earlier.

Traits in Action

Although Li & Fung originally restricted its role to directing processes, it has recently started owning some critical links in the process—a change that we would argue has been driven by an Outside-In focus.[62] For example, in some cases the company has begun to offer raw materials to its suppliers. As Li & Fung grew to understand its customers' needs more fully, the company realized that many customers were increasingly focused on procuring higher-quality materials at the best possible price. If Li & Fung could insert itself effectively in the raw materials acquisition process, these ends might be better served—as indeed they have been.[63]

But the customers' needs for quality control had other implications as well, and here's where the richness of Li & Fung's ecosystem—and its willingness and ability to be Eco-Driven—pays off in a big way. The company's extensive network of relationships allows each element of a finished garment to be handled by subcontractors with core strengths in that area. As one study puts it:

> *A down jacket's filling might come from China, the outer shell fabric from Korea, the zippers from Japan, the inner lining from Taiwan, and the elastics, label, Velcro, and other trim from Hong Kong. The garment might be dyed in South Asia, stitched in China, then sent back to Hong Kong for quality control and finally packaged for delivery to The Limited or Abercrombie & Fitch.*[64]

Rather than being simply a "trader" or a "manufacturer," the company has made a conceptual leap. It has drawn upon the power of its ecosystem to become an *information company* with manufacturing expertise. Again, this aptly illustrates the Eco-Driven mentality. It also gives the company increased agility. If one node in the value network is unable to deliver, the company can substitute another manufacturer with minimum disruption to the larger process.[65]

This agility reflects and enables a strong Fighting Trim mentality. Today, customers can make adjustments to their orders right up until the last minute at various stages in the production process. Until the fabric is dyed, for example, the customer can change the color. Until it's cut, the customer can change the design. The order can even be cancelled altogether before the material has been woven. As Ada Liu, a Li & Fung division manager, explains, "There are generally fewer mistakes and disputes now when changes are made, because communication is clearer."[66]

Again, Li & Fung did not launch initiatives to achieve Fighting Trim or become more Outside-In. Rather, by *thinking* Outside-in, it realized that its customers would appreciate more flexibility to change their orders. The company's Fighting Trim mind-set allowed it to meet this goal in an efficient, flexible, and cost-effective way.

Customer focus has been a Li & Fung hallmark for generations, but the company's rapid expansion in recent decades has challenged its longstanding techniques for maintaining close relationships with its most important customers. In order to protect those key relationships even as the company is building new ones, Li & Fung has adopted a novel structure that, we suggest, reflects a House in Order mentality. Today, senior managers run ninety smaller divisions of the company as separate companies, thus allowing more individual focus and greater

ORGANIZATIONAL STRUCTURE AND THE FRONTIER

The case of Li & Fung raises the perennial issue of the "centralized, decentralized, autonomous or not" organizational structure debate. This question is contextual with no single "fits all" answer. However, what is clear is that the information frontier requires greater coordination between units and a more interdisciplinary understanding of how to deliver value regardless of how a company is organized.

agility. While the larger corporate structure offers the benefit of central-ized IT, administrative, and financial support from the company's Hong Kong base, the independence of the smaller units allows faster response to seasonal fashion shifts and rapidly changing customer needs.[67]

Li & Fung and the Internet

Realizing that advanced communications were necessary to imple-ment broader growth strategies, the company moved to adopt Internet technologies on a large scale in the mid-1990s. According to group chairman Victor Fung: "The Internet is not black magic, there is no need to be afraid of it. Yes, it is a disruptive technology, but so what? Disrup-tion comes from the real world, not cyberspace."[68]

Once the company committed itself to embracing the best in digital systems, progress came quickly. In 1997, the organization began im-plementing a full browser-enabled intranet that facilitates the instan-taneous exchange of current prices and order-status information. It also provided unexpected benefits, such as the instantaneous transmis-sion of high-resolution product photographs. In the past, a suspected quality-control problem in Bangladesh (for example) would have re-quired the mailing of fabric swatches to Hong Kong for analysis—and often to the customers as well. Today, a color digital photograph can be electronically transmitted and analyzed almost instantaneously, dra-matically shortening response times. Time elapsed? Virtually none. Transaction cost? Virtually zero.[69]

Building on this capability, a major 2000 initiative involved develop-ing comprehensive extranet capabilities for each of Li & Fung's ten major customers. These extranets allow for the instantaneous exchange of catalog descriptions, order-status information, payment-status infor-mation, and current prices. The extranet service has enhanced customer relationships and increased service levels, thus raising the bar for their competitors.

The success of the extranets seemed to prepare the ground for StudioDirect.com, Li & Fung's B2b Web portal aimed at small- and medium-sized retailers in the United States. ("B2b" nomenclature indi-cates a relationship between a big-B business and many small-b busi-nesses.) This was a market historically not served by Li & Fung, but rather by import agents. The company initially had high hopes for the portal, which was based on the concept of marrying technology pathways to the company's broader business interests. Through careful study, they developed an understanding of how a digital business-to-business trading arrangement would support its fundamental commercial goals. The site launched in February 2001.[70] According to William Fung, group Managing Director:

> Our starting point was a defensive posture. Would we get "amazoned" by someone who will put together all of the information about buyers and factories online? After a lot of research, we realized that the Internet facilitates supply chain management, and we weren't going to be disintermediated. The same reason why we were not disintermediated by the offline guys is going to be the reason why we're not going to be disintermediated by the online guys.[71]

Even with the careful research and planning that went into this initiative, and despite the success of its extranet forerunners, Studio Direct.com so far has only limped along—perhaps due in part to the economic downturn that more or less coincided with the site's launch. The jury is still out, and Li & Fung has drastically modified its approach to both ownership and rollout of the concept.[72]

The lesson of StudioDirect? Sometimes doing almost everything right still may not be enough. Although the traits we've defined can help organizations set and achieve important goals, the fact that an initiative is consistent with a trait won't ensure its success. Out there on the frontier, *some bets will fail.* But incorporating the traits—though by no means a guarantee—can certainly improve the odds and maximize the value of the hand you hold. And even a frontier option not profitably converted may be valuable in terms of the institutional learning it generates. As Robert Sutton, a professor of management and engineering at Stanford University, states in his recent work, "Rather than rewarding success and punishing failure, reward both but punish inaction."[73]

Bringing It All Together: Building Trait Objectives

Now it's time to start putting the traits to work for you and your organization. The following exercise is designed to help you begin to:

- Assess where your organization is relative to each trait.

- Think about where you would like to be with respect to traits.

- Establish some tangible objectives toward further infusing traits into your organization.

To guide you as you work through the exercise, we provide a summary version of each Trait Meter with sample trait gap results in figure 3-7.

Figure 3-7: Summary of Trait Meters with "Gap" Results

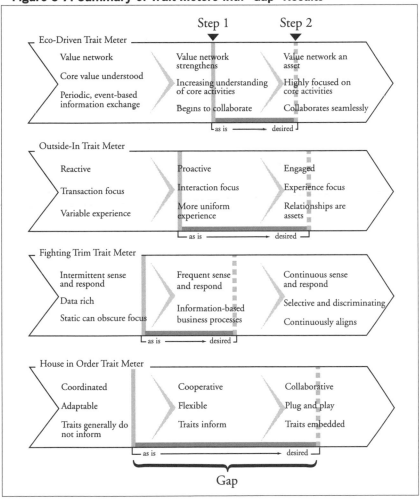

Step 1: Based on your understanding of your company, its practices, and its value network, draw a solid vertical line through the meter *where your company is today,* with respect to embracing each trait. This will be referred to as your "as is" assessment.

Step 2: Next, plot *where your organization should aim to be*—given factors including placement in the industry and markets served—moving toward infusing traits. Do this by drawing a dotted vertical line through each of the Trait Meters. This plot will be referred to as your "desired" target.

By establishing your as-is and desired placements for each trait on the Trait Meters, you've done two important things. You've evaluated the relative priority of the traits for your organization, and you've set relative end-points that define trait objectives for your organization. Simply put, the distance between the as-is (solid) lines and the desired (dotted) lines (annotated as "gap" in figure 3-7) sets the parameters for your trait objectives. Although the Trait Meters provide useful information toward your organization's formulation of traits, up until this point the meters represent generalized, cross-industry practices. To make traits even more relevant and useful, the Trait Meters can be customized for your industry. By giving traits this additional context—that is, more ties to a company's specific industry and circumstances—they become even more tangible and actionable.

In other words, start with the general principles and hold them up against the filter of your industry, your market, and your business context as a whole. For example, say your company is a manufacturing firm competing in an industry segment that has made progress toward collaborative product development. The Eco-Driven meter would be customized to reflect the specific benchmarks and requirements for collaborative product development in this specific industry.

By establishing tangible, industry-specific Trait Meters, companies can develop plans for achieving the next level of desired performance. In the process, traits evolve from a relatively general and intangible mind-set to a concrete series of goals and activities for the organization to pursue.

The Power of Traits

Traits are mind-sets that help companies prosper on the information frontier. You can think of them as a form of psychic provisioning. Of course, just thinking about traits isn't enough. Traits are valuable because once you start thinking about the world differently, you then make choices about how to *act* differently. To summarize, traits and the trait meter tool help companies in these primary ways:

- By understanding the traits and including them as a third, explicit intention, companies are more conscious of this previously elusive objective.

- Since each company's strategies and tactics are likely to change as it continues to evolve, traits provide an *underlying power of constancy*. Sailors steer by the North Star and the Southern Cross; settlers can steer by the traits.

- Trait Meters help companies focus, communicate objectives, and gauge progress toward achieving them.

- By reshaping existing projects to achieve multiple intentions— short-term and trait objectives, for example—the investment delivers greater value by fulfilling a business need *and* demonstrating adaptive, frontier-driven behavior.

With the traits defined and Trait Meters explained, let's next look at some additional tools that can help you achieve greater alignment between your company's portfolio and its objectives.

4 the alignment workshop

Life consists not in holding good cards
but in playing those you hold well.

JOSH BILLINGS (1818–1885), HUMORIST AND LECTURER

Think of your project portfolio as a poker hand—the cards you have been dealt. So what are you holding? And what is the best way to play your hand? Our alignment tools will help your organization play its cards well—using its project portfolio to best effect on the information frontier. That's what this chapter is all about.

We call this chapter an "alignment workshop" because it introduces, in an accessible way, the remaining principles and tools of our alignment approach. It shows you how you can actively shape your project portfolio into frontier currency.

Again, our recommended route toward development of the traits, or organizational mind-sets, is not one of radical transformation. It's not about stopping the presses and reconsidering all that you do. Instead, we believe the way to develop traits is to bring them to life by playing your hand in a systematic and purposeful way, with one eye on fostering greater alignment of your current objectives and actions and the other on preparing for the future.

You'll recall from our first chapter that aligning your company's portfolio is a multifaceted proposition, as shown in table 4-1.

Table 4-1: Facets of Alignment

Facets of Alignment	Purpose
Aligning projects with intentions	Each project, and the portfolio as a whole, delivering on what the organization is working to achieve
Aligning projects with other projects	Projects working more effectively with one another
Aligning the organization and portfolio for frontier living	Using projects as vehicles to promote trait development and to build a more adaptable organization

Long-Term Objectives

Short-Term Objectives

Trait Objectives

● = Project

Following is a conceptual overview including case examples and benefit descriptions for the remaining six of our alignment tools that, together with the Trait Meters, address this multi-faceted endeavor. Then, in chapters 5 and 6, we move beyond conceptual discussion, and those of you who like diving into details can walk through an example of how these new tools are applied in a corporate setting. You decide: If you are interested in the practical details, read straight through. If you prefer to stay on the conceptual level, after reading this chapter, skip to our summary, chapter 7.

Starting Point: The Project Portfolio

The idea of viewing a company's collection of projects as an "investment portfolio" grows out of finance theory about how to maximize the return on a stock portfolio. This school of thought originated in the early 1950s, when economist Harry Markowitz first introduced what became known as Modern Portfolio Theory.[1] The theory gained adherence and momentum, and eventually earned Markowitz and others a Nobel Prize. Among the key principles of this theory:

- An optimal portfolio generates the highest possible return for a given level of risk.

- Expected risk has two sources: (1) investment risk—the risk of the stock itself and (2) relationship risk—the risk derived from how a stock relates to the other stocks in a portfolio. Diversification

FROM ONE PORTFOLIO TO ANOTHER

Modern Portfolio Theory (MPT) says, in a nutshell, that out of a universe of risky assets, an efficient frontier of optimal portfolios can be constructed that offers the maximum possible expected return for a given level of risk.

Modern Portfolio Theory argues that there is no single right portfolio. Rather, given the level of risk the investor wishes to bear and careful consideration of the combined value and risk of different assets within a portfolio, an efficient portfolio can be compiled to deliver the maximum benefit to that investor.[2]

reduces the overall portfolio risk by minimizing the relationships between the different investments and overdependence on any one investment.

As outlined in the list that follows and depicted in table 4-2, these principles are extended to a company's project portfolio in the following ways.

- Individual projects are analogous to stocks. Projects are investments the company makes in its future.

- Risk for individual projects is defined broadly. It includes a failure to obtain full projected benefits (both financial and nonfinancial), delays in implementation timelines, and budget overruns.

- The expected risk of the portfolio is a combination of investment risks: the individual project risk, the risk of how projects relate to one another, and the overall complexity of the portfolio. For example, projects may depend on one another, so their implementations must be properly sequenced to succeed. Similarly, with lack of effective coordination, two projects might call upon the same limited resource at the same time. Risk can only be fully understood—and mitigated—by looking at all the projects together as a portfolio.

- Companies, like individuals, choose from among multiple optimal portfolios. A company's preference for risk/reward is driven by its competitive context and the risk profile of its leadership.

The practice of using investment portfolio management techniques to manage project portfolios has been around for decades. (As noted in the preface, author McFarlan advocated this approach more than twenty years ago.[3]) Most large organizations, however, still manage their portfolios as a *collection* of projects, rather than as an integrated portfolio. In fact, according to a Gartner Group survey, "only 10 percent of large enterprises use portfolio management as a value-planning tool."[4] Consider your own organization for a moment. Does your portfolio management process consist of a spreadsheet where projects are itemized for budgeting purposes and intermittent project tracking? Or does it include an active process of balancing and recalibrating the project portfolio as changes in business context—shifts in intentions, competitive conditions, innovations, resource contention, and so on—warrant?

Table 4-2: Summary Comparison of Financial and Project Portfolios

	Financial Portfolio	Project Portfolio
Assets	Various financial instruments with distinct characteristics	Various projects with distinct characteristics
Diversification	Employing multiple financial instruments can reduce risk	Many project variables— scope, approach, vendor, project manager, etc.— can reduce risk
Goals	Income and capital gains	Profitability and growth
Asset Allocation	Invest according to investment goals	Invest according to organizational intentions
Connection	Correlation	Interdependency

Managing projects individually or managing the portfolio as a collection of projects rather than as a cohesive whole causes multiple problems—benefits are often double counted, opportunities for reuse and idea-sharing are lost, and duplication proliferates. We've seen many cases where several projects within the same portfolio are actually working toward opposite ends. As a result, the overall portfolio risk rises and, reciprocally, the return on investment falls. Losing value is never a good thing, and on the frontier, the cost of expending scarce resources on avoidable inefficiencies is especially high.

Returning to Alignment

It's 10 P.M. Do you know where your project portfolio is?

If your organization is like most, your honest answer is probably "yes and no." Assuming that you occupy a senior management perch, you probably have a grasp of the organization's major initiatives. You may have a clear (or fuzzy) picture of *how many* projects are out there, and *how much* is allocated to some or all of them. You may even know *how* and *why* they got started. The question, though, is how well you understand how these projects fit together, delivering on today's objectives while also preparing for tomorrow's.

Our approach brings your intentions and your portfolio into greater alignment—with each other and with frontier realities. Through alignment, we increase the portfolio's currency value by reshaping it to achieve four general goals: (1) improve its direction, (2) increase its efficiency, (3) reduce its risks, and (4) enhance its flexibility. An ambitious assignment, right? Yes and no. Yes, in the sense that the alignment effort ultimately will have major impact on your organization. But no, in the sense that our approach breaks the alignment challenge into bite-sized pieces, which you can take on at a pace that's appropriate for your particular circumstances.

Well, that all sounds good enough, but just what are these general goals?

Direction is where the portfolio outcomes take the company. By better aligning the portfolio to intentions, the organization more rapidly and deliberately progresses toward where it wants to go. *Efficiency* is increased by eliminating redundancy, tapping synergy, and sharing common components, thus producing a greater "bang for the buck." The tools also *reduce the risk* of the portfolio's implementation, thereby enhancing return on investment. And finally, the portfolio becomes more *flexible* by building in options or choice points that allow the organization to be more adaptive in dealing effectively with an unfolding future.

In addition to the Trait Meter tool discussed in chapter 3, there are three additional diagnostic tools—Intentions, Sides, and Right Brain—that uncover alignment issues. And a second set of tools—Common Threads, Project Chunking, and What-if Planning—equip the portfolio to be more adaptive to frontier living. All these tools are summarized in table 4-3.

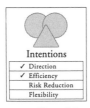

Intentions Tool

The Intentions tool is the second of our four diagnostic tools designed to reveal gaps between the direction the company intends to go and where the portfolio is actually taking it.

It is, in essence, the compass for our alignment approach. It evaluates how well the outcomes of individual projects as well as the portfolio as a

Table 4-3: Alignment Tools Summary

Tool	Description	Ways Tool Improves Alignment
Trait Meters	Assesses, plans, and measures trait development	Direction, flexibility
Intentions	Assesses alignment of portfolio to intentions	Direction, efficiency
Sides	Removes bias and finds synergies by sorting projects into main business activities	Direction, efficiency
Right Brain	Identifies change capacity issues	Efficiency, risk reduction
Common Threads	Finds common, reusable components	Efficiency, risk reduction, flexibility
Project Chunking	Structures projects into bite-size pieces that deliver incremental, stand-alone value	Risk reduction, flexibility
What-if Planning	Develops contingencies for varying scenarios	Risk reduction, flexibility

whole will meet the company's objectives and priorities. This tool converts the project dots you plotted in chapter 1's alignment warm-up (and illustrated in table 4-1) into a more precise and measurable assessment. This activity delivers both project- and portfolio-level alignment results. Projects that are not working toward the organization's intentions provide the starting point for better focusing the portfolio.

Unfortunately, there is little (if anything) that is static on the information frontier. Using the Intentions tool, a company might see an increasing gap between the portfolio and the company's intentions. But it is not always the portfolio that's the problem. Often, it is the company's intentions that are outdated or, for whatever reasons, don't reflect changes in the marketplace.

While Intentions is primarily a *diagnostic* rather than a *prescriptive* tool, the benefit derived from it can be immediate—especially for companies that are migrating their collection of projects into an integrated portfolio for the first time. Consider the case of ITT Fluid Technology and Specialty Products in Upper Saddle River, New Jersey. After assembling the initial portfolio, the company realized it had similar projects underway in numerous departments. As Dan Vantucci, the vice president of IT, commented, "The biggest benefit to us was being able to spot redundancies." By combining the duplicative projects, the project database saved $4.5 million. "Instead of doing the project [many] times over," Vantucci explains, "we did it once, and rolled it out to [multiple] organizations."[5]

In summary, the Intentions tool provides the touchstone for alignment. By measuring individual projects against the company's intentions, both the nature and magnitude of the alignment opportunity are revealed. This creates the imperative for action, opportunities for immediate changes, and input for the application of additional tools.

Sides Tool

Our next tool for looking at the portfolio is called "Sides." What do we mean by "Sides"? Companies consist of three broad functional areas: sell-side, inside, and buy-side. Almost all of the activities and interactions within an organization can be assigned to a single side. (However, the walls between these sides are soft and porous. For the purpose of our analysis, we consider the *primary affiliation* of each project.) The exceptions—

Table 4-4: Side Definitions

	Side Definition	Representative Projects
Sell-side	Sell-side generally describes customer-facing touchpoints, including marketing, selling, and servicing activities.	• Customer and channel strategy • Customer acquisition and retention process redesign • Customer relationship management (CRM/eCRM) • Customer experience design • Brand development
Inside	Inside generally focuses on two sets of the enterprise's internal activities: (1) manufacturing and service delivery activities and (2) administration and support activities including human resources, finance, and information technology.	• ERP implementation • Flexible manufacturing design • Business process redesign • Merger and acquisition integration • Shared services creation • eLearning implementation • Human capital development and management
Buy-side	Buy-side represents activities that work with the enterprise's supply chain and procurement processes.	• Logistics improvement • Vendor management • Purchasing process redesign • Supply chain optimization • eProcurement implementation
Multi-side	Multi-side describes activities that provide integration and cooperation across sides.	• Knowledge management • Collaborative product commerce • Digital assets and rights management • Regulatory compliance

those activities that impact, or transcend, more than one side—are tagged as "multi-side."

When organizations analyze the portfolio through Sides, they are frequently surprised. They often find that the way they *intend* to focus their efforts, as a whole, is not how they're *actually* focusing those

THE JOYS OF SIDES THINKING

- Minimizes departmental and organizational bias
- Links to income statement
- Subaggregates the portfolio
- Promotes traits

efforts. Often the drivers of this misalignment include an inward focus, silo-thinking, individual agendas, or even good old human nature—especially when people are vying for scarce resources. Through Sides, these distortions are simply put on hold, allowing organizations to see the whole more clearly.

Let's explain. Above a certain level of organizational complexity, companies are *compelled* to aggregate individual projects in the portfolio in some way—turning 1,500 projects into, say, eight aggregated categories—if only to make the overall portfolio comprehensible and manageable. As a result, organizations frequently categorize their portfolios along internal corporate dimensions—for example, by department, business unit, functional area, or cost center. Breaking down a complex reality according to these criteria makes some sense, because that breakout maps to existing organizational structures and budgeting processes.

Through the Sides analysis, the departments and functional areas are pushed off the table, at least for the moment. Instead, it asks you to think of the fundamental activities—sell-side, inside, buy-side—that cut across those kinds of functional boundaries. See figure 4-1 for an illustration of projects mapped to sides.

Sides in Action

Let's take a moment to illustrate Sides in action. True story: When a multinational looked across its e-business project portfolio, it saw hundreds of projects—totaling hundreds of millions of euros—spread out across multiple business units in more than a hundred countries. Each unit had launched its own initiatives in response to a changing environment. Although senior management appreciated their organization's desire to be proactive in a changing environment, they were increasingly

Figure 4-1: Example of Projects Mapped to Sides

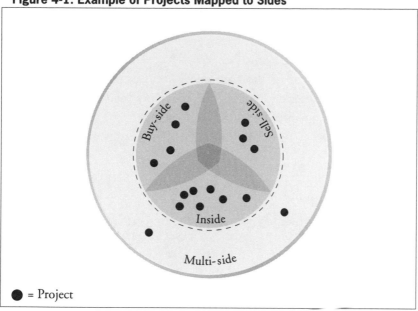

concerned about an overall lack of coordination. They couldn't see how all these projects fit together, and it certainly looked like the company was investing in a lot of duplicative efforts.

Management experimented with rearranging the organization's portfolio by Sides. The move worked, reducing costs and increasing interoperability among business units. Many projects within each side were consolidated into a "hub" project that, once completed, was customized by each business unit. The hub project eliminated redundant efforts, created the core engines the company needed, and focused the organization on delivery of a comprehensive solution to the constituencies of each Side. The basic portal included single sign-on, common search, and catalog functionality, all of which were tailored and extended into "spoke" portals that were eventually developed for each business unit. Additional, more sophisticated capabilities were developed for online transactions, where appropriate.

The Sides model did not diminish the power of the business unit, but it did significantly reduce longstanding organizational bias, since no one business unit or geographical area could claim ownership. This allowed a broad spectrum of the company to participate in the development efforts. And because this development proceeded on fairly equal footing, the "not invented here" syndrome was mitigated.

Is this important? Well, a significant and growing percentage of the company's revenue is currently derived from electronic commerce, and several million euros of the company's total purchases are executed through its procurement portal. The company believes that these are interim numbers, which will ultimately grow to 50 percent for both the revenue and procurement sides and deliver substantial profitability growth.[6]

As this case study illustrates, looking at the portfolio by Sides presents multiple benefits. It creates a perspective less driven by internal hierarchy and better tied to both shareholder value and to the organization's intentions. It's only logical, when you think about it: The drivers of shareholder value—or at least the parameters of the income statement—are revenue (sell-side) and cost (in- and buy-side.) If the stated intentions of the organization are to promote growth, then finding that a majority of projects fall within the inside functional area indicates a disconnect between where the company is investing and its intentions.

Another key point: Sides adds another level of value to the portfolio in that it reinforces traits. Sides are trait-friendly. The Sides tool puts all customer-facing, or sell-side, projects side by side, in a way that more or less compels the organization to explore its success at developing the Outside-In perspective. The map of diverse projects for different constituencies on a given side begs the question of how they contribute to a value chain or ecosystem—which, in turn, spotlights the degree to which the company is internalizing Eco-Driven principles.

As we'll see in chapter 5, a constituency's articulated and unarticulated needs can both be explored as a natural extension of Sides. Armed with this understanding, a company can better deliver on its promise to serve its constituencies. The inside view also shines light directly on House in Order issues, and—given the right types of analysis—the state of an organization's Fighting Trim.

Another major reason to use Sides analysis is that it puts in close proximity projects that, on a superficial level, may appear to be very different, but which at a fundamental level are actually related in intention. As you'd expect, putting these close cousins in the same conceptual rooms tends to illuminate contradiction and redundancy along with opportunities to maximize good ideas and capture synergies.

Consider this (true) example. The CEO of a Yellow Pages company had always thought of a now-completed and somewhat star-crossed database redesign project as inside, invariably referring to it as an "infrastructure project." He had an interesting reaction when he learned about our Sides tool. He told us that, had this analytical tool been available to him at the time the project was being implemented, he would have labeled it "buy-side."[7]

After all, he explained, the project was a critical building block for a major supply-chain initiative, and therefore was essential to the way the organization thought about and operated its business. But it was only after the project had been completed that they recognized its real potential. Not only did it make the company much more efficient, but it also enabled entirely *new businesses on the sell-side*. If he *had* labeled it buy-side, the CEO told us, the project would have had a different project sponsor, a different priority status, and very likely, a different outcome. It certainly would have moved along with a greater sense of purpose and efficiency.

One of the most dramatic features of the information frontier is what we've referred to as "role blurring"—your customer may also be your partner or your competitor. Getting a handle on the needs— unique and shared—of your many constituencies, and understanding how they relate and overlap, is critical to maintaining today's increasingly complex business relationships. The Sides tool helps shed light on the unique challenges that this new business reality presents.

We will take this notion a step further in chapter 5, but for now, let's move on to our next tool: Right Brain.

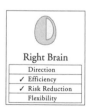

Right Brain	
Direction	
Efficiency	✓
Risk Reduction	✓
Flexibility	

Right Brain Tool

Today, it's pretty well understood that getting people to change how they do things constitutes a major risk for most projects. Armed with this understanding, many companies adopt *project-level* change management programs. But Modern Portfolio Theory reminds us that to fully understand and manage risk, a *portfolio-level* perspective is also needed. The Right Brain tool takes this counsel to heart. It looks across the portfolio and identifies and aggregates the demands it makes on people, ultimately asking the question: "Can our people really do all this?" In this way, it serves as a heads-up that the organization is imposing an imbalance of effort, unrealistic expectations, conflicting directives, or other stresses on particular constituencies. By more deliberately managing the projects contending for the finite resource of change capacity, the Right Brain tool improves implementation success rates, thus reducing risk and better achieving intentions.

We've borrowed the "right brain" metaphor from the realm of brain physiology. Neuroscience research has demonstrated that the two hemispheres of the human brain are responsible for very different modes of thinking. The left brain focuses on logical thinking, analysis, and accuracy. It structures and stores information in a linear, precise, and exact manner. It deals with things that are empirical and can be measured, weighed, and verified objectively. It uses deduction to arrive at conclusions, and moves from the general to the specific, from cause to effect.

The right brain, by contrast, focuses on aesthetics, feelings, and creativity. It works in a nonverbal manner and excels in visual, spatial, perceptual, and intuitive information. For the right brain, processing is nonlinear and nonsequential.

Our apologies to neuroscience for using its research as a metaphor. But we believe that human capacity for change—intellectual and emotional—is a crucial element of portfolio planning and management. To quote Andy Grove, chairman of Intel, "Change happens on human time."[8]

Just how big is the right brain risk? The most common reasons that projects fail to fully achieve their goals are people-related, and as pointed out in chapter 1, approximately *40 percent of all projects fail to deliver their expected return.*[9] This fact has been well documented for almost every wave of business change over the past decade. Whether you consider business process reengineering, enterprise resource planning (ERP), or e-Business—to name just a few—the data all support the same conclusion: People-related issues are the most common cause of project failures. (See table 4-5.)

This is not news, of course, and most projects today include at least some change management. It is beyond the scope of this book to address best practices for managing organizational change. Fortunately, there are abundant other resources available on this topic. Amazon.com lists more than 2,200 business books with the word "change" in their titles.[10] One of our favorites is *Heart of Change,* John Kotter's latest work with Dan Cohen.

Table 4-5: The Extent of Right Brain Challenges

Type of Change	Finding
e-Business	59 percent of respondents cite politics/culture/ communication as the premier e-business issue, not integration.[a]
ERP Second Wave	Prior to ERP go-live, 62 percent of issues are people issues and post go-live, 51 percent of the issues are people-related. Compare this to technology issues post go-live which are 19 percent.[b]
Reengineering	82 percent of CIOs say organization resistance to change is biggest barrier to reengineering success.[c]

[a] Demir Barlas, "Fixing the IT Unit," *Line56,* 7 December 2001.

[b] Deloitte Consulting ERP, *Second Wave* (New York: Deloitte Consulting, 1998–1999).

[c] Deloitte Consulting, *Eighth Annual Survey of North American Chief Information Executives* (New York: Deloitte Consulting, 1996).

No amount of spreadsheet recalculation, incentive manipulation, or good old-fashioned scolding will make organizational change happen if key constituencies lack the capacity to absorb the scale or scope of the required change. What companies often fail to realize is that project-level efforts to manage change can actually *increase portfolio-level risk* and the associated project-failure rates.

How can this be? Almost all classic approaches to project-level change management emphasize activities such as communicating regularly, engaging those impacted by the change in the project, training people in new skills, modifying reward systems, and most important, leading change from the top. (Do any of these sound familiar?) And for any single project, these approaches are rational and logical. But consider what happens when a company with a robust portfolio (many companies have literally thousands of active projects at any given time) performs these important activities energetically:

- Employees are barraged with communications.

- Operations managers are beset with requests to pull employees off the line to participate in project activities that "engage those impacted by the change."

- Reward systems become so complicated that employees are no longer sure just which goals and behaviors are supposed to drive their compensation.

- Managers, who are supposed to "walk the talk" of change, discover that they can't possibly model all the new behaviors.

Right Brain in Action

When project-level efforts are aggregated, they may exceed people's capacity for change. Consider, for example, GE's experience with implementing e-business. In e-business, as in most things, General Electric is considered a world-class role model. But the company's initial goals to conduct 30 percent of its revenue over the Internet by 2001 had to be scaled way back. Why? It turned out the customers and suppliers both couldn't and wouldn't change fast enough to enable GE to meet this aggressive goal. As Lloyd Trotter, head of GE's industrial systems unit put it, "A lot of our customers were not ready for what we were trying to do out there." Although their achievement of 5 percent of business conducted over the Internet is admired by many, the way they expended resources may have been different if this constraint had been recognized at the outset.[11]

To gauge the change requirements of the portfolio, we approximate the change capacity each project demands. The four variables we assess are: (1) the *magnitude* of the proposed change; (2) people's *ability* to make the change; (3) people's *willingness* to make the change; and finally, (4) the *timing* of the change. (See figure 4-2.)

These are not common metrics for an organization to employ as it assesses its portfolio. There are generally two reasons for this omission. First, many organizations consider these "soft" Right Brain issues to be either nonquantifiable or of secondary importance to (or represented

WHY IS IT?

Although many projects have change programs, it is far less common to see change levers employed at the portfolio level—the place where the organization's capacity and need for change are best managed.

Figure 4-2: Key Variables to Assess Change Requirements

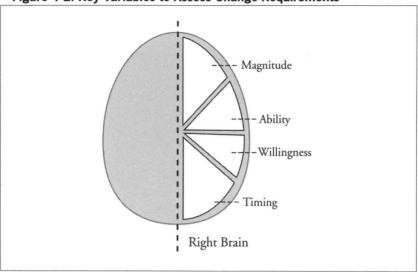

within) more quantitative projections—ROI, machine uptime, productivity gains, and the like. But magnitude, ability, willingness, and timing are fundamental linchpins in the alignment process and collectively are a key contributor to an organization's success.

Second, as noted, managers most often think about and plan for change at a *project* level. They devise workshops, assemble update meetings, schedule training sessions, and so on—all worthy endeavors, of course. Change programs sponsored at the *enterprise* level are also common. But in our experience, it's very rare for an organization to think about the dynamics of change at a *portfolio* level. And skipping this crucial level of analysis can wreak havoc.

Constituencies are asked to engage in too much change too soon, and all at once. For example: Imagine that three different functional areas have initiatives underway that will eventually require new training for your call center representatives (CSRs). These employees are going to be taken away from their phones for hours in a few cases, and days in other cases, for each type of training. Contingency plans may or may not be in place to handle the workload during each training period. In the case of one company we are familiar with, uncoordinated project-related training resulted in scheduling CSRs to be off the floor *almost three months out of the calendar year*.

In this example, it's tempting to discount Right Brain project issues as the result of "poor planning," but we believe that these issues derive more from a lack of deliberate attention to Right Brain considerations. The truth is that human capital is rarely managed as carefully as financial capital.

Let's consider a second customer-service example, this one pertaining to a call center. The goal of such a center is to process as many calls—sales or service—as quickly as possible, with the lowest number of dropped calls or mistakes.

One company's leadership decided that its three-hundred-agent call center needed to depend more heavily on technology to (1) more actively manage its call volume, and (2) radically improve customer service. Management implemented new telephony, voice response, and sophisticated call-tracking systems. Weekly training was provided to the call center's team leaders to support them in making these changes toward greater measurement and accountability. In the midst of this change, digital reader boards were mounted on walls to show how many calls were waiting and for how long. They were programmed to flash when call wait times had gotten too high. The tote boards and their attendant technologies were touted by their designers as "the perfect system."[12]

But the resistance of the workers to what was being thrust upon them was greater than expected, and management wasn't prepared to deal with the issue. The call center actually ended up with *decreased* productivity and lower morale. And the reader boards? As one observer pointed out after touring the facility, "They scrolled the message, *Have a nice day.*"[13]

What happened here? Simply put, *information overload*—the change demanded by the array of call center–related projects—was just too much. The managers couldn't get their heads around why time measurement was so important, nor were they willing to deal with the strong resistance of the workers to such a publicly measured environment. Their own fear of failing at the new management approach, moreover, left them with emotional resistance to change.

So, if the portfolio as a whole makes too many demands on folks—for their time, energy, and spirit—what can a company do? Using the Right Brain, organizations are able to maximize the finite change capacity of the organization by:

- Looking for ways to extend the capacity for change by creating more effective portfolio-level change management tools.

- Identifying opportunities to consolidate change management efforts, making them both easier to understand and more effective.

- Adjusting the timing of the portfolio's implementation to better map to the constituencies' change capacity.

- Identifying and addressing issues where a constituency or subgroup is a bottleneck for the overall portfolio or a portion thereof.

In summary, the portfolio as a whole may look great on paper, but if it can't be implemented successfully, it won't pay off. By considering the Right Brain challenge at a portfolio level, you have a better chance of seeing the potential disconnects between how much change you're anticipating the group can handle, and what in reality they're able to achieve.

From Diagnosing to Creating Options

The diagnostic tools examined here and in chapter 3—Trait Meters, Intentions, Sides, and Right Brain—are analytics that define trait objectives and uncover alignment opportunities. Each of the remaining tools—Common Threads, Project Chunking, and What-if Planning—provides similar benefits for improving the portfolio's efficiency and direction and reducing portfolio risk. But they also provide an additional benefit: options. Like their financial distant cousins, portfolio options create more choices for the future. They allow you to be *more adaptive*, providing flexibility and working as a hedge against the unforeseen.

Common Threads

Direction	
✓	Efficiency
✓	Risk Reduction
✓	Flexibility

Common Threads Tool

It's one of those truths of organizational life that we're so accustomed to, we hardly notice it any more: Lots of efforts duplicate one another. With the Common Threads tool, we counter this complacency with compelling opportunities for greater efficiency. Common Threads finds commonalities, often hidden, among projects that can be reused, extended, or leveraged for added value.

By promoting reuse, Common Threads creates options or choice points for the portfolio. For example, once a reuse library exists, a project that previously was too expensive may become affordable, because much of it can be built with existing components. Reuse also allows projects to use proven components—reducing risk—while increasing the speed of development. Furthermore, interoperable components can be reconfigured to create new leading-edge innovations. Remember our Hallmark example in chapter 3? In this case, a very simple technology component—moderated chat rooms—emerged as an innovative way to be more Outside-In.[14]

There are two types of Common Threads: (1) up-to-date information that is held in common and (2) reusable components. The first of these is already fairly prevalent in large organizations. Take, for example, the ERP system. One of the many features of ERP is that multiple users in diverse parts of the organization can share data.

Although there are likely additional opportunities to share common data, we'll focus on the second type of Common Thread, reusable components, in describing the tool's use. It's all too common to find several projects in a portfolio expending resources to build project components that essentially duplicate one another. For example, each project might build its own Web site from scratch as a way to share information with stakeholders, or several separate programmers might code an object to extract financial data from the accounting system.

The Common Threads tool is, in a sense, a liberal adaptation of Carliss Baldwin and Kim Clark's work on modularity. Projects in the portfolio are first deconstructed into their composite parts. This deconstruction makes it possible to see common activities in areas such as

ON BALDWIN AND CLARK'S MODULARITY

Modularity involves building a complex product or process from smaller subsystems that can be designed independently, yet function together as a whole.[15]

Figure 4-3: Common Threads Illustration

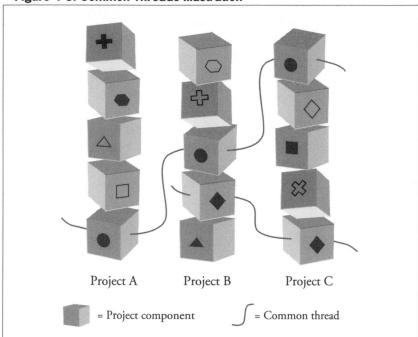

Project A   Project B   Project C

= Project component   ∫ = Common thread

change management, business processes, or technology. By building these components once and then reusing them, Common Threads are born.

Figure 4-3 illustrates the idea of "looking sideways" and deconstructing projects in order to identify similar components that become candidates for reuse.

Common Threads is not about moving at the speed of the "slowest" common denominator; rather, it is *sharing and coordinating at market speed.* Common Threads strikes a balance between the benefits of collaboration and the benefits of quick, independent action. With these goals in mind, a word of caution is in order. When organizations see project pieces that appear similar, the natural reaction is to simply combine them. But taken to an extreme, combining projects threatens to add bureaucracy, demand greater coordination, and create monolithic projects. We recommend evaluating opportunities against a simple benefit/cost hurdle, so that Common Threads can be leveraged wisely. Reusable components span the full range of activities that projects entail, ranging from technology infrastructure, data, and application function-ality to parts of business processes, the development of relationships, skills training, or even corporate policy making. While reuse of software and programming routines is an accepted practice in many IT organiza-tions, many projects have other, less commonly recycled components that Common Threads can identify.

Common Threads in Action

Let's consider some examples, beginning with a global $25 billion manufacturer. More or less simultaneously, several of its divisions started to streamline their division-specific processes for managing product design changes. Almost inevitably, they began duplicating one another's efforts. At the same time, the divisions began to find that their inwardly focused change processes were not adequate, in terms of both speed and efficiency, for an organization that had to coordinate design changes across a broad global ecosystem of contract designers, contract manufacturers, and the company's own divisions.[16]

The company's leadership determined that to get the most out of its efforts, a common process was needed. The question was: To what depth should the process be standardized in order to make it successful? If it lacked enough commonality, it would leave money on the table. But if it was "too common," it could fall victim to bureaucratic standardization. In such a case, the process would be a straitjacket, denying the divisions enough flexibility to meet their unique requirements.[17]

The result, ultimately, was a set of common process activities (and supporting technology) that the divisions collectively identified, devel-oped, and reused. Beyond this, each division defined its own subordi-nate activities.[18]

Activities such as skills training, communication, and recognition programs are also often duplicated across the portfolio. As we saw in Right Brain, many constituencies are buffeted by different project teams seeking changes in the way the constituencies operate. Common Threads not only helps leverage change management techniques, but also unifies the way people *experience* change, so that each change is more familiar and therefore more readily accepted.

Dow Chemical presents a good case in point. In 1999, Dow realized that although two technicians might complete the same training class, training content and results often differed widely, depending on whether those two technicians were trained in (for example) Cairo, Egypt, or Greenburg, Louisiana. So it launched Learn@dow.now, a $1.3 million e-learning system that delivers standardized online training around the world. So far, the site has already delivered an estimated total cost savings of $100 million by putting health and safety training online.[19]

When it was launched, Learn@dow.now offered fifteen course titles. Currently, over two hundred thousand courses have been taught to sixty thousand users around the world. Every week another five thousand to ten thousand courses are completed.[20] But its value has *gone beyond the time and dollars saved.* Dow Chemical is able to use this tool to respond quickly and flexibly to unforeseen business circumstances.

When hundreds of Dow employees were caught sending offensive e-mails over company servers, then CEO (and now chairman) Bill Stavropoulous mandated that all employees around the world receive six hours of training on workplace respect and responsibility. Rather than having to launch worldwide workshops, which would have required considerable investment and coordination in course material, handouts, classrooms, and trainers, Dow simply delivered the program through Learn@dow.now—and saved nearly $2.7 million in the process.[21] "We demonstrated commitment from the senior leadership to protect our values of respect for people and to take swift and decisive action where those values are compromised," says David Wilkins, Dow's director of global diversity.[22]

Even many IT departments can go beyond merely using code libraries to making reuse a part of the way they work every day. At Charles Schwab & Co., for example, "recycle and reuse" is the mantra by which the IT group lives. For instance, it reused a feature that allows domestic U.S. customers to trade before the market opens, providing the same functionality to foreign customers.[23] To its credit, Schwab recognizes that technology reuse is not as much a technical problem as a *mind-set* issue. Notes Ron Lichty, Schwab's vice president of Java Object Services, "Whether you're a small company or a large one, it's the same problem. Getting teams to recognize that leveraging other people's work, and sharing their work before moving on to other projects, is very important."[24]

Project Chunking

Direction	
Efficiency	
Risk Reduction	✓
Flexibility	✓

Project Chunking Tool

The information frontier's increased velocity has dramatically heightened expectations. Businesses are expected to deliver results ever faster and ever better. Project Chunking responds to these rising expectations. It breaks projects into manageable "chunks," each of which delivers incremental benefits. This tactic has several merits. First, risk is reduced because projects are smaller and less complex; moreover, later chunks learn from earlier ones and thus have faster response times to new information. Second, incremental benefits are realized earlier and more reliably (which is, of course, the flip side of lower risk—better return). Finally, Project Chunking provides more frequent choice points, making it easier to change project direction, scope, or budget when needed. In this way, it makes the portfolio more flexible.

To better understand how Chunking does all this, consider figure 4-4. It represents an ambitious, large-scale project scheduled in a traditional phased approach over several time periods.

The x-axis represents time, and the y-axis shows the net benefit of the overall project. As with most projects, this one requires some period of up-front investment. Then, over time, the benefits accrue and (expectedly) exceed the initial investment. With each phase of the project, the investment-to-benefit ratio changes, as indicated by the circles and the squares. Projects usually have one to several phases of net investment before net benefits are realized.

'chənk-ing\ :

> Breaks projects into smaller pieces, each of which delivers stand-alone benefits. At the end of each chunk, a "choice point" occurs where project scope, direction, budget, and other elements are modified as needed.

Figure 4-4: Traditional Project Cost/Benefit Curve

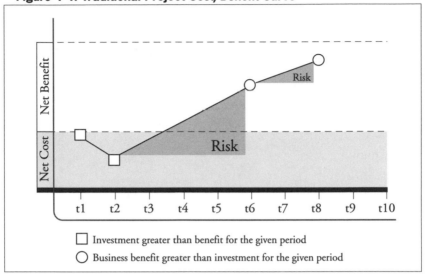

So what's wrong with this picture? Well, nothing really. It's a picture of a well-designed project that has properly-scoped phases and will achieve benefits over time. But *the loftier the project goal, and the longer the time to implement, the greater the risk*—as represented by the shaded triangles underneath the investment curve. Remember that we're talking about life on the information frontier, where unpredictability lurks around every turn.

So what is the alternative? An incremental or "chunked" approach, as depicted in figure 4-5.

Let's take a closer look at the risk triangles in figures 4-4 and 4-5. In the traditional scenario, captured in figure 4-4, there are only two opportunities to capture value. The long time frame pushes the realization of benefit far into the future, and the corresponding "triangle" of risk is larger. In the chunked diagram, each triangle is smaller than those in the traditional model, because the organization is incurring less risk at each stage of investment. There is less risk in part because there is less investment at any given time and because each chunk realizes benefits— but also because *there is more information available stage by stage*. When Chunking is applied, information from earlier chunks is available to

Figure 4-5: Chunked Project Cost/Benefit Curve

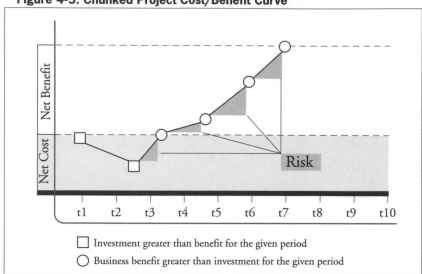

subsequent ones. Each chunk can also take advantage of *new* information the company gains—about its markets, its competitors, or a new technology, for example.

Think about it. Companies are constantly gaining new data and clarity about conditions in the market. This data should be used to shape (or reshape) current projects, as well as assist in future funding decisions. On the information frontier, good ideas can age rapidly, and the art of the possible changes with remarkable speed. Having more opportunities to act on new information improves project results.

Chunking also builds opportunities to "bring the Right Brain along." Since Chunking has more frequent choice points, constituencies who will be affected by a proposed change can participate more often in project decisions. This is yet another reason why the triangles of risk are smaller in figure 4-5 than in figure 4-4.

So what does this all mean? Although there are times when the Chunking outcome would deliver a lesser net benefit than the best-outcomes result of a traditional project implementation, in the same time frame, it may still be the preferred approach, especially when one factors in (1) the probability of a best-outcomes result, and (2) the associated reduction in overall project risk. In fact, a study by the Standish

Group concluded that the smaller the duration and team size of a project, the greater its chances of success (which it defined as being on time, on budget, and with all features and functions as originally specified). A typical project with a team of six and a six-month time frame, for example, had a 55 percent success rate. This stands in stark contrast to the 8 percent success rate enjoyed by projects of more than 250 people and an average duration of twenty-four months.[25] In other words, best outcomes are seldom achieved, or may only be achieved through relatively high-risk scenarios. Most of the time, you are better off Chunking.

Two important caveats about Chunking. The first, implied above, is that it isn't *always* appropriate. For example, you generally wouldn't use Chunking to build a large-scale transaction-processing system. (This is a big bet with a long timeline where the scale needs to be built in early before benefits can be produced.) However, there are probably more opportunities to employ this tool than you might think.

The second caveat: Chunking requires a clear road map and an explicit understanding of where the end-state lies. Companies that apply Chunking without well-constructed plans risk contracting "disassembly fever" and winding up with a patchwork portfolio. This constitutes a good idea gone wrong. As one auto industry executive noted, "Without a roadmap, the result is a rag-tag collection of smaller projects without common direction or outcome."[26]

A Chunk of Savings Example

Does Chunking really work? Does it make sense, out there in the real world, to break bigger projects into smaller ones?

The real-world evidence suggests that the answer to these questions is yes. Let's look at the case of Carlson Hospitality Worldwide, which is the company that manages Radissons and other high-visibility hotel properties. When Carlson's managers asked their board of directors to authorize a complete overhaul of the company's central reservation system, the board rejected the $15 million request as being too much, too fast.

End of story? No. Carlson's managers then adopted a Chunking approach, which featured flexible "choice" points at which the board could elect to stop the project but retain benefits already gained.[27]

The team set up a number of guidelines to help design the chunks. Stand alone benefits at the end of each one were, of course, a must. But they also focused on minimizing rework and keeping mutual dependencies to a minimum. (In other words, if one chunk was cancelled, others could still go forward.) Another requirement was to work with legacy systems, since these would still be in place during some of the early chunks.[28] With these plans in hand, the management team sought funding for the first chunk—which the board soon approved.[29]

Chunking also let Carlson respond flexibly to new information not known at the beginning of the project—for example, how important connecting to the Internet would become. As information became available, some chunks were cancelled and others added.[30]

The pay-off? The new system was voted best reservation system in the industry and handles over 7.9 million room nights per year.[31] The voice-reservation chunk alone has already generated $40 million in annual revenue.[32]

In summary, Chunking:

- Is a "get benefits as you go," results-focused approach.

- Offers more frequent decision points at which the company can elect to change or modify the project's course.

- Helps leverage new information and learnings, thereby contributing to risk reduction.

- Also reduces risk by shortening time frames and reducing complexity.

What-if Planning Tool

In order to understand What-if Planning, let's think for a moment about the experience of organizations that regularly come face-to-face with extreme uncertainty. What do armies, sports teams, and disaster-relief agencies have in common? In one way or another, they devise contingency plans for facing a reality that is different from what was expected. By being prepared for different outcomes, they can quickly change course. What-if can be thought of in a similar light. It is *contingency planning for the project portfolio.*

WHY WHAT-IF PLANNING?

What-if Planning raises awareness about how invested an organization is in its current context and provides a measure of how adaptively it can respond to a change in context.

As we've seen, Common Threads and Project Chunking put the organization in a position to react nimbly to change. But this alone will not ensure success on the information frontier. Being ready to move quickly is only wonderful if you can move in the *right direction*.

The chairman of a $9 billion services company recently addressed this challenge with his management team. "We have been neither optimistic nor pessimistic in our forecast," he reported, "but forward visibility in today's market is treacherous, at best."[33]

This begs the question: How do you prepare your organization to make good decisions quickly— to take the right fork at the crossroad that you're approaching at high speed? Put simply, the answer lies in *anticipating volatility and articulating a responsive game plan*. In What-if Planning, this is done first by building scenarios of possible alternative futures. Then the portfolio of projects is tested against each scenario to see if the project would be accelerated, maintained, or slowed/stopped under those circumstances. These test results provide insight into how well the portfolio can meet future possibilities.

What-if Planning builds directly on the foundation you've established using the other alignment tools. You've gotten new insight into how projects relate by Sides, what Right Brain aspects to consider, where commonalities exist among projects within the portfolio, and how structuring projects into chunks can make their implementation and extension more manageable. With this knowledge at your disposal, you're well positioned to anticipate change.

To illustrate What-if Planning, let's revisit the diagram that we developed in the context of Chunking and modify it slightly, as shown in figure 4-6.

What-if Planning considers the future direction of a project based on different likely scenarios. For example, in this picture, the three dotted circles represent three different trajectories of a project based on

Figure 4-6: Possible Future Project Trajectories

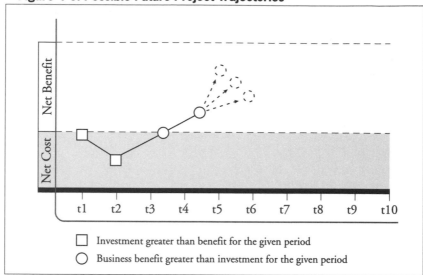

Net Benefit

Net Cost

t1   t2   t3   t4   t5   t6   t7   t8   t9   t10

☐ Investment greater than benefit for the given period

○ Business benefit greater than investment for the given period

varying scenarios. The top-most dotted circle represents a scenario in which the project is accelerated to deliver value faster. The middle circle might represent the expected direction of the project. The lowest circle may indicate a scenario in which the project is delayed or slowed down. And as we know from Chunking, a final option exists—the option not to continue with the project at all.

In our experience, many organizations informally consider hypothetical situations. For example, Agilent CIO Marty Chuck and his team challenge themselves with questions like, "What if we only had $1 to spend—how would we spend it?" Or, "What if our budget doubled—what could we achieve?" Similar questions are often asked when setting priorities, but they also make for fruitful management dialogue when moving the team toward thinking about multiple possibilities rather than a single target destination.[34]

In What-if Planning, we build on this foundation, formalizing the process by crafting scenarios that consider alternative futures. Of course, there's an infinite range of possible scenarios against which we could test the portfolio. For demonstration purposes, we'll discuss What-if Planning using two scenarios: a business expansion and a business contraction. In a business expansion, growth and innovation are the prime priorities—though a company must, of course, keep its eye on profitability. In a business contraction, the focus shifts to efficiency and cost control, though companies may make some investments to prepare for future growth when the contraction moderates.

By examining different scenarios from the current vantage point, the company gets information on how it is positioned to respond and can make adjustments today to better position itself for tomorrow. What-if Planning gives you a qualitative view of your organization's ability to respond given a significant change in its business context. It raises your understanding of how invested you are in the current context, and how adaptable you are to what's happening out there on the frontier. It further informs an organization about projects or decisions that might "lock out" options. And most important, it helps you see which projects are most fungible.

For example, projects that would be maintained or accelerated across the board, in all or most scenarios, are likely delivering relatively more value to your organization. So when you do whatever reckoning you do, they probably deserve some extra credit.

What-if Planning is not limited to the existing portfolio. Depending on the scenarios, new projects may also be introduced. During times of rapid growth, new sales and marketing projects may be added, while downtimes may call for efficiency or rationalization projects. Let's take a look at a real-world example.

ORIGIN OF WHAT-IF PLANNING

What-if Planning is a practical offshoot of strategic flexibility, a discipline that formulates multiple scenarios and connects to and dynamically monitors corporate strategy. Rather than starting with strategy formulation and scenario development, What-if Planning tests the current project portfolio against several to many likely, preformulated scenarios (e.g., growth and cost-cutting). This advance planning provides a ready course of action for work underway should a rapid shift be warranted.

What-if Planning Case in Point

Ellipsus Systems AB, located in Vaxjo, Sweden, is a software design company whose products link corporate computer systems to mobile phones.[35] The company's success depends on making the right technology decisions, especially around the standards and protocols its software uses. As wireless and mobile devices continue to take hold, there are two major emerging technical standards. One standard is WAP (Wireless Application Protocol). The second standard, Java, is based on Internet programming standards created by Sun Microsystems.

Rikard Kjellberg, one of Ellipsus's founders, was facing a conundrum: which standard to use? Two scenarios were possible. In one, WAP was dominant; in the other, Java was dominant. Although WAP was the first to the market, and the initial demonstrations indicated sufficient interest (more than a thousand people downloaded a free trial), it produced very few sales. As it turns out, some negative perceptions were developing about systems based on the WAP standard. Due to the slow response, a Swedish newspaper ran a story titled, "WAP Is Crap."[36]

Kjellberg's solution was to have projects in his company's portfolio *based on both standards.* Ellipsus built early prototypes of both systems and took them to a trade show, with both systems sitting side by side. "We knew within an hour which way to go," says Douglas Davis, the COO.[37]

No, we won't presume to tell you how to reshape your portfolio. (Nothing takes the place of sound management judgment.) But What-if Planning creates the practice drills and contingency plans that identify both the opportunities and limitations inherent in your portfolio.

Alignment Tools Summary

The process of aligning the portfolio is part art and part science. As we've demonstrated in this chapter, alignment's power is derived from looking at the portfolio in new and complementary ways, and acting on those insights.

The alignment process is also an iterative one. Each time a change is contemplated, the organization needs to consider the potential impact of the proposed change on the overall portfolio. For example, a company may decide that it wants to shift the focus of the portfolio more toward the short term and traits. But after reviewing the impact of this proposed change across the portfolio, it may conclude that putting greater emphasis on the short term may have the unwelcome effect of exacerbating Right Brain issues—perhaps to the extent that the cons of the proposed change outweigh the pros.

We've now presented the main concepts, primary benefits, and quick case studies for all seven alignment tools: Trait Meters, Intentions, Sides, Right Brain, Common Threads, Project Chunking, and What-if Planning. Now let's move down a few levels of specificity. In chapters 5 and 6, we show how these tools are put to productive use by looking at an example of a composite company working toward greater alignment.

5
through the looking glass

*Men who wish to know about the world must
learn about it in its particular detail.*

HERACLITUS (c. 535–475 B.C.), GREEK PHILOSOPHER

You might well ask: why start with old Heraclitus? The answer is that he reminds us that the present—and therefore the future—is in the details. Now it's time to dive into the details. Building on the conceptual overview and cases in chapter 4, we apply our alignment tools to a composite company.

Since an application of each of the tools doesn't fit comfortably within one chapter, we further describe and apply the four diagnostic tools—Trait Meters, Intentions, Sides, and Right Brain—in this chapter. In chapter 6, we'll see how the three options-oriented tools work with the same company portfolio.

With the exception of Trait Meters, which were discussed in chapter 3, we provide guidance for each tool's use through examples, analysis, and insights delivered in this and the following chapter. We also provide a "Turning up the Dial" section, wherein we present a second level of activity for more robust analysis.

Remember, these tools *complement* your company's current ways of managing its collection of projects. Each is designed to integrate easily into your existing processes, allowing for quick implementation. So the choice of which tools to use, and the order in which to use them, is left up to your good judgment in your particular context.

Let's now introduce you to a company we call Fairland Products. Because no one company "does it all," at least in a way that lends itself to easy summary, Fairland is a composite that brings together many of the real experiences of the companies we've studied and worked with in recent years.

Fairland is a $1.2 billion division of an $8 billion global consumer products company. This global giant is a conglomerate that makes a wide variety of household snack products, such as chips, chocolates, and candy. The Fairland division manufactures and markets a subset of these products.

Meet our protagonist, Ellie Anderson, division chief and senior VP of Fairland Products. For our purposes, Anderson has purchased and read this book. She has been thinking through its particular implications for Fairland and is now acting on its lessons. Her coconspirator is Brendan Burkley, Fairland Product's CIO, who shares both Anderson's inquisitive nature and her pragmatism. As CIO, Burkley sees his role as ensuring that IT both influences and delivers on Fairland's business goals.

The Price of Admission

Before we visit Anderson's particular realm, let's agree upon a set of seven ground rules. They're designed to put you in a frame of mind that will make the discussion productive and easier to follow.

First, *check your guns at the door.* When you start looking at your own portfolio, dismiss any preconceived notions since this natural response impedes a critical and objective assessment. Ask yourself the hard questions and be willing to answer them honestly.

Second, *check your slide rule at the door, too.* We present the math for these examples as a fait accompli, so we can focus on the ideas behind the exercises. When you apply the tools in your organization, start at a level where the process doesn't bog down in quantification and detail.

Third, *don't get overloaded.* We're presenting a comprehensive set of tools. As just noted, however, you don't have to apply them all, or all at once. At a minimum level of intervention, you can become familiar with the approach and think about how your organization might better promote traits. Each level of investment has a payoff.

Fourth, *the 80/20 rule applies*. According to this old business maxim, you often get 80 percent of the value from 20 percent of the effort. Beyond that, it may be a case of half-steps-to-the-wall. With this in mind, think of your first pass through this material as a directional assessment, rather than an expansive analysis. We're pragmatists. We have designed our approach to provide the maximum value for a minimum amount of effort, and there are a number of ways to apply these ideas quickly. One way, for example, is to apply a tool to the 20 percent of your projects that represent 80 percent of expenditures. Once you see the value a particular tool offers, you can choose to expand its use.

Fifth, *look for opportunities to act*. Incomplete information is no excuse for inaction. You never have *all* the facts, and you don't need all the information to act and derive value.

Sixth, *look for opportunities to "turn up the dial."* Turning up the dial is structured so that each tool can be applied at a number of levels of detail, with even the lowest level of effort delivering value.

And finally, when it comes time to make decisions and act, *let the Trait Meters be your guide*. These meters give form to your business context and can help you adapt and capitalize on its opportunities.

Anderson's World

Ellie Anderson is living with some of the same worries as the bank CEO whom we introduced at the outset of chapter 1. She is anxious about a shifting competitive landscape. She has a growing sense that the old tricks aren't necessarily cutting it.

Like many in the consumer products industry, Anderson is passionate about growth. However, the recent economic slump has made *profitability* her highest priority. Because of increased competition and a slowing economy, Fairland and its retailers were largely unable to pass cost increases on to the consumer, and margins are suffering along with relationships between Fairland and its retailers. Anderson wants to increase profitability quickly, while also setting the stage for strong growth once margins recover.

She and her divisional leadership have set ambitious objectives, both for the short term (i.e., to be achieved within a year) and the long term. These objectives are as follows.

Short-Term Objectives

1. *Achieve $20 million in efficiency improvements this year.* The consumer products industry is extremely competitive, and the company needs to preserve competitive prices while maintaining attractive margins for Fairland and its retailers. The division is looking for opportunities to trim costs. It is expected that these efficiency improvements will propel the division to greater profitability and prepare it for growth.

2. *Enter one emerging market.* While the company is increasing advertising and spending on core brands in its traditional markets, it can't afford to neglect new geographic opportunities. The division has selected one South American market to enter this year. This scale of expansion will be a pattern for the foreseeable future.

3. *Launch one to two new core products.* As part of its continuing commitment to increase revenue, the division is relying on innovations and new-product launches. As competition continues to intensify, product innovation is exploding. Fairland must keep pace with the market. Product launches used to take place once every few years; now the division plans to introduce at least one new core product each year.

Long-Term Objectives

1. *Achieve a 25 percent increase, to $1.5 billion in revenue, through internal growth in three years.* Given this stretch goal—as well as the division's ambitious plans to enter new markets and accelerate the rate of product launches—the company is going to need new levels of innovation, efficiency, and implementation excellence.

2. *Increase gross margin by 2.5 percent in two years.* In order to generate additional cash and create financial flexibility, the company is looking to cut costs by $35–$45 million in two years. The company will also continue to launch distinctive new products to avoid commoditization and maintain premium pricing.

3. *Become the industry employer of choice.* Fairland recognizes that its long-term success depends heavily on hiring and retaining great people. As a result, the division will continue to invest in leadership

training and management development so that it can attract the best and the brightest.

Trait Meters
✓ Direction
Efficiency
Risk Reduction
✓ Flexibility

Using the Trait Meter Tool

This list of short- and long-term objectives completes the first prerequisite. The second prerequisite is to identify the company's trait objectives using the Trait Meters tool. Anderson, who has thought a lot about trait-related issues, has come up with the following observations about traits, relative to her organizational and industry context.

- *Eco-Driven.* The industry as a whole does a good job with end consumers, retailers, and distributors. For example, the consumer products industry invented the integration of point-of-sale data and inventory, and perfected methods of collaboration with retailers and distributors. However, most companies in the industry, including Fairland, are vertically integrated from product development through manufacturing. Anderson believes that Fairland is at competitive parity with others in the industry. All in all, therefore, Eco-Driven is important, but it is not one of Fairland's most pressing priorities.

- *Outside-In.* Along with the retail fashion industry, consumer products is one of the industries most intensely focused on external constituencies, particularly retailers and consumers. From developing new snacks to match every taste to creating packaging that meets every conceivable product use, the industry is focused on innovative ways to meet customer needs. Fairland, in particular, has pioneered new techniques—such as rapid focus groups and market prototyping—to gather data from consumers and understand their needs. So, the company seems to be in good shape in terms of its Outside-In traits.

- *Fighting Trim.* Although the organization understands its consumers' needs very well, *acting* on that information has proven to be a bigger hurdle. Even though Fairland often has new information and insight ahead of its competitors, the company is generally slower to act in the marketplace. Individual functions often focus too narrowly on their specific objectives rather than on larger organizational goals, a mind-set that needs to be expanded.

- *House in Order.* Getting the company's internal systems and processes to be more flexible and better able to respond to market shifts and changes has proven an elusive goal. Anderson recognizes the urgent need to inculcate a House in Order mind-set into her division.

Based on these observations, Anderson plotted Fairland on the Trait Meters illustrated in chapter 3. The solid lines in figure 5-1 represent Fairland's as-is condition, and the dotted lines represent its desired goals.

Figure 5-1: Fairland's Trait Meter Results

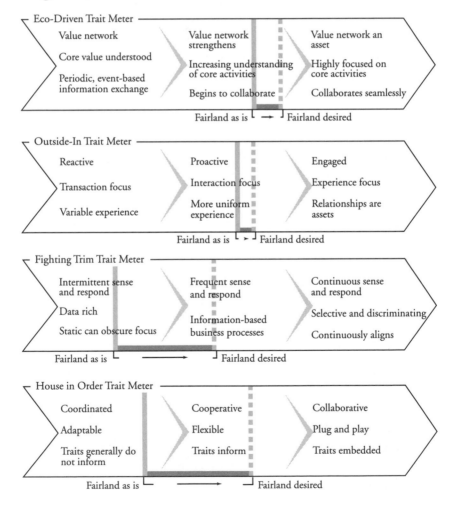

ALIGNMENT APPROACH PREREQUISITES

- Articulate short- and long-term objectives.
- Understand traits.
- Prep the portfolio.

Although the company has aspirations for all the traits, Anderson concludes that her most immediate trait objectives are Fighting Trim and House in Order. Fighting Trim, in particular, emerges as a major priority, since Fairland suffers from a relatively slow speed to market. If not corrected, this shortcoming will jeopardize the company's future competitive position. But Fairland's Fighting Trim target can't be reached if its House in Order trait doesn't sufficiently support it.

Prepping the Portfolio

Anderson now begins the process we call "prepping the portfolio." As we've mentioned before, the project portfolio is where it's happening. The portfolio already has an infrastructure in place. Investment is happening there; it commands management attention; and whether it's viewed this way or not, the project portfolio is an agent of change.

We encourage you to think about your own sample portfolio as we work through Fairland's. Pick off, say, a half-dozen to a dozen representative projects and note important information related to each one, including sponsor, budget, project benefit/outcome, schedule, and deliverables. If a project portfolio list doesn't exist in a usable form—mental or physical—start thinking about how you might pull one together.

What you're doing, in other words, is *painting a selective portrait* of your portfolio. It's selective in two senses: (1) you're using a representative sample of projects, and (2) you're focusing on a reasonably short list of key project parameters. In this chapter, we're not going to ask you to do any heavy lifting. We're going to do the work for you. But eventually, we expect, you'll work through these exercises with your own portfolio in mind, and you'll be better able to wield the tools that follow.

A Sample of Fairland's Project Portfolio

Back at Fairland, Anderson compiles a selective portrait of the division's project portfolio. She views this initial work as a precursor to engaging her senior team in aligning the full portfolio. Table 5-1 shows Anderson's sample portfolio.

In order to follow our discussions in this chapter and in chapter 6, you'll need to understand some fundamentals about each of Fairland's projects. Here's an overview.

Overview of Fairland's Representative Projects

1. *Market Research Redesign.* As indicated on the Outside-In Trait Meter, Fairland is very good at focusing on end consumers and understanding their needs. The Market Research project is designed to push the company to even higher levels of performance by complementing focus groups and surveys with more "in the moment" interactions with consumers. It includes online chat rooms where consumers discuss their needs and frustrations and on-location observations of how Fairland's products are used.

2. *Sales Force Automation.* As noted, the company is looking to extend into new markets, but a recent benchmarking study found that Fairland's sales force is not as productive as several of its competitors which may prevent cost-effective expansion. The Sales Force Automation project is designed to automate administrative activities, such as time keeping, expense tracking, contact management, and lead management. This project's goal is to better leverage the time and energy of the sales force, thereby increasing sales productivity.

3. *Retail Promotion and Inventory Improvement (Retail Promotion).* This project is designed to better support Fairland's retailers and their category managers as they manage store inventories, sales, and promotions. This is an important way to obtain more preferential shelf space for Fairland's products. The extranet-based system will analyze historical point-of-sale (POS) data and provide profit optimization tools to deliver additional profits for the retailer. Armed with this information, the retailer's category manager can better design and execute special promotions and pricing strategies.

Table 5-1: Fairland's Representative Portfolio

Project	Project Sponsor	Budget (in millions)		Status
		Lifetime	Current Year	
Market Research Redesign	VP Marketing	$4	$2	Starting second year
Sales Force Automation	VP Sales	$2	$2	Underway
Retail Promotion and Inventory Improvement (Retail Promotion)	Director of Customer Support	$5	$3	Just starting
Supplier Rationalization	Director of Purchasing	$2	$1	Underway
Division Level Enterprise Resource Planning (ERP)	CIO	$14	$3	Year three of a four-year effort
eLearning	VP Human Resources	$3	$1	First year
Legacy HR Upgrade and Migration (Legacy HR)	Director of Human Resource Systems	$5	$2	Just starting
Benefit Portal	Benefits Manager	$3	$2	Underway
Legacy Data Integration	CIO	$5	$3	Not started
Regulation Compliance	Governmental Affairs	$1	$1	Just starting
Total Budget		$44	$20	

4. *Supplier Rationalization.* Colloquially referred to as "supplier bash-
ing," this strategic sourcing project seeks to cut costs quickly.
Launched when the company realized how many suppliers it would
need to transfer into the new ERP system, the goal of Supplier Rationalization is to reduce the number of suppliers and negotiate better
deals from those remaining. To deepen relationships with suppliers
who emerge as "top tier," Fairland plans on providing extranet capability for these favored suppliers, enabling them to recoup some of
their margins through efficiency gains. The project is anticipated to
involve a year of negotiation and recontracting, and Fairland expects
to begin seeing savings next year.

5. *Division-Level Enterprise Resource Planning (ERP).* Fairland is in
the third year of a four-year ERP system implementation. So far, the
division has spent $8 million of $14 million in planned division-
level spending. While corporate is directing the enterprise-wide ERP
implementation, each division is responsible for its own customization. After implementing the basics of shop floor and materials
requirements planning (MRP), Fairland recently decided to implement two final modules: Financials and Business Intelligence. Next
year, Fairland will begin the process-redesign efforts—commonly
referred to as ERP Wave 2—that are necessary to complete the project. The ERP project is the foundation on which the company hopes
to meet its long-term margin improvement objectives. The new unified platform is expected to reduce the overall costs of running the
business as well as yield considerable savings from new, more efficient processes.

6. *eLearning.* In order to train and retain key people and achieve its
desired standing as "employer of choice," Fairland is undertaking an
eLearning project. This project automates many of Fairland's existing basic and advanced management development courses so that
24/7 self-paced learning is available to its managers. Fairland views
this project as a way to invest in and upgrade the division's human
capital.

7. *Legacy HR Upgrade and Migration (Legacy HR).* The current HR
system—payroll, benefits, and employee data—is an older legacy system that is generally considered to be a tried-and-true workhorse, but

one that has outlived its useful life. The HR and IT groups at corporate want to upgrade it, which will require a reinstall of the entire system. The expected benefits include lower systems maintenance costs, faster access times, and better and easier access to data for analysis.

8. *Benefit Portal.* This project is designed as part of an overall plan to create the "paperless office" inside Fairland. The company intends to move all administrative processes into online portals, both as a way to drive down costs and make the organization more nimble. The Benefit Portal will recast enrollment and benefits administration activities as a self-service model. Because the Benefit Portal is being implemented in the same time frame as the Legacy HR, it is designed to draw data from the legacy system initially, and later interface with the new HR system.

9. *Legacy Data Integration.* To Anderson, this project is a complete cipher. It arose mainly out of past frustrations. Often when she or a colleague came up with a new idea, especially in the selling and promotion of products with consumers and retailers, she'd be told that it wasn't feasible because, despite ERP, the company's systems still "couldn't talk to each other." In addition, each time she tried to introduce new HR policies and options for employees, she met with the same resistance. The technologists would argue that the data needed to be "normalized."

Today, most people look at this project—intended to clean up the information flows in the marketing, sales, and HR areas—as an effort to fix past mistakes, but most can't articulate exactly how that's supposed to happen. And although many opportunities are not pursued because of the problems this project proposes to solve, it is nevertheless an unglamorous effort with no strong advocates among senior management, admittedly because it isn't well understood. It hasn't yet been assigned a start date. Anderson decides to include this project in the analysis, mainly to see if she can gain insight into whether or why it is important to the company.

10. *Regulatory Compliance.* Because of a heightened emphasis on security in the United States and around the globe, the government and several industry associations have issued new guidelines designed to better ensure food safety and protection of consumer products.

These new regulations require additional levels of security, testing, and monitoring. Fairland has launched this project to comply with these guidelines.

That's it—Fairland's sample portfolio. It includes projects that represent many of the key challenges in today's business context and will help ground our application of the alignment tools. Again, we suggest that you consider your own portfolio as you read the following pages and begin thinking about how these ideas might be useful to your organization.

Now, with Fairland's intentions and representative portfolio in hand, Anderson and Burkley start with the Intentions tool.

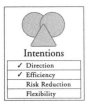

Intentions

✓ Direction
✓ Efficiency
Risk Reduction
Flexibility

The Intentions Tool

The Intentions tool is a diagnostic lens that helps you look at your portfolio from a variety of angles. It reveals gaps between intentions and projects, unveils additional opportunities and synergies, and offers new ways to evaluate and set priorities among initiatives. The result is a portfolio that is more efficiently heading in the right direction.

The Intentions tool maps the selected projects against the organization's intentions. To begin, Anderson and Burkley first estimate the organization's optimal resource allocation between short- and long-term objectives and then compare this optimal allocation to the actual allocation of effort in the portfolio. (We'll deal with trait objectives shortly.)

There are two ways to measure how the portfolio aligns to intentions: (1) the *effort*, usually measured by budget, and (2) the *expected outcomes*, or results. We'll start by using effort/budget as the measure for our Fairland example. Later, we'll illustrate how to incorporate expected outcomes.

As mentioned earlier, Anderson feels that growth is the lifeblood of consumer products and remains a key organizational priority, though in the short term, Fairland is compelled to focus on profitability. As a result, Anderson skews the optimal allocation of effort more heavily toward achieving short-term objectives, allocating 70 percent of effort toward these objectives and 30 percent toward longer-term objectives.

CHECKLIST OF FAIRLAND'S INTENTIONS

SHORT-TERM OBJECTIVES (CURRENT YEAR)

- Achieve $20 million in efficiency improvements this year.
- Enter one emerging market.
- Launch one to two new core products.

LONG-TERM OBJECTIVES

- Achieve 25 percent revenue growth in three years.
- Increase gross margin by 2.5 percent in two years.
- Become industry employer of choice.

TRAIT OBJECTIVES

- Focus on trait development with an emphasis on Fighting Trim and House in Order.

To determine the actual allocation of effort in the project portfolio, Anderson asks Burkley to score each of the projects in the portfolio, since he is closer to what each project is contributing. Burkley distributes each project's current year budget across three buckets—short-term objectives, long-term objectives, and "unallocated." The unallocated bucket is for resources being expended that, although they may be necessary, do not map to either objective.

Having allocated the budgets for all the projects, Burkley then (1) totals the scores for the portfolio and (2) determines the percentage of the portfolio's effort for all three buckets. His goal is to compare these percentages to the optimal resource allocations Anderson has already identified: 70 percent short term and 30 percent long term.

To complete the intentions analysis, Burkley assesses each project's contribution to developing the established trait objectives, using a high, medium, low, or no scale. For example, the Regulatory Compliance project does not improve Fairland's speed to market or ability to make decisions, nor does it make systems and processes more flexible. So although he recognizes that the compliance project is necessary and nonnegotiable within the portfolio, Burkley scores the project "N" or no in terms of its contribution toward the trait objectives.

FOUR STEPS FOR THE INTENTIONS TOOL

1. Determine the *ideal* allocation of effort/budget (and/or expected outcomes) to short-term and long-term objectives.

2. Assess the *actual* level of effort against objectives.

3. Estimate how well each project furthers trait objectives.

4. Compare the results and evaluate them for opportunities.

Table 5-2 shows the result of Burkley's assessment of projects relative to the company's Intentions.

Remember the alignment warm-up exercise from chapter 1? In that exercise, you mapped a sample of your portfolio to the Intentions Framework (see "Alignment of Projects to Intentions"). In the worksheet shown in table 5-2, Burkley has completed a more in-depth analysis that provides greater detail and clarity regarding alignment opportunities.

Let's take a moment to interpret Burkley's results. Keep in mind that we are looking for insight into how well the project portfolio is aligned to the optimal resource allocation of Fairland's short- and long-term

ALIGNMENT OF PROJECTS TO INTENTIONS— SAMPLE TEST RESULTS

Short-Term Objectives

Long-Term Objectives

Trait Objectives

● = Project

Table 5-2: Fairland's Projects/Intentions Analysis— Effort/Budget Method

Project	Current Year Budget (millions)	Optimal Allocation	Budget (in Millions) Short-term %	$	Long-term %	$	Unallocated %	$	Trait Contribution (H, M, L, N)
Total Budget	$20	*Optimal Allocation*	70%	$14.0	30%	$6.0	0%	$0	—
Market Research Redesign	$2	—	60%	$1.2	40%	$0.8	0%	$0.0	M
Sales Force Automation	$2	—	40%	$0.8	30%	$0.6	30%	$0.6	L
Retail Promotion	$3	—	20%	$0.6	80%	$2.4	0%	$0.0	M
Supplier Rationalization	$1	—	20%	$0.2	80%	$0.8	0%	$0.0	L
ERP	$3	—	40%	$1.2	60%	$1.8	0%	$0.0	M
eLearning	$1	—	30%	$0.3	70%	$0.7	0%	$0.0	L
Legacy HR	$2	—	20%	$0.4	60%	$1.2	20%	$0.4	L
Benefit Portal	$2	—	30%	$0.6	70%	$1.4	0%	$0.0	H
Legacy Data Integration	$3	—	30%	$0.9	70%	$2.1	0%	$0.0	H
Regulatory Compliance	$1	—	0%	$0.0	0%	$0.0	100%	$1.0	N
Total Budget	$20	Actual Compared to Budget	31%	$6.2	59%	$11.8	10%	$2.0	—
		Portfolio Gap	-39%	-$7.8	29%	$5.8	10%	$2.0	—

H= High; M= Medium; L= Low; N= None

objectives, and how effectively it promotes traits. Based on this analysis, it looks like there are significant opportunities to better balance efforts.

- There is a gap between the optimal and actual resource allocation. Anderson indicated that 70 percent of the portfolio's effort should be allocated to short-term objectives. Based on the actual effort calculated, it appears about 31 percent of the portfolio's effort or budget is allocated to short-term objectives, resulting in a 39 percent variance from the desired allocation. Obviously, there is a parallel imbalance on the long-term side, with long-term objectives commanding 59 percent of the portfolio's budget against a desired allocation of 30 percent.

- Currently, about 10 percent of the portfolio's resources are not delivering value or results in line with Fairland's stated short-term and long-term objectives. While this sounds like an immediate area for improvement, Fairland's options are limited since, as mentioned earlier, the Regulatory Compliance project is mandatory.

- When reviewing the trait objectives, Burkley and Anderson note that only two projects score high, which leaves a significant opportunity to perhaps reshape other projects to promote greater progress toward achieving these objectives.

Given this information, what can Anderson and Burkley do? We've argued that our tools provide insights into ways an organization can reshape its portfolio, better aligning it with intentions, creating greater "bang for the buck" from each project, and increasing the portfolio's overall efficiency. True in this case? We think so. For example:

- *An opportunity to increase traits.* The eLearning opportunity aligns with short- and long-term objectives, yet scores low on traits. The current curriculum basically consists of digitized versions of existing materials. This appears to be a good opportunity to introduce and promote traits. By building traits into the curriculum, the project can promote the mind-sets that the organization needs for continued success.

- *A hidden gem uncovered.* Every organization has projects that appear to be "house cleaning," or nonstrategic. When viewed through

INTENTIONS TOOL INSIGHTS

- Discover opportunities for greater intentions/portfolio alignment.
- Improve balance of resource allocation between short- and long-term objectives.
- Identify ways to enhance trait development.
- Find places to improve the direction and efficiency of the portfolio.

the perspective of traits, however, some of those projects may emerge as hidden gems. In Fairland's portfolio, the Legacy Data Integration effort appears to be such a project. Designed to streamline the information flows in the sales and HR areas, it is a "building block" project that—if executed successfully—will promote more House in Order. This, in turn, will promote improved responsiveness through better internal coordination, advancing Fairland's development of Fighting Trim.

- *Finding places for greater efficiency and alignment.* The Sales Force Automation and Legacy HR projects are both opportunities for greater efficiency and alignment. These projects have resources that are not fully allocated toward intentions and don't contribute to traits. Also, despite the organization's standardization and implementation of ERP, the Legacy HR project is investing, along with corporate, in an upgrade to a stand-alone system. This decision—as well as the relationships among the ERP and Legacy HR projects—needs to be better understood to see if restructuring to realize savings can be accomplished.

- *Accelerating value creation.* The Supplier Rationalization project isn't scheduled to deliver the majority of its value until next year, but since the project is designed to wring costs out of Fairland's procurement processes, it may make sense to accelerate it. This would be consistent with Fairland's short-term objectives of achieving greater efficiency and short-term profitability.

Having said this, let's reiterate that the Intentions tool is a diagnostic, rather than a prescriptive, tool. Although it may uncover some low-hanging fruit, the primary benefit of the Intentions tool is to establish a baseline understanding of current alignment and provide hints about where to dig deeper using the other diagnostic tools.

Turning up the Dial on Intentions

So far, in the calculations of the Intentions tool, we have used the effort method. As promised, we now turn to the expected-outcomes method. Each method has both benefits and drawbacks. Let's take a moment to consider these. Then we'll complete an exercise using the expected-outcomes method.

Measuring effort/budget of each project presents several advantages over measuring outcomes. First, most organizations know their project budgets, so there is no need to do a lot of research. This approach also creates a level of discipline. Since there is a finite budget for each project, the allocation between short- and long-term objectives is a zero-sum game. In other words, you can't allocate one dollar to multiple objectives.

However, measuring by effort/budget tends to create a bias in favor of large-budget projects. In addition, relative efficiency and the overall cost versus benefit can be obscured when you measure by budgets alone. What happens, for example, when two projects have equal budgets of $1 million, but one has the potential to deliver $10 million in benefits, while the other has the potential to deliver $20 million? Obviously, this critical distinction would be lost if budget were the only measure.

Furthermore, using effort/budget as the sole measure does not fully support the concept of moving projects into the intersections of the intentions shapes. For each dollar allocated to one objective, the fixed budget inherently means it is removed from the other objectives.

Measuring by expected outcomes solves many of these problems. Because this method measures outcomes rather than budgets, it eliminates the larger project bias. Furthermore, projects can be given credit for achieving multiple goals, so there is no trade-off or fixed total when assessing the impact of projects.

However, measuring by expected outcomes also has its limitations. First, trying to score perfect alignment on all three objectives is unrealistic, so reasonable targets need to be developed. Second, without a quantified cost or budget, outcomes don't reflect the relative size of each project. Finally, expected outcomes suffer from "benefit inflation." Advocates of particular initiatives overpromise against objectives, leading to the very real possibility that the project will not deliver as promised.

Here are the steps for the expected-outcome method:

1. Assuming a total of 30 points to allocate for each project (with a maximum of 10 for each intention category), evaluate how well the expected outcomes of each project meet each of the company's three types of objectives: short-term, long-term, and trait. A 10 would indicate that the project's outcomes are *very* consistent with the objective category and have a *significant impact* on meeting the goal.

2. Next, total (horizontally) the points for each project. Then subtract this total from the total possible—30 points (three objectives, each with 10 points possible). This calculates the gap between the maximum (30) and actual contribution each project is making toward intentions.

3. Based on the size of the gap, review individual projects to see if there are potential ways to reshape each, individually or together, to better align with the company's objectives.

Table 5-3 is the result of the expected-outcomes method applied to Fairland's portfolio. As illustrated, the measure of value for each of Fairland's projects is totaled across the three objective categories. Projects that rank higher are delivering greater value across multiple intentions. Projects that rank particularly low across the three columns provide Anderson and Burkley with another view of how well (or poorly) individual projects, as well as the portfolio, are aligned.

Through the expected-outcomes analysis, you can see the overall contribution of a project to intentions by looking at the total points scored. You can also see projects that may be designed to deliver on one of the company's short- or long-term objectives, but don't support traits. This analysis thus provides a potential guideline for reshaping efforts.

By viewing both the expected-outcomes and effort/budget methods together, an even richer picture can emerge. Expected outcomes provide a clear view of which projects are *expected* to contribute and which are not. The budget allocation process then provides a sanity check. First, it provides the relative cost of each project, so a cost/benefit understand-

Table 5-3: Fairland's Projects/Intentions Analysis-Expected Outcomes Method

Project	Expected Outcomes for Company Intentions (10 Point Maximum)			Total Scores		
	Short-term Objectives	Long-term Objectives	Trait Objectives	Potential Score	Actual Score	Gap
Market Research Redesign	8	6	7	30	21	9
Sales Force Automation	5	3	2	30	10	20
Retail Promotion	5	8	6	30	19	11
Supplier Rationalization	2	5	7	30	14	16
ERP	6	7	7	30	20	10
eLearning	5	7	2	30	14	16
Legacy HR	2	4	4	30	10	20
Benefit Portal	6	9	8	30	23	7
Legacy Data Integration	3	6	9	30	18	12
Regulatory Compliance	0	0	0	30	0	30
Total	42	55	52	300	149	151

ing can be gained. Second, it provides insight into whether projects can truly deliver on the promises made by looking at the amount of resources actually applied to each objective.

By now, you can probably see several ways to modify this analysis and turn up the dial for your own purposes. We encourage you to set the level of granularity and quantification where you can gain insight without getting mired in overly complex analysis.

The Sides Tool

In chapter 4, we described how the Sides tool helps you look at the portfolio with new eyes. Sides reduces organizational bias from the portfolio analysis, dampening self-interested perspectives and politics that all too often contribute to portfolio misalignment. Also, by grouping projects around major business activities, waste, redundancy, and even conflicting objectives in the project portfolio are easier to see, thereby setting the stage for improved efficiency. Furthermore, each Side of the business correlates to a section of the income statement, providing a high-level link between the portfolio and shareholder value. And finally, because each Side relates to specific constituencies both inside and outside the organization, using this tool provides a perspective of the portfolio that promotes traits.

Applying the Sides tool to a portfolio is a fairly simple process, requiring two project-level data points. The first data point, as you'd expect, results from assigning each project to a particular Side. The second results from indicating the project's primary impact, relative to the income statement. After adding these two data points, the portfolio can be sorted by Side and reviewed.

The Sides tool provides a view along three different dimensions. First, the allocation of resources by sides can be compared to the company's intentions to provide another perspective on the allocation of resources vis à vis intentions. Second, the projects in each side can be reviewed to see how well they relate to each other and to the Side in question. This dimension is where overlapping objectives, conflicting approaches, and differing outcomes may first be uncovered. Finally, the sides view can be taken to another level of granularity, considering the

SIDES IN A NUTSHELL

SELL-SIDE includes activities that relate to the marketing, servicing, and selling of products and services. Its principal goal is to maximize the value of customer relationships over time.

INSIDE is everything that happens within the enterprise. Generally composed of two parts, operations and administration, inside seeks to coordinate and streamline internal processes and information flows.

BUY-SIDE is any part of the organization that works with the supply chain. The goal of this side is to optimize the value network.

MULTI-SIDE refers to projects and activities that span more than one of the sides, often providing integration and cooperation across them.

impact on constituents' needs, both articulated and unarticulated.

To see the Sides tool in action, let's go back to Fairland Products, where Anderson and Burkley add a column to the portfolio for sides and tag each of the individual projects by the appropriate area (see table 5-4). Note that they have also mapped each project to its primary impact on the income statement, based on the business results each project is expected to produce in the coming year.

After sorting by sides, Anderson and Burkley notice some interesting relationships between the portfolio and Fairland's intentions. While Fairland's current focus is short-term profitability, its longer-term goal is to grow revenue. Anderson and Burkley immediately see the result of their trade-off between short- and long-term objectives, with the realization that 65 percent of the portfolio's budget is going to inside and buy-side. This may not leave sufficient investment in sell-side to establish their foundation for future growth.

This relative balance is confirmed by mapping the projects to the company's income statement. From this perspective, the majority of effort also appears to go toward efficiency or margin improvement. This brings into clear focus the strategic decisions that have been made. It raises questions such as: "Are our objectives too heavily skewed toward cost reduction and margin improvement?" "Can we do a better job of having projects that contribute to both of these business priorities,

Table 5-4: Sides View of Fairland's Representative Portfolio

Project	Side	Link to Income Statement	Short-term %	Short-term $	Long-term %	Long-term $	Unallocated %	Unallocated $	Contribution to Traits (H, M, L, N)
Market Research Redesign	Sell-side	Revenue	60%	$1.2	40%	$0.8	0%	$0.0	M
Sales Force Automation	Sell-side	G&A	40%	$0.8	30%	$0.6	30%	$0.6	L
Retail Promotion	Sell-side	Revenue	20%	$0.6	80%	$2.4	0%	$0.0	M
Percent of Budget: Sell-Side	**35%**			**$2.6**		**$3.8**		**$0.6**	
ERP	Inside	COGS	40%	$1.2	60%	$1.8	0%	$0.0	M
eLearning	Inside	G&A	30%	$0.3	70%	$0.7	0%	$0.0	L
Legacy HR	Inside	G&A	20%	$0.4	60%	$1.2	20%	$0.4	L
Benefit Portal	Inside	G&A	30%	$0.6	70%	$1.4	0%	$0.0	H
Legacy Data Integration	Inside	G&A	30%	$0.9	70%	$2.1	0%	$0.0	H
Regulatory Compliance	Inside	G&A	0%	$0.0	0%	$0.0	100%	$1.0	N
Percent of Budget: Inside	**60%**			**$3.40**		**$7.20**		**$1.40**	
Supplier Rationalization	Buy-side	COGS	20%	$0.2	80%	$0.8	0%	$0.0	L
Percent of Budget: Buy-Side	**5%**			**$0.2**		**$0.8**		**$0.0**	

Total Budget= $20 million   H= High; M= Medium; L= Low; N= None

THREE STEPS FOR THE SIDES TOOL

1. Assign each project to a side and map it to the income statement.
2. Sort projects by sides and gauge level of effort allocated to each side.
3. Analyze how projects relate to one another and to intentions.

rather than one or the other?" At the end of the day, they may be satisfied with the result, but the choices are now clearer and more deliberate.

The third step in the Sides analysis is a look at how projects interrelate. Could they be working more closely together? The first observation is that each project "stays within the borders" of its respective owners. As mentioned, our approach creates new value by breaking down the "silo thinking" that so often permeates projects and organizations. Most often, the solution is *not* to take a heavy hand and combine projects, but rather, to figure out the coordination points, and see where resources can be better leveraged and greater value can be delivered.

Upon some reflection, Anderson and Burkley decide that both the Legacy Data Integration and ERP projects may be similarly misconceived (or at least, mislabeled). Although these projects appear to be inside, they can *be considered as key enablers of the sell- and buy-sides of the business.* For example, both of these projects create "normalized" data, solve the problem of "systems not talking," and enable activities as diverse as the retail promotion, benefit portal, and future e-procurement projects.

Could changing how these projects are conceived further encourage trait development? For example, could ERP make Fairland more House in Order by promoting information sharing and more for-the-common-good behaviors? By creating the ability to link standardized data, could legacy data make the organization more Eco-Driven? How would these projects change if they were (accurately) labeled "sell-side" or "buy-side" (depending on the module)? Would they deliver enhanced outcomes and better promote trait mind-sets?

Anderson and Burkley also turn back to some of the nagging questions that came to light with the Intentions tool. They start by grouping

INSIGHTS FROM THE SIDES TOOL

- Reduces organizational bias.
- Allows portfolio to be mapped to intentions and the income statement.
- Creates opportunities to spot both redundancy and improvements for how projects work together.

their sell-side projects together and begin critically reviewing them (as shown in table 5-5).

In particular, the sides view looks at the level of integration, the match to trait objectives, and alignment to the desired allocation of effort.

- The level of integration looks at how well the project is integrated with other projects in any given side. In Fairland's sell-side portfolio (see table 5-5), for example, two-thirds of the projects are stand-alone sell-side systems.

- From a traits perspective, looking at projects by sides reveals whether they encourage stronger interrelationships between different units inside the company as well as external organizations.

- Finally, by combining this view with information from the Intentions tool, an imbalance in resource allocation may surface.

As a result of these three different views, Fairland can see an opportunity to further integrate the sell-side projects. Both the Market Research Redesign and the Retail Promotion projects build revenue. Market Research drives product innovation—a pull-based strategy. On the other side, Retail Promotion grows revenue by helping retailers optimize promotions and product mix—a push-based strategy. Right now, Retail Promotion is using only historical data, while Market Research uses prospective data.

Consider the concept of bringing together the "push" of Retail Promotion with the "pull" of the forward-looking Market Research data. Through reshaping the Market Research effort—by collecting and analyzing real-time data on customer promotional and pricing

Table 5-5: Fairland's Sell-side Portfolio Review

Project	Project Sponsor	Level of Integration	Fit with Trait Objectives	Alignment to Optimal Allocation of Efforts
Market Research Redesign	VP Marketing	Stand-alone project	Project moves Fairland closer to customers and furthers Outside-In trait	Project close to allocated effort across short- and long-term objectives
Sales Force Automation	VP Sales	Stand-alone project	Efficiency project automates existing expense submission process, contributing to House in Order trait	Project not fully aligned with short- and long-term objectives
Retail Promotion	Director of Customer Support	Project integrates with back-end operations and ERP projects	Project moves Fairland closer to retailers, promoting Eco-Driven, Outside-In, and Fighting Trim traits	Project fully allocated (though not fully aligned with optimal allocation) across short- and long-term objectives

preferences—new value could be delivered directly to the retailer, thereby enhancing the Retail Promotion project. The traditional scope of Market Research could expand to include promotions, integrating push and pull. Linking these two sell-side projects might well yield more value while promoting stronger traits-thinking. Thus, the customer, the retailer, and Fairland would all benefit.

An even more expansive idea would be to integrate Market Research, Retail Promotion, and the recently completed call center. Fairland would thus integrate its customer information flows throughout the company. This information could form the basis of decision making for new product development, retail support, and even manufacturing forecasting.

More important, this sell-side change would help promote traits. Up until now, Market Research has been a stand-alone project that didn't improve Fairland's ability to *respond* to new information. But if Market Research were linked with the Retail Promotion project, the organization would improve its ability to act on new information, creating a more sophisticated "sense and respond" enterprise and furthering its Fighting Trim objectives.

With this first-pass analysis complete, let's see what turning up the dial has to offer.

Turning up the Dial on Sides

Earlier, we stated that the sides are trait-friendly, because they are oriented toward specific constituencies. Turning up the dial extends these categories to the constituency level, uncovering additional insights and opportunities for the portfolio. We can break projects down by constituencies, just as we did for sides. Consider table 5-6.

In turning up the dial, we look at how the project portfolio is meeting the needs of these constituencies. The more an organization gains clarity on its constituencies' needs, the greater the effectiveness of project outcomes. With that in mind, considering both the *articulated* and *unarticulated* needs of your key constituencies sheds new light on how well your portfolio is delivering value. Let's explore this a little further.

Table 5-6: Constituency Groups within Sides

Sell-side	Inside	Buy-side
Customers	Employees	Logistics
Channel partners	Recruits	Procurement
Influencers/information brokers	Subcontractors	Suppliers
Service providers	Investors	Vendors
Brokers/agents	Staff augmentation	Expeditors/intermediaries
Wholesalers	Alumni	
Retailers		
Alliance partners		
Multi-side		
	Government	
	Regulatory agencies	
	Industry associations	
	Rating agencies	
	Press/media	

Articulated needs are those that are readily identified, understood, and easily communicated by a constituency. These needs generally reveal themselves through goals, focus groups, surveys, and business requirements.

Unarticulated needs include the assumptions, inferences, and expectations people are often unaware of as they choose among alternatives. For example, customers may subconsciously associate the loudness of a motor as an indication of its power, or an employee may assume that each step in his workflow is essential and not be able to conceptualize improvements to it. These needs are rarely articulated and do not reveal themselves except through careful observation. Nevertheless, these latent, unexpressed needs remain a building block toward constituency satisfaction and represent ways to build closer relationships, increase performance, and engender loyalty. Some companies go to great lengths

DEFINING NEEDS

ARTICULATED NEEDS are the expressed wants or requirements of a particular constituency.

UNARTICULATED NEEDS are the latent requirements of the constituency.

LATENT NEEDS include the assumptions, inferences, and often the subconscious expectations a constituency makes when evaluating its choices.

to identify and understand these needs. Case in point: To get the right smell in their new cars, Nissan Design International tested more than 90 samples of leather for the Infiniti J-30 before selecting three.[1] Looking at a constituency's articulated needs builds a strong foundation and provides clear direction for projects and their outcomes. Taking time to gather the articulated constituency needs for given projects—as well as the portfolio overall—and understanding how they relate and overlap creates greater confidence that the portfolio is maximizing the return from a constituency perspective. Recall the Duke Energy example in chapter 3. By asking customers what they needed, Duke quickly prioritized its Web site functionality and saved time and money by eliminating features its customers didn't value.[2] This is an example of project-level articulated needs.

The market research nudists. What does the search for unarticulated needs look like? Well, let's return to Moen for a colorful, extreme example. When Moen was looking to break into the showerhead market, the company wanted to learn exactly how people showered. To move up the learning curve and design their new product line, researchers not only conducted focus groups and observed how people bought showerheads, *they even watched how people showered.*[3]

Moen installed waterproof cameras in volunteers' homes. (To find subjects willing to be observed in the shower, Moen recruited nudists.) By understanding a constituent's unarticulated needs, Moen learned that the shower is not just a place to get clean. Their research showed it was also a warm, silent, and private place to think, meditate, and even pray.[4]

This insight, along with more pragmatic observations, helped Moen design the new showerhead with innovative features. For example, Moen learned that the shower is generally dark because the shower curtain blocks the light. They also learned that many people, particularly those with glasses, can't see well in the shower. In response, Moen designed the massage settings dial to be large and easy to adjust and then placed it below the showerhead for easy access.[5]

The result was the Moen Revolution showerhead. From the larger settings of the dial, to the engineered size of the water droplets, to the weight of the showerhead, the Revolution was designed to meet both the articulated and unarticulated needs of the showering consumer market.[6]

While companies can go to great lengths to understand a company's articulated and unarticulated needs, as Moen illustrates, valuable insights can often be gained just by putting yourself in your constituency's shoes—in their context—and asking some simple questions:

- What does the constituency need to be successful? What is the ultimate solution it is trying to achieve? What is its underlying motive?

- Does the constituency have the tools, skills, and information needed to achieve its goals? What are the frustrations that prevent success?

- What measurements would the constituency use to grade its experience with this project? Are there ways to influence those measurements?

- What does the constituency buy from or sell to the organization? Is this part of a bigger solution it is trying to achieve?

- Why does this constituency choose to interact with you? What are the "pain points" that the constituent faces when interacting with the organization? What can you do to improve the interaction?

- What is the emotional state of the constituency? How does the experience created by the project either fulfill, change, or improve that emotional state? Are there different cues (verbal, visual, tactile, and audio) that influence a constituency's experience?

- What is the context of the constituent? Are there underlying assumptions that this constituency demonstrates or has communicated?

Focusing the portfolio on meeting the articulated and unarticulated needs of multiple constituencies also promotes the Outside-In trait through project design. Furthermore, a constituency analysis provides greater shape and purpose to projects and to the overall portfolio.

A Few Parting Thoughts on Sides

Although sides may appear to divide the organization along somewhat arbitrary lines, in fact, the effect is quite the opposite. Sides creates a manageable *starting point for action.* Too often, when looking at the entire organization, companies bog down in politics and the sheer magnitude of the changes at hand. By looking through sides, projects are grouped by common interest, constituencies, and areas of impact. The Sides tool creates more manageable ways to foster collaboration and cooperation—but again, it does so one step at a time. Done right, it generates momentum for a mind-set shift and creates opportunities for synthesis and action that can transcend either a centralized or decentralized organization structure, flagging opportunities for greater cooperation, and value creation.

Right Brain

Direction	
✓	Efficiency
✓	Risk Reduction
	Flexibility

The Right Brain Tool

Is there any circumstance in which a portfolio that is perfectly aligned to the company's intentions is effectively valueless? The answer—as you may recall from chapter 4—is yes. It's the circumstance when the constituencies simply can't implement the changes that are required of them. With the Right Brain tool, we look at how to better allocate the capacity for change—for the organization overall, as well as the impacted constituencies—to lower the risk and enhance the implementation success of the *entire* portfolio. This portfolio-level analysis and coordination is rare, despite its obvious implications. It is our aim to remedy this shortcoming, which robs portfolio value, by putting companies in the habit of routinely and

RIGHT BRAIN RECALLED

The term *right brain* is borrowed from neuroscience research. The right brain focuses on aesthetics, feelings, and creativity. The left brain, by contrast, focuses on logical thinking, analysis, and accuracy.

directly considering and addressing these issues. Through Right Brain, companies can examine questions like these:

- What is our overall appetite for change, and how does it match our capacity?

- If limited capacity for change is a significant constraint on the organization's ability to achieve its intentions, how might that capacity be expanded?

- Are there specific time frames in which a specific constituency's capacity for change is especially overtaxed? How might projects be reshaped to resolve this issue? (Reshaping might include changing their timing, scope, or both.)

- Are there opportunities to coordinate change management activities across projects more effectively? If so, where are they, and how could this kind of coordination be implemented?

Applying the Right Brain Tool

Let's go back to Ellie Anderson and Fairland Products. As she was compiling her sample portfolio, Anderson was struck by the magnitude of the changes underway. Now, as she starts thinking about Right Brain issues, she ponders this again. Between the ERP system and other various projects, the technologies and processes of the company are changing fundamentally. The question in Anderson's mind is, "Can our people keep up?"

To evaluate whether change requirements and change capacity match, it's helpful to assign the people in the organization and its

FOUR STEPS FOR THE RIGHT BRAIN TOOL

1. Identify key constituencies.
2. Evaluate each project's impact on the constituencies, including the magnitude of the change, the willingness and ability of each constituency to make the change, and the timing of the change.
3. Assess overall match between change requirements and change capacity.
4. Identify opportunities for leveraging change activities across projects.

ecosystem to constituency groups and then evaluate the demands of the portfolio on each group. As step 1 then, Anderson sits down and writes a list of key constituencies:

- Corporate headquarters

- Employees

- Consumers

- Retailers

- Suppliers (including Fairland's distribution partners)

- Government regulators

For the purpose of making our points, we'll look at Right Brain from the perspective of Fairland's employee constituency. (On her own, Anderson will complete the Right Brain exploration for other key constituencies.)

In step 2, Anderson examines the demands of the portfolio, as currently constructed, on Fairland's employees. How is this done? Unfortunately, there's no one universally applicable answer, since measuring and assessing a constituency's capacity for change is part art and part science, and our approach does rely partly on managerial judgment. But in our experience, we find that organizations benefit from considering the *collective change capacity* that is or will be required at the *portfolio level.*

DETERMINANTS OF CHANGE CAPACITY

- Magnitude
- Ability
- Willingness
- Timing

By looking at the portfolio, the impact of multiple projects on each constituency can be reviewed. This, we argue, is something that is too broad to be done on the project level.

Change capacity is the extent to which people can move from one way of doing things to another *in any given period of time*. To estimate how much change capacity a project uses, four variables are assessed.

1. *Magnitude of change.* Small changes generally (though not always) use less capacity than large ones.

2. *Ability of constituency to change.* A change that people are able to make using existing skills takes less capacity than ones that require new skills.

3. *Willingness of constituency to change.* Change that is resisted uses up more change capacity than change that is welcomed.

4. *Timing.* Changes that occur in the same time frame compete for capacity, and an overload of change can consume even more capacity due to the confusion and frustration that are likely to arise.

Rather than revisit all of Fairland's projects, Anderson and Burkley consider the projects that create the largest change demands on employees (again, the constituency group we are focusing on). Since projects are likely to affect (for example) the sales force differently from the Market Research group and the IT department, they include constituency subgroups. We encourage you to include similar subgroups in your analyses as warranted.

Table 5-7 shows what Anderson and Burkley's evaluation reveals.

Table 5-7: Fairland's Right Brain Employee Analysis

Project	Magnitude	Ability	Willingness	Timing	Notes
ERP	Large	◑ (Medium)	○ (Low)	Continuing through next two years	Significant displacement of workers from existing roles. Employee attitude is "just get it over with."
eLearning	Medium	◑ (Medium)	◑ (Medium)	Ongoing	Many managers are excited, though some are resistant. None know where they'll find the time.
Legacy HR	Medium	No impact	No impact	This year	Project is largely transparent to employees.
Benefit Portal	Small	◑ (Medium)	● (High)	Midyear through year-end	Employees very much want self-service.

● = High   ◑ = Medium   ○ = Low

Anderson now takes some time to figure out what this chart is telling her. Her goals are: (1) to develop actions that will make sure there is enough change capacity to support the activities of the portfolio at any point in time (step 3), and (2) to ensure that opportunities to coordinate change activities are exploited (step 4). Her conclusions are as follows.

- The ERP project, in its third year of a four-year effort, represents major ongoing changes for affected employees. The learning curve for the modules already rolled out has been steeper than expected, and people are struggling to learn new processes and systems, identify and fix problems, clarify roles, and generally figure out who's supposed to do what in the wake of the restructuring. For example, managers at Fairland are quite good at "managing by the numbers," but don't have the same feel for the new numbers as they had for the old. What reports do they come from? What do they really mean? What's the right action? These employees are weary, and get even more discouraged when they look to the future and see two more years of tumultuous change ahead for them. All these factors combine to create *risk* for the portfolio. Therefore, other projects that call upon the same employee base to absorb change may need to be rescheduled to free up enough capacity to finish the ERP implementation and deliver the expected results.

- Second, the eLearning project appears to be a very good investment, but managers are hard-pressed to make full use of this new resource while the ERP implementation continues. At the same time, several of the projects will attempt to instill some common skills in a core group of managers, so there appear to be opportunities to combine training using the eLearning infrastructure. Finally, since eLearning will not be a plug-and-play implementation, ensuring its effectiveness will require careful monitoring and follow-up.

- The Benefit Portal is welcomed by employees and, as such, is more likely to add to (rather than detract from) the overall change capacity. The "word on the street" is that through this effort, the company is acknowledging its obligation to pay attention to employees' needs during a time of substantial change.

- The Legacy HR sounds like a project that would have broad implications for the entire organization, but it is largely transparent to most employees.

It is also helpful to view key constituencies' change capacity through sides. Bottlenecks sometimes pop up and demand to be counted. For example, when Anderson looks at the sell-side projects and their impact on affected employees, she sees the results shown in table 5-8.

As Anderson considers this sell-side portrait, she notes that the sales force is overextended. Retail Promotion and Sales Force Automation are scheduled to occur in the same time frame, possibly jeopardizing both projects. One response, of course, would be to delay Sales Force Automation by a year. But Anderson has been adamant that it move ahead, in part because benchmarks show that Fairland's sales force is less productive than others. She needs to rethink this now, given its Right Brain risks.

So what else might help? Because the sales force is more accepting of the Retail Promotion project, perhaps this project can—in addition to its current objectives—help the sales force become more technology-literate. Building on this foundation, Sales Force Automation might have a better chance of success.

This exercise helps Anderson spot and think about an organizational "cow path." It appears that many in the organization, including but not limited to the sales force, have trouble accepting new technology. Anderson would like to get people off that specific path and, more generally, help people become more resilient and receptive to change. Progress toward this outcome could be woven into both the Retail Promotion and Sales Force Automation projects. Anderson makes a note to engage the VP of sales and the rest of the management team in a dialogue about these issues.

As we've seen, the Right Brain represents a reality check for the organization. For Anderson and her leadership team, the challenge lies in implementing an aggressive series of changes in the organization without overtaxing constituencies. Using the Right Brain tool, she's gained insight into the change capacity issues that her company faces, and she's identified some possible solutions, such as delaying the Sales Force Automation implementation. She's also generated ideas about

Table 5-8: Fairland's Sell-Side Employee Analysis

Project	Magnitude	Ability	Willingness	Timing	Notes
Market Research Redesign	Small	◑	●	Implement this year	Market Research is pushing hard for this project and has the needed skills.
Sales Force Automation	Large	◑	○	Begins roll out at end of year	IT wants this project. Sales force opposes the project—it doesn't want corporate checking up on it.
Retail Promotion	Large	○	●	Just starting	Sales welcomes this project, but to help its retail accounts use the new tool, it will need new skills.

● = High   ◑ = Medium   ○ = Low

RIGHT BRAIN TOOL INSIGHTS

- The project portfolio is an underused but logical place to measure change requirements and capacity at both the organizational and constituency levels.

- Change capacity is determined by each project's impact on individual constituent groups along the dimensions of magnitude, ability, willingness, and timing.

- Right Brain analysis uncovers constituents' change capacity and possible responses, and over the longer term, expands the organization's change capacity.

creating some two-for-one synergies, such as using the eLearning infrastructure to deliver some of the ERP training. Finally, she's spotted a weak link in the organization's change capacity—the sales force—and started thinking about how to address the larger issues this raises.

Turning up the Dial on Right Brain

There are two primary ways to turn up the dial on the Right Brain tool. The first is to consider additional constituencies or subgroups. The second is to better quantify the capacity of constituencies to change.

First, it can be beneficial to consider additional and/or smaller segments of constituencies. For example, if you have both business and retail customers, recognize that the portfolio often puts very different change demands upon these groups, which can have quite different change capacities. Conversely, one constituency's change capacity can impede changes for another. If there are multiple projects that adversely impact the sales force, to illustrate the point, their lack of change capacity may constrain the desired impact to your customers, regardless of the customer's capacity for change. And from another angle, if your business has multiple projects that impact your sales force, their lack of change capacity may constrain the portfolio as a whole.

We encourage you to *stay realistic* in this realm. Big companies have lots of constituency subgroups. (We've seen a *six-page* list of constituencies associated with a single project!) By instinct and training, good managers are tempted to worry about *each and every one* of them. But this level of detail doesn't help you see the big picture of the portfolio, which is critical to the effective use of the Right Brain tool. To determine the right level of detail, keep the list of constituencies to a manageable number and stay focused on the groups that are most important to the successful implementation of the portfolio.

These groups will change as the composition of projects in the portfolio changes. For example, the current Fairland project portfolio has multiple initiatives that require extensive involvement from HR, including Legacy HR, eLearning, and the Benefit Portal. In past portfolios, there were not as many simultaneous HR projects, and it was less critical to check the pulse of this particular employee population. Today, it makes a lot of sense for Anderson to keep an eye on this subgroup.

Another way to turn up the dial is to augment the simple analysis presented earlier with more information from, for example, formal skills assessments, change-readiness and employee attitude surveys, and dialogue with key constituencies. These quantitative assessments more fully measure the key determinants of change capacity, especially magnitude, ability, and willingness.

For example, a formal skills assessment determines how many of the needed skills employees already possess, and therefore how steep their learning curves are likely to be. It removes managerial bias in estimating ability—minimizing the influences of both the manager who always thinks her people can do anything and the manager who always assumes his people are slow adapters with little desire to learn.

Similarly, employee attitude surveys can contribute to the assessment of willingness. This can be especially important if those reviewing the portfolio are quite removed from the constituencies under consideration. For example, in many companies senior management is too far removed from employees on the front lines to gauge their willingness to change.

If your organization has a history of projects that miss goals because of people-related issues—especially issues associated with a particular constituent group—then turning up the dial is likely to have real benefit. The data from existing surveys often turns out to be very useful in developing a more refined, accurate, and quantitative view of change capacity.

In many cases, a couple of questions can be added to an existing survey, minimizing the demands being placed on the surveyed population while improving information quality. But don't forget that there are likely to be trade-offs associated with ferreting out more information. Be selective, if you go this route, since more surveys often translate into "more disruptions."

It is also useful to track the overall results of the portfolio by conducting post-implementation reviews of projects to see whether they achieved their goals—and if not, why not. The trends in project portfolio performance provide an excellent guide to how much emphasis and effort to invest in Right Brain. It is beyond the scope of this book to walk through how to conduct skills assessments, employee attitude and change readiness surveys, constituency dialogues, and post-implementation reviews, but there is abundant information readily available on these topics.

Summary of Diagnostic Tools

At this point, we've illustrated each of the diagnostic tools in action. Now let's step back and summarize the insights derived, both individually and in combination.

We started with the Trait Meter tool. Fairland used this tool to evaluate where Fairland is vis à vis its industry in developing trait mind-sets. This assessment highlighted Fairland's slow speed to market as a key competitive issue, thereby establishing Fighting Trim and House in Order as its trait objectives. Having set its trait objectives and completed its Intentions Framework, Fairland was ready to begin using the diagnostic tools.

First we presented the Intentions tool, which set the agenda by outlining the overall nature and size of the alignment opportunity. We then moved to the Sides tool, where the portfolio was recast to remove organizational bias and reflect both the company's income statement and external constituencies' experiences.

Finally, the Right Brain tool measured one of the most overlooked aspects of portfolio success: the portfolio's required change versus change capacity at both the organizational and constituency levels. The observations that Anderson and Burkley have made about Fairland's portfolio so far are summarized in table 5-9.

Table 5-9: Summary of Fairland's Diagnostic Findings

Tool	Summary of Observations
Trait Meters	**Trait Objective Insight** • Fairland is at or near parity with its industry in Eco-Driven and Outside-In. • Fairland's slow speed to market is jeopardizing its competitiveness, making Fighting Trim and the enabling trait of House in Order key trait objectives.
Intentions	**Portfolio-level Insight** • Effort is overallocated to long-term objectives and underallocated to short-term and trait objectives. • About 10 percent of the portfolio's effort doesn't map to intentions, but regulatory requirements make it a necessary cost of doing business. **Project-level Insight** • The eLearning project can be used to educate managers and actively promote traits. • The Legacy Data Integration project is a "building block" project for long-term and trait objectives. • The Sales Force Automation and Legacy HR projects do not appear to fully align with intentions. • Accelerating the Supplier Rationalization project would help achieve Fairland's short-term priorities.
Sides	**Portfolio-level Insight** • Currently 60 percent of the portfolio is classified as inside, illustrating Fairland's short-term profitability priorities and clarifying the trade-offs with other growth-related objectives. **Project-level Insight** • It may be possible to view ERP as more of a strategic tool and a launch pad for enabling sell-side and buy-side projects rather than as an inside systems project. • There is an opportunity to gain additional benefit by linking the Market Research Redesign and Retail Promotion projects. This move would also promote trait development.

Tool	Summary of Observations
◖ Right Brain	Portfolio-level Insight • The level of expected change reflected in the portfolio, which includes the impact of the multiyear ERP project, is creating an organizational weariness with change. • The sales force seems to be the weak link in the organization's change capacity, and the Sales Force Automation project may be delayed to help "bring them up the curve," using the Retail Promotion project as a lever. Project-level Insight • The Benefit Portal will be well received by the general employee group, but is creating some friction inside the HR and benefits departments. • There may be an opportunity to leverage the eLearning infrastructure for ERP training.

As they talk their way through these observations, Anderson, Burkley, and other senior Fairland managers start a dialogue about a few specific observations. First, they discuss the Legacy HR project. Because HR uses an old system, IT and HR—at the corporate and divisional levels—are both advocating its replacement. Information Technology wants to lower its systems maintenance costs, and HR wants faster system response times and better access to real-time data to support decision making.

But as they continue their discussions, Fairland's senior management team isn't convinced by these arguments. This project is transparent to end users (employees), and it does not appear that other projects, including the Benefit Portal, are dependent on the upgrade. So what is the value inherent in this project? Although upgrading the system may produce some efficiency benefits, can the same dollars be spent elsewhere to produce a greater benefit? And judging from Fairland's work with the tools so far, implementing both the Legacy HR and the Benefit Portal risks pulling too many HR resources away from day-to-day operations.

A second area of discussion is the Supplier Rationalization project. If the benefits of this project could be moved forward, the project would be better aligned with the immediate needs of the organization. For Fairland's management team, the challenge is whether and how to accelerate this project. Since resources are scarce, do they reallocate resources from other projects, resulting in potential delays, or is there a way to rethink the implementation of this project to accelerate some value creation?

Anderson and Burkley will bring all of these thoughts with them as they begin to use the tools in chapter 6.

6
taming the future

*The unpredictability inherent in human affairs is
due largely to the fact that the by-products of a
human process are more fateful than the product.*

ERIC HOFFER (1902–1983), U.S. PHILOSOPHER

Why is the information frontier so unpredictable? In part because frontiers are opened by *people,* and—as Hoffer implies—the unintended consequences of human processes are profound and often more significant than the intended consequences. But unintended consequences aren't created solely by a myriad of actors. They're also the result of an unprecedented ubiquity and transparency of information. This, too, generates daunting levels of static and confusion in today's business context. What's the best response to all this confusion? Well, to *deal* with it. When the horizon is obscured, put one foot in front of the other and take appropriate steps to *keep your options open.*

The tools described in chapter 5 provide insight into how to define and improve the alignment between a company's portfolio and intentions *today.* But there remains another challenge: setting the table so that the organization can adapt in ways that maintain or increase alignment over time. In this chapter, we focus on building flexibility, or *options,* into the project portfolio. In this way, alignment becomes dynamic rather than static. This posture also helps develop traits, another key to prospering on the frontier.

Specifically, this chapter focuses on three tools: Common Threads, Project Chunking, and What-if Planning (see table 6-1).

You may recall from chapter 4 that the portfolio gains flexibility through Common Threads by maintaining shareable, up-to-date information (through repositories such as ERP) and by creating reusable components. Both the information and the components can be leveraged over multiple projects.

In Project Chunking, we work to create options by "chunking" projects into smaller-scope, shorter-length projects. Chunked projects are more likely to deliver pay-as-you-go benefits—with less risk and more frequent choice points. In What-if Planning, we evaluate the portfolio against possible future scenarios and use the information gained to modify the portfolio so it can better respond to any outcome.

In keeping with our "turning up the dial" design, the tools are modular and scalable. Keep in mind, however, that although these tools provide value when used independently, they provide an even greater return when used together. For example, Common Threads can help chunk projects more effectively, and What-if Planning helps inform when and how a company could change a project's direction as chunks are implemented.

Let's take a closer look at each of the tools. Along the way, we reintroduce our traveling companions—Ellie Anderson and Brendan Burkley of Fairland Products—to continue the practical illustration of the tools we present.

Common Threads Tool

The central idea of Common Threads is that project components can be reused, replicated, extended, or better leveraged—improving both the efficiency and flexibility of the portfolio. This is not a novel idea, of course (think program code libraries), and companies often initiate projects designed to create common usage. ERP is such an example, and it is a good model, but it's not the only model. Within the project portfolio, there are less

Table 6-1: Tools That Promote Options (highlighted)

Tool	Description	Ways Tool Improves Alignment
Trait Meters	Assesses, plans, and measures trait development	Direction, flexibility
Intentions	Assesses alignment of portfolio to intentions	Direction, efficiency
Sides	Removes bias and finds synergies by sorting projects into main business activities	Direction, efficiency
Right Brain	Identifies change capacity issues	Efficiency, risk reduction
Common Threads	Finds common, reusable components	Efficiency, risk reduction, flexibility
Project Chunking	Structures projects into bite-size pieces that deliver incremental, stand-alone value	Risk reduction, flexibility
What-if Planning	Develops contingencies for varying scenarios	Risk reduction, flexibility

obvious but worthwhile reusable project components, including operational processes and policies, change management activities such as training and communications, and even constituency experiences.

Using our Common Threads tool, we break down a company's projects into their component parts and then search across these components to identify shareable components, or threads. Once found and developed as "shareware," these components are cataloged and available for reuse by multiple initiatives.

This approach not only creates efficiencies, it also makes the portfolio more flexible. In chapter 4, we noted Dow Chemical's response to the unforeseen event of employees abusing their e-mail privileges: The company's reusable e-learning component provided an effective platform for a rapid, far-ranging, and relatively inexpensive response to a serious organizational challenge.[1]

Using Common Threads also reduces risk. Since components in the library are known to be effective (each has a proven track record), implementation risk falls for those efforts that recycle these existing components appropriately. As libraries become robust, the interoperability of the company as a whole grows, facilitating more flexible configurations of the business and also promoting traits.

Recall from the discussion of Outside-In in chapter 3 that constituencies don't view the world from a process perspective; instead, they look at it from an experience perspective. For example, a business customer and a channel partner both view their interactions with a software company—sales, customer support, and accounts payable—as part of their total experience with the company. Yet many companies—either because of merger integration issues or simply because they've been operating from an inside-out perspective—define discrete business processes for each of these activities (acquire customers, service customers, and collect payments).

To illustrate the point, consider your telephone/high-speed Internet access provider. Although your provider often sells its services as one integrated package, you likely receive multiple bills. When you need customer service, you are also likely to be transferred to multiple service desks, where you have to repeat the same information. The experience for the customer is neither coordinated nor seamless.

The Common Threads tool helps companies move toward this total experience, or Outside-In, perspective because component reuse can also make the constituency experience more uniform. For example, if the call center and the Web site reuse the same content, then the information customers receive is more consistent. The reuse of a user interface across multiple interactions is another example. Not only is this an efficient use of corporate resources, but it's easier for the users of the applications because they only need to learn how one interface works.

Like our other tools, Common Threads should be adopted in a practical way that reflects a company's particular circumstances. Common threads should be chosen judiciously, using conventional cost/benefit measures. But our experience suggests that there is a lot of low hanging fruit to pick, as you get comfortable with Common Threads. So with both the promise and caveats of this tool on the table, let's look at its applications.

Applying the Common Threads Tool

Let's consider GMAC Commercial Mortgage Corporation, a commercial mortgage lender. In keeping with the company's goal of trying to achieve paperless processes by the end of 2001, people within the unit developed a digital-signature component that they now reuse in multiple processes, ranging from loan approvals to employee benefit enrollments.[2]

In this simple example, the digital signature became a common thread, as both the technology and business processes for digital signatures are reused across the organization. GMAC now plans to leverage its learning from working with paperless processes inside its own four walls to develop similar processes for doing business with customers and suppliers.[3] In this way, GMAC believes, it can make quick, efficient processes part of the benefits it delivers to constituencies, promoting both Eco-Driven and Outside-In traits. As we'll see in "turning up the dial," the reuse of components can ultimately be extended across the value network.

As stated earlier, technology elements are already being used by many companies to drive commonality across their project portfolios.

Divisions and departments of companies routinely share major technology infrastructure elements, such as servers, networks, storage devices, and fiber optic backbones. But even in IT, reusable components can be hidden. Consider the case of Northwest Airlines, which was interested in developing portable workstations that would allow gate agents to leave their stations so that they could better serve passengers. The VP of information "discovered that the maintenance department was (already) certifying a wearable computer for recording nonroutine maintenance needs." Rather than implement a new technology, the IS organization seized upon this "battle-tested" computer and rolled out the portable units to the gate agents in record time.[4]

As the example illustrates, even in technology applications—where reuse is more common—there are unnoticed opportunities in the portfolio. By and large, the major strategic applications—such as ERP and customer relationship management (CRM)—are common at least across divisions, mainly due to their expense and complexity. Smaller applications, especially those perceived as less strategic, may "fly under the radar screen," yet still have potential reuse value. Applications like product data management (PDM), computer-aided design (CAD), and statistical analysis packages, for example, often get overlooked. At one Fortune 50 manufacturer, the CAD package was selected for the entire organization, and each division had to adhere to it. When it came to the PDM package, however, each division—and sometimes each product group within the division—came up with its own PDM solutions.

Let's take a moment to illustrate the relationship between common threads and average-sized projects. Most companies' portfolios are bimodal with a multitude of small- to mid-size projects and a few very large projects. While large projects tend to be top-of-mind when searching for common thread opportunities, most companies have only a handful of projects of this size. At the same time, opportunities to reuse elements can often be found across the myriad of smaller and midsized projects proliferated across the company. As figure 6-1 illustrates, it is not simply the size of the project that matters when it comes to employing the Common Threads tool, but also the number of projects underway.

The big point here? Since most project funding occurs at a department level or lower, few projects put much energy into creating solution

Figure 6-1: Bimodal Distribution of Average and Large Projects

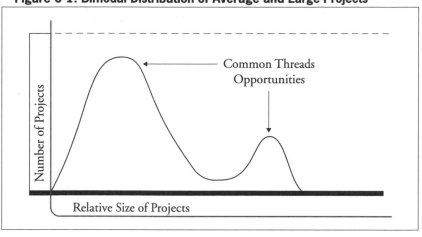

components that can span across the entire company. This, again, is lost opportunity that is likely to be "found" when Common Thread thinking is employed.

Fairland Gets Back to Work

Sometimes a savvy general manager can spot reuse opportunities based solely on a reservoir of personal knowledge about the activities going on inside the portfolio. More often, though, the detection of common threads requires a systematic delving into the details, discovering duplications that aren't obvious on the surface. That's why the first step of Common Threads is to find project specialists.

STEPS FOR THE COMMON THREADS TOOL

1. Gather appropriate expertise.
2. Use expertise to break projects into components.
3. Identify common components across the portfolio.
4. Evaluate coordination cost versus benefits of reusability (the cost/benefit hurdle).
5. Build, catalog and share reusable components.

Let's return to Fairland Products, where Ellie Anderson and Brendan Burkley are eager to begin putting Common Threads to work. As their first step, they engage other key specialists in the division. These specialists are the primary people who will accomplish the second and third steps—breaking the projects into components and finding commonalities among their projects.

Conceptually, figure 6-2 shows how Fairland's selective portfolio looks when decomposed into project components.

Figure 6-2: Common Threads and Fairland's Sample Portfolio

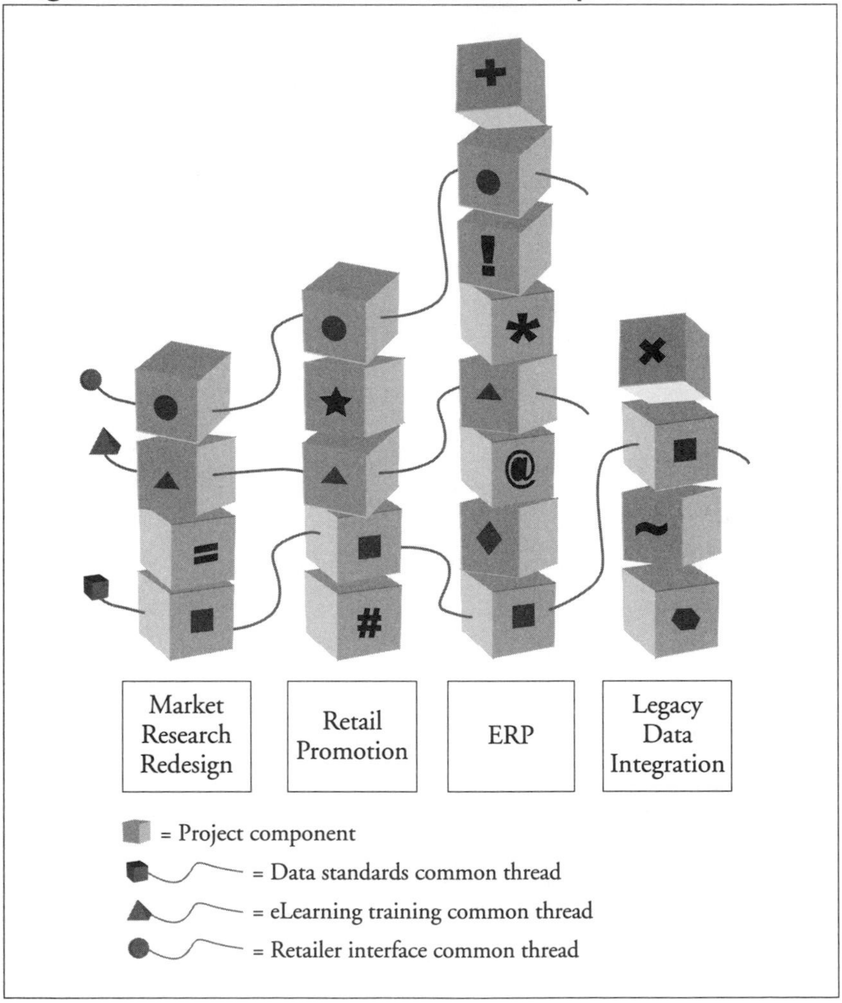

To implement the second and third steps of Common Threads—using the specialists' expertise to deconstruct projects and find reusable components—Burkley organizes a working session. The manager of each project in the sample portfolio is invited to send one or more delegates, each of whom has a solid understanding of the major components of the project. To facilitate the discovery process, Burkley provides the teams with a set of questions designed to help break down the projects into component parts. By starting with this information, the discovery process is accelerated. The general questions are as follows:

- *Business process and constituency experience.* What are the business process and constituency experience components of the project? Which components are candidates for reuse?

- *People and organization.* Do the projects include human capital investments, human resource policies and practices, or change management tools? If so, which components can be thought of as "common"?

- *Technology.* What are the infrastructure, applications, data schemas, code objects, presentation layers, and similar attributes of the projects? Are there any that should not be considered as "common," and if so, why?

- *Project management.* What management processes do the projects follow? Is there an opportunity to share a common process and vocabulary to facilitate understanding and promote the use of Common Threads? If so, how? And if not, why not?

Once projects are broken into components, the work groups look for commonalities and then report back to Anderson and Burkley. Their reports suggest, among other things, that there appear to be several common threads among four projects: Market Research, Retail Promotion, ERP, and Legacy Data Integration. Table 6-2 shows the work teams' results in a matrix form.

Let's take a moment and interpret this data set, which although limited, still has interesting aspects.

- The Market Research, Retail Promotion, and ERP projects all exchange information and analysis with retailers, a key constituency

Table 6-2: Fairland's Common Threads Findings

Select Project Components	Market Research Redesign	Retail Promotion	ERP	Legacy Data Integration	Summary of Potential Common Threads
Retailer Interface	Interface with retailers for information exchange	Interface with retailers for information exchange	Captures point-of-sale (POS) data from retailers	Not Applicable	Reusable, Common Retailer Interface
Training	Train retailers and employees	Train retailers and employees	Train retailers and employees	Not Applicable	Leverage eLearning Training
Data Definitions	Sets standards for new data	Sets standards for new data	Sets new standards for data in all ERP modules	Sets standards for sharing data across legacy systems	Consolidate Data Standards

group. For example, each project has been planning to interview retailers to develop the user-experience and interaction processes. In addition, each project is also planning to train retailers in the new processes. By reusing a common "retailer interface" component, the projects could save time and money and eliminate multiple interactions with the retailer. This, in turn, would improve the retailer's experience of doing business with Fairland and contribute to a better overall relationship.

- They also discover that extensive energy will be invested in training retailers. The work teams point out to Anderson and Burkley that, using the Right Brain tool, the organization has already spotted the opportunity to leverage the eLearning infrastructure to support a more effective rollout of ERP. Now the work team also suggests that they consider further leveraging this framework to provide coordinated, cost-effective, and high-quality training for retailers.

- Finally, it is not surprising to see that the ERP project is driving major change in the data standards for much of the information that Fairland uses to run its business. Market Research and Retail Promotion, however, both contain data not found in the ERP modules, so both of these projects also include a data standard–setting activity. In addition, the Legacy Data Integration project is driving standards to connect to Fairland's legacy systems. Fairland has experienced a steadily growing need to share data from different parts of the business, and it is especially critical that these three applications share data seamlessly and work smoothly with the retailers' extranet. To ensure the flexibility needed to meet future requirements, Fairland's experts recommend consolidating the setting of data standards into one of the four projects.

Now, with the identification of common threads complete, it's time for the work teams to tackle the fourth step: testing these components against a cost/benefit hurdle. Their charge is to determine whether the benefit of reusing these common components exceeds the extra cost of coordinating the elements across multiple projects.

The costs of coordination include additional management time and effort, especially where components are in the design phase and requirements that satisfy multiple constituencies must be considered. The benefits include immediate cost savings from the elimination of duplicate efforts, the value of future reuse and the associated flexibility interoperability brings, and of course, constituency value.

After looking at the cost/benefit hurdle, Anderson and Burkley determine that all three possible common threads clear the hurdle. Having decided to move ahead with each of the project components described above, Fairland moves to the fifth and final step, reshaping the projects and the project management process to build the common threads. Typically, one project—called the "hub" project—hosts each common thread. Subsequent projects that leverage the hub project are called "spokes." In future development efforts, spoke projects can themselves be candidate hubs for the next generation of projects.

The hub project is accountable for building for the "common good" by designing the component to be reusable. This responsibility includes understanding the requirements of other projects, modifying the component's design for reusability, and creating the documentation and training that enable reuse. For a large or complex reusable component, spoke projects may send delegates to work on its development and bring back knowledge about the component's application. Conversely, experts from the hub project can move to spoke projects once the reusable component is developed.

A caution: We don't recommend that companies build components "on speculation." Initially, at least, components should be developed for a specific project and purpose. To ensure the greatest possible leverage, the common components should be developed through existing efforts, as part of projects whose benefits are already validated. Over time, a company may want to fund selective common component projects

HUB AND SPOKE

HUB PROJECTS provide common components and knowledge that can be used by a number of other projects.

SPOKE PROJECTS use the common components and knowledge developed by the hub project to develop a "leveraged" solution.

whose value is derived solely from the elimination of duplication and the accompanying increase in portfolio flexibility. There are numerous questions to consider in selecting the hub project:

- Should ownership of the hub project lie within an existing project? Which project has the most expertise to contribute to the component's development? Which project's time line needs the component first? Will development of the common component distract the team's focus from its project mission?

- Do some project resources need to be reallocated or shifted to the project that becomes the hub?

- How will coordination between the hub and spoke projects be managed?

At Fairland, Burkley assigns the reusable component of data standards to ERP and the process for building a link to retailers and training of retailers to the Retail Promotion project. The Market Research effort becomes a spoke for all three threads.

Last, but not least, the success of Common Threads depends on the ability of other projects to know where and how to access the existing (or newly formed) library of reusable components. The technology standards are an extension of an existing reuse library, and will be placed there. Creating the "learning reuse" library is assigned to the head of training and development, and the task of setting up the retailer experience library will be turned over to the head of marketing.

Yes, this is an investment of time and energy. But over time, as Fairland's library of reusable components grows, subsequent projects will be cheaper, less risky, and have a greater probability of interoperability. As a result, they will create flexibility along multiple dimensions.

Turning up the Dial with Common Threads

If your organization is just starting with Common Threads, it makes sense to work initially with a single thread. Then—as we like to say— turn up the dial as you gain experience and comfort with this tool. If your company has already laid the path by using the technology common thread (e.g., code libraries, joint use of servers, and object-oriented programming), this may be a good time to expand into the other threads. One place to start is to build a library of reusable components related to business process and constituency experience.

Another way to expand Common Threads further is to look to the value network to see where building common threads across organizations can enhance the interactions of all involved. As you look across this broader landscape, it's usually not hard to spot opportunities for productive collaboration. These may range from the standards-setting work of industry associations to shared development and integration between companies and their individual partners.

Start the process simply by looking at the current workflows and information exchanges between constituencies and your organization. Are there places where the handoffs could be automated or improved if common protocols or practices were implemented? Stated in a more Outside-In way, which parts of the value network have similar goals, objectives, or constituency needs? Are there ways to leverage common threads in achieving those objectives? The goal, in all cases, should be to start incrementally, then seek to build strong threads based on earlier success.

Although tying together and building common threads across the value chain can be difficult and time-consuming, you don't need to tackle the entire value chain at the same time. Start by picking a few key customers and/or suppliers with whom to collaborate, and accumulate benefits and learning as you jointly develop and deploy a reusable component. This might be as simple as building an extranet to update and cross-list part numbers, or creating a virtual meeting space to share product design plans and better integrate the design process. As you gain confidence and experience, expand the solution vertically by including more applications, or horizontally, by including more customers and suppliers, or both.

Common Threads is a powerful tool for alignment. By leveraging shared data and reusable components, the organization gains efficiency and responsiveness. Working from standard components also allows faster integration between different units of the organization. This interoperability creates higher levels of House in Order, which, in turn, makes the organization more responsive and facilitates the development of other traits.

Project Chunking

| Direction |
| Efficiency |
| ✓ Risk Reduction |
| ✓ Flexibility |

Project Chunking Tool

Simply put, Project Chunking involves taking larger projects and breaking them into smaller bundles that reduce risk, realize benefits sooner, and increase flexibility by providing more choice points. In this way, Project Chunking weaves the traits into the very fabric of the portfolio.

As the speed of business escalates, companies are working to deliver positive results on a more consistent basis with shrinking margins for error. Project Chunking is a tool that responds to these rising expectations by both delivering incremental value and shortening the reaction time in response to change, so that results arrive on schedule, even in uncertain times.

Variations on the theme of Project Chunking are known by several names, including time-boxing, time-pacing, and fast-tracking. All of these approaches share the same conceptual underpinnings: how to respond to uncertainty and velocity by building choice points and delivering value more quickly. We like the term "Project Chunking" because in a visceral way, it captures one central idea of this tool. "Chunks" are bite-sized and more easily "consumed" by the organization.

Chunking helps managers develop trait mind-sets. In chapter 4, we described Carlson Hospitality's approach to chunking the development of a new central reservation system. Their team had a "plan not to be wedded to the plan," as one observer put it. They embraced the idea that there could be no perfect system—and that, in fact, it was probably "not

PROJECT CHUNKING DEFINED

- Each chunk results in benefit capture.
- Choice points about future project direction occur at the end of each chunk.
- Chunks have relatively short cycle times, often between 90 and 120 days.
- Change in overall project—including cancellation—doesn't undo benefits already realized.

> "Chunking a project allows you to be more flexible as time goes on, as business priorities change, as you learn more about what you're doing. . . . If you try to do the whole project all at once, often you'll find that functions you focused on weren't what you really should have been focusing on."
>
> —Steve Medina, Carlson Hospitality's director of application development[5]

even a good idea to aim for one."[6] This is exactly the right mind-set— one that accepts unpredictability and makes it work for, rather than against, the portfolio.

As noted in chapter 4, there are situations in which Chunking may not be appropriate, such as a large infrastructure upgrade or the implementation of multiple modules of a packaged application. For example, in the case of some infrastructure projects, Chunking might reduce volume-purchase discounts. Even more problematic, a new infrastructure might not work with the old, so a partial implementation wouldn't be possible. In the case of a multimodule package implementation— such as multiple supply-chain modules in an ERP implementation— Chunking might prove too costly. If every module were rolled out as a chunk, expensive interfaces to older legacy applications would likely be needed. And in many cases, building "throwaway" interfaces simply isn't cost effective.

In these and other cases, economies of scale and rework costs may exceed the benefits that Chunking provides. But don't write off Chunking prematurely. In our experience, there are more opportunities to employ this tool than you might think.

Consider for a moment how unpredictable an environment most projects operate in today. An eighteen-month project is likely to go through a multitude of disruptions, from changing business priorities to implementation challenges such as new technology partners. When long projects are confronted by all this change, they tend to get longer. What begins as an eighteen-month project becomes a twenty-four- or even a thirty-month project. The result? The realization of benefits is pushed further into the future.

WHEN TO USE PROJECT CHUNKING

- When project does not have significant economies of scale, as do ERP and many infrastructure projects.
- When project does not have significant incompatibilities between existing or new software or hardware.
- When rework costs are small to moderate. (Moderate rework is OK, because cost is offset by benefits of risk mitigation.)

While project delays can be the result of mismanagement, in a traditional project design, delays can also be noble and necessary. As John Parker, VP of information systems for Northwest Airlines, puts it, "It comes down to either not doing what we want in order to protect some time line, or coming in late and over budget because we [have to] accommodate the change. People tend to appreciate that we take the time to stay competitive."[7]

Chunking seeks to reduce four main sources of risk in a project: the overall size, the technical complexity, long time lines, and the amount of organizational change. By making projects more incremental across all four dimensions, Chunking increases the chances of success. As you may recall from chapter 4, a study by the Standish Group confirmed that the smaller the duration and team size of a project, the greater its chances of success.[8]

Our point? On the frontier, change is going to happen—and *quickly*. Projects and project sponsors shouldn't be taken by surprise. They shouldn't be without options when changes happen. Phrased from the other direction: How many projects anticipate and plan contingencies for a major change in competitor action, technology capability, the loss of a key executive sponsor, or a reorganization of the part of the business the project impacts? Not many—and yet these kinds of things happen every day, often affecting multiple projects. Even well-run projects often end up with delayed time lines and budget overruns. Project Chunking anticipates the likelihood of these changes and gives projects and therefore the portfolio, the flexibility to respond to them.

WHAT'S THE DIFFERENCE BETWEEN
A PROJECT *PHASE* AND A PROJECT *CHUNK*?

Phases are project life-cycle steps, such as define requirements or test system. Project chunks are short activity periods that culminate in implementation and benefit realization. Key differences include:

- BENEFIT CAPTURE. Project chunks, by design, always plan to capture end-project benefits. In phasing, many phases (plan, design, and test) do not capture stand-alone benefits.

- CHOICE POINTS. At the end of each chunk, project direction is revisited. In phasing, project direction generally remains the same through the final implementation phases.

- PHASES INSIDE OF CHUNKS. Traditional project phases occur, in miniature, inside a chunk and often follow a rapid application development (RAD) approach.

To summarize: Chunking creates option value by allowing you to stage investments and benefits in an incremental fashion. Other benefits include:

- A "pay as you go" approach that better matches the benefits to the investment.

- Frequent decision points, which both increase flexibility and reduce project risk.

- The ability to make decisions with better information and leveraged learning.

- The reinforcement of common threads, discussed in preceding sections, and promotion of trait development within the organization.

Applying Project Chunking

When selecting projects for chunking, consider the following factors:

- *Project scope and sponsorship.* A project with a moderate scope and high-quality sponsorship is a good place to start. If the project scope

STEPS FOR THE PROJECT CHUNKING TOOL

1. Select project for chunking-based implementation.
2. Build a project game plan, divvying up activities, deliverables, costs, and benefits into chunks and defining project decision points.
3. Implement first project chunk.
4. Evaluate implementation, capture learnings, revise game plan, and continue forward accordingly.

is too small, there may be only one logical increment. Too large a scope, and there may be too many increments to experiment with an unfamiliar technique.

• *Quick wins.* Projects that are strong candidates for Chunking are those that both serve an immediate need and aspire to a larger vision. The immediate need can be addressed in the first (or early) chunk, garnering support from the organization and visibly demonstrating the benefits of Chunking. The larger vision provides a solid foundation for developing a chunked-project game plan.

• *Cost/benefit hurdle.* Some projects, such as infrastructure upgrades and large-package software implementations, don't chunk well. These projects typically require economies of scale to generate ROI, or they touch so much of the business that the effort has to be done all at once.

Once a project has been chosen for Chunking, it is time to *build the chunked project game plan.* What is a "game plan?" It's a high-level view of the activities and deliverables for each chunk of work, including a vision of how each new chunk builds upon previous ones to form a coherent whole.

In coming up with the game plan, the project team makes initial decisions about what project activities, costs, and benefits will map to each chunk and the order in which the chunks will occur. The game plan also helps each chunk "think ahead" by anticipating what future chunks are likely to be, which helps minimize rework over the life cycle of the project.

The game plan is not static, rather it defines decision points for review and revision. At the conclusion of each chunk—and sometimes more frequently—it's revisited and changed to match whatever the new reality is.

The trick to shaping a successful Chunking game plan is to *keep it on middle ground* across a number of dimensions, such as level of detail, amount of work invested, and emotional attachment. If the game plan is too detailed, too much effort is expended. In Chunking, we assume the game plan is going to change, and we limit our investment in it correspondingly. A game plan aims to be directionally correct, rather than precisely targeted. If the game plan starts to resemble the traditional "requirements definition" phase of a long project, you've overinvested in it. Why? Because in many cases, the lessons and result of a previous chunk influence the development of subsequent ones.

One more thing: Remember our discussion of Right Brain issues in previous chapters? When large amounts of time and effort are invested in the game plan, team members and sponsors become increasingly committed to it. Commitment is a good thing, of course—except when it creates resistance to changing a plan that *should* change. Again, avoid the kind of "overengineering" that would limit the very flexibility that Chunking promotes and you are working to develop.

At the other extreme, of course, are chunked projects that are not well conceived beyond the first chunk. Without a clear sense of project direction, the series of project chunks often ends up in unintended places, failing to create the alignment you are striving to achieve.

The goal of Chunking is *not* to make planning obsolete. Rather, its goal is to help make planning flexible and fluid so that it can better keep pace with the frontier. The project's vision, business case, and scope are the best starting points for thinking about how to chunk a project. Like much of business decision making, there's no substitute for common sense when it comes to Chunking. So we offer the following tips, which mainly augment your own good sense:

- *Pain points or immediate needs.* In the first or early chunks, tackle immediate needs, such as a "pain point" or an easy-to-seize opportunity. Traditional projects often bundle immediate requirements with

TIPS FOR CREATING CHUNKS

- Tackle immediate needs—pain points and easy-to-do-opportunities—first.
- Benefits are a must. Chunks should deliver discrete and stand-alone value.
- Minimize rework.
- Plan for learning.

midterm and longer-term requirements, and a pain point is left unaddressed for months while the full functionality is being built. Meanwhile, the company forfeits the benefits of solving the pain point as it waits for the project to complete.

Consider what happened when J.P. Morgan Partners launched a major overhaul of their partnership management and accounting systems. They broke the project into more than twelve chunks. One early chunk was automated global deal-tracking. Prior to implementing this chunk, according to Marcia Bateson, chief administrative officer and CFO, "Someone would send an e-mail inquiring about a particular industry, for example, and people from all over the world would respond by sending back spreadsheets, which the recipient would put together and try to manipulate."[9] This chunk was an early one because it was easy to automate, was welcomed by users, and required minimal training—all of which meant that it could deliver immediate benefit while building momentum for the full project.

- *Benefits are a must.* In an ideal world, Project Chunking means that costs and benefits are matched in each chunk. Practically speaking, however, the first chunks of some projects may bear the burden of up-front investment, making their cost/benefit ratio lower than subsequent chunks. The key is to *make sure that each chunk optimizes its level of benefit,* even if the ratio of costs to benefits varies across the chunks over time. This way, if the project is later altered or cancelled, at least some sustained benefits have been achieved to offset project costs.

- *Minimize rework.* This is often easier said than done. Some rework may be a necessary cost of Project Chunking. The cost of a little rework, though, is usually more than offset by the multiple benefits of Chunking, especially risk reduction in cases where the confidence level of being able to achieve a "best outcome" through more traditional methods is not high. Rework should be kept within reasonable bounds, of course. At times, a chunk may need to be longer or shorter than other chunks, in order to manage rework costs appropriately.

- *Plan for learning.* If you move forward with the expectation that you'll learn as you go, some decisions can be intelligently delayed until more information is available from earlier chunks. That's a fundamental part of the design of Chunking—making full use of lessons learned.

How long should a chunk be? What makes sense, of course, varies widely based on the nature of the project in question. The key is to *live up to the spirit of Chunking,* rather than adhering to any arbitrary guideline. For example, if a systems project that originally required eighteen months to implement is broken down into three six-month chunks— each of which delivers discrete benefits, minimizes rework, has the support of constituencies, and allows for incremental learning—we'd call that a win. The company has two decision points it didn't have before. Benefits can accrue sooner and be captured regardless of whatever changes may be made at each choice point.

So is the answer always "18 divided by 3"? Of course not. Another company might choose to chunk a similar project into quarterly cycles or hundred-day wins, based on how it defines gain and forward progress.

Returning to Fairland Products

Let's return to Fairland Products. Anderson and Burkley are particularly interested in the opportunities for Chunking since this tool may give them a few ideas for how to accelerate some of the expected savings from the Supplier Rationalization project. Initially, though, they decide to experiment with the Benefit Portal, because this effort has a positive impact on all employees—completing the first step. As they get a little experience under their belt, they will revisit the opportunity Chunking may have for Supplier Rationalization as well as other projects.

The original project scope for the Benefit Portal was a one-year effort that was going to result in a "big bang" rollout at the end of that year. All the functionality was to be completed and launched at one time, with the promise that each component part would work together. Yes, this is an orderly and logical way to implement a project. But it takes a *lot of time*—all components must wait for the longest lead-time (or slowest) component—and it fails to match incremental investments with benefits.

Anderson and Burkley share their information on Project Chunking with the project team and ask them to recommend a game plan for Chunking the portal project. This begins step 2. The team, which includes representatives from key constituencies for the portal project, identifies three functionality chunks:

- Paid time off (PTO) inquiry

- 401(k) management

- Benefit enrollment and employee manual

The project team quickly begins sequencing the chunks. First, they designate PTO processing as the initial chunk. Why? Because it appears to be (1) the easiest to implement and (2) the most immediate pain point for employees. (It currently takes the HR department about a week to process questions around available PTO days, and employees have long complained about "lost" PTO days.)

The team also knows that the potential benefits of online benefit enrollment exceed those of the 401(k) management process—which employees can already accomplish using a telephone integrated voice response (IVR) system—so they sequence these projects accordingly. Here's the high-level game plan the team develops for the portal project:

Chunk 1

- Functionality: PTO inquiry

- Primary constituency: All Fairland employees

Chunk 2

- Functionality: Benefit enrollment and employee manual

- Primary constituency: All Fairland employees

Chunk 3

- Functionality: 401(k) management

- Primary constituency: All Fairland employees

Simple but still powerful, because this new game plan is poised to deliver online benefits administration in incremental, regular cycles. Pain will diminish faster and gain will arrive on the doorstep sooner. Figure 6-3 illustrates this concept.

Anderson and Burkley approve the plan, and the team moves ahead with step 3: implementing the first chunk. The first chunk is implemented on schedule, and the portal is well received. But there is also a good deal of feedback from employees about the need to improve the cumbersome user interface.

Bad news, right? Well, no; *good* news. This information can now be built into subsequent chunks. So Anderson and Burkley commend the project team and celebrate the delivery of the first Benefits Portal chunk. At the same time, they move to step 4, asking the team to review their game plan in light of the learning derived from this chunk. With necessary adjustments made, they move onto the next chunk.

As the team prepares to move on to chunk 2, Anderson finally finishes her exhaustive search for a new VP of human resources, and so a new executive joins the Fairland team. Understandably, this new VP wants a few weeks to get his hands around the operation and make recommendations about future direction. So chunk 2 of the portal is placed on hold for eight weeks. While this is not exactly good news (what do they do with the project team for those eight weeks?), there is *some* benefit in that (1) there's a strong new player on board, (2) this delay has zero impact on the benefits of the PTO inquiry that have already been rolled out, and (3) the delay is easier to accommodate through the chunked game plan.

In this example, Project Chunking has allowed the more immediate realization of benefits from a given project. Referring back to the game

Figure 6-3: Fairland's Traditional versus Chunked Benefits Portal Implementation

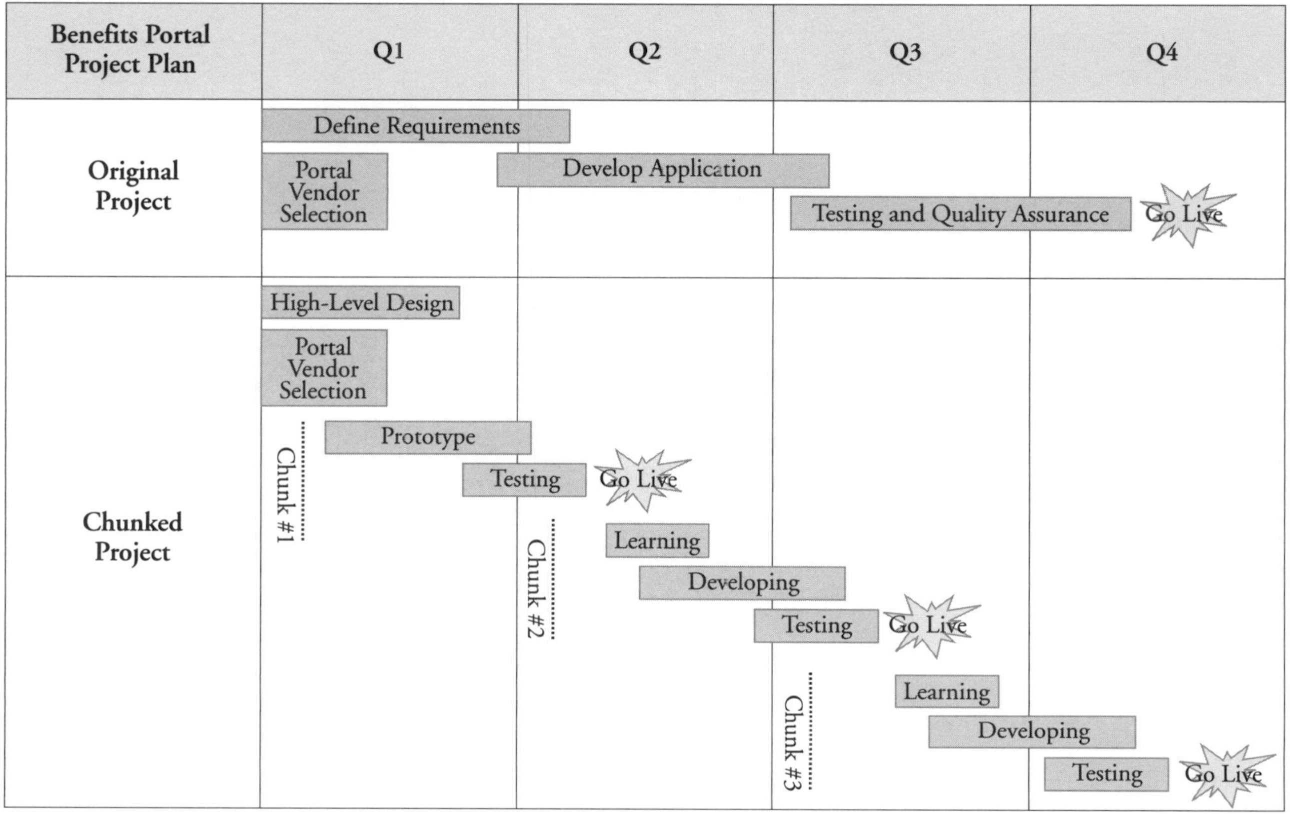

Benefits Portal Project Plan	Q1	Q2	Q3	Q4
Original Project	Define Requirements / Portal Vendor Selection	Develop Application	Testing and Quality Assurance	Go Live
Chunked Project	High-Level Design / Portal Vendor Selection / Prototype	Testing / Go Live — Chunk #1 / Chunk #2 / Learning	Developing / Testing / Go Live / Learning — Chunk #3	Developing / Testing / Go Live

CHUNKING TOOL BENEFITS

- Realize incremental benefits sooner.
- Reduce risk.
- Increase flexibility.
- Promote traits.

plan, we see that PTO inquiry was delivered by the end of Q2, providing incremental benefit to employees six months earlier than in the original schedule. In addition, the project team and sponsors are better able to validate the benefits through constituency feedback, understand the adoption curve within the organization, compile "lessons learned" for folding into subsequent chunks, "prove" the technology platform and user presentation design, and revise the project ROI (or similar cost/ benefit analysis). In addition, the PTO chunk also creates several re- usable components—remember Common Threads?—such as portal look-and-feel, which can be leveraged in subsequent chunks.

Finally, the increased number of decision points improves flexibility while adding sustainable value along the way. For example, in the tradi- tional approach, if—due to factors beyond the project's control—the project was terminated at the end of the second quarter, Fairland would have completed the overall Benefits Portal design, but would not have delivered any finished product. Through the chunked method, by con- trast, the PTO portion of the portal is in place. Even if a bolt from the blue terminates the project at this point, the organization has realized value from the project.

Turning up the Dial on Project Chunking

In most cases, the best way to get into Project Chunking is to pick a suitable project and take the plunge. Once you have some experience with Chunking, the pool of chunked projects in your portfolio can con- tinue to expand. "Turning up the dial" means applying Project Chunk- ing across a broader and broader base. For some companies, Chunking becomes an important part of how they do business. Cisco, for example, requires projects to deliver value on quarterly cycles that mirror the company's financial planning and budgeting timelines.

The last word? Project Chunking significantly increases the flexibility of the portfolio, thus giving organizations more options over time. Chunking enables the organization to focus on *adapting,* preserving the ability to move in different directions as an uncertain future unfolds.

Try it. You'll like it.

What-if Planning
Direction
Efficiency
✓ Risk Reduction
✓ Flexibility

What-if Planning Tool

We've been working to create options for companies by making the portfolio more adaptable to change. We've demonstrated how both the Common Threads and Project Chunking tools enable more flexible alignment choices.

But these steps alone can't ensure success on the information frontier. What-if Planning is about thinking through likely scenarios *in advance,* rather than waiting to react to an unfolding future. As Louis Pasteur once said, "Chance favors the prepared mind." We've argued in favor of creating the organizational capacity to move quickly. But moving quickly is only wonderful if you can *move quickly in the right direction.* The What-if Planning tool provides this "direction finder," making the portfolio more flexible.

What-if asks and answers a key question—"What happens to my portfolio if significant changes occur in my business context?"—thereby heightening the organization's awareness of how invested it is in its current context. What-if Planning evaluates how readily the portfolio can adapt to major change. It helps companies better understand how decisions today may "lock out" (or open) options for tomorrow. And finally, What-if helps companies see which projects are most fungible.

Applying the What-if Planning Tool

The first step is to identify scenarios against which we will test the portfolio. What do we mean by "scenarios"? Scenarios are simply descriptions of alternative directions or constraints the portfolio may face due to changing priorities and the business environment. Each scenario needs to be sufficiently considered, in terms of the impact to the portfolio, to contribute to decision making. For example, in chapter 4 when we first introduced the What-if Planning tool, we illustrated Agilent's examples of two scenarios: reducing the portfolio's budget to a (figurative) single dollar and doubling the budget.

Because the number of alternative directions and constraints that may impact a portfolio—from technology trends to consumer trends to global macroeconomic factors—is infinite, the number of potential scenarios is also unlimited. Managers can't worry about—or even conceive of—all possible scenarios. The boundaries are generally crafted by selecting a few alternative futures.

In the Ellipsus case also discussed in chapter 4, the key driver for the future of that company's business was marketplace adoption of a technology standard. Ellipsus had to develop scenarios based on the marketplace success of either Java or WAP.[10] This is a very specific What-if Planning scenario.

Generally, as companies think about possible scenarios, there are two dimensions along which portfolios can be reshaped: (1) changing the priorities or direction and (2) modifying the budget or resources available. These two dimensions, while related, are *independent* events. For example, a company seeking efficiency might increase the size of its budget to achieve the efficiency gains (a reengineering situation). Conversely, a company might model a high-growth scenario but have limited resources (a start-up situation). Scenarios are basically built on these two dimensions.

Figuring out Fairland

Back at Fairland, Anderson and Burkley—relative newcomers to What-if Planning—decide to begin by considering two shifting business priorities: focus on growth and focus on efficiency. In both situations,

STEPS FOR THE WHAT-IF PLANNING TOOL

1. Identify scenarios to test portfolio.
2. Assess portfolio against scenarios.
3. Evaluate and adjust portfolio.

they assume the budget is fairly fixed. For the first step of What-if Planning, they describe the two scenarios after determining reasonable boundary conditions. In a high-growth scenario, the conditions and priorities mimic what Fairland may face if the business environment were robust and expanding. While efficiency is always important, Anderson and Burkley also build a low-growth scenario that reflects the cost-cutting and efficiency priorities associated with a contracted or slow-growth environment.

To make these scenarios a more useful guide for testing the portfolio, Anderson and Burkley engage their leadership team, and together they add more specificity to the high- and low-growth scenarios by detailing the likely new priorities, direction, and budget constraints of the portfolio for each situation.

With Fairland's scenarios in hand, they move on to step 2: Testing the impact of the scenarios when superimposed on the portfolio. Generally speaking, scenarios impact the projects in the portfolio in one of three ways:

- *Accelerate/enhance.* Speed up project implementation and potentially enhance its scope.

- *Maintain.* Keep the project time line, resource base, or scope "as is."

- *Slow/stop.* Scale back or stop the project.

Rather than testing the entire portfolio, at least initially, we suggest limiting What-if Planning to key projects. By "key projects," we mean those that consume a disproportionate share of resources, are higher-risk, and/or are critical to achieving the company's intentions.

But for the sake of illustration—and given the relatively small size of Fairland's sample portfolio—we will continue in our discussion using the company's full suite of projects.

Armed with their tailored two scenarios, Anderson and her leadership team think through the implications each scenario would have on their portfolio. They come up with the plans shown in table 6-3—which hold the portfolio's budget constant—as they consider possible shifting priorities.

Anderson and her team evaluate the results of their analysis. They look at whether or not there is balance in the portfolio to ensure an adequate response to either scenario. They particularly look to see if some

Table 6-3: Fairland's What-if Planning Results

Project	Side	High Growth	Low/No Growth
Market Research Redesign	Sell-side	Accelerate/enhance	Slow/stop
Sales Force Automation	Sell-side	Accelerate/enhance	Accelerate/enhance
Retail Promotion	Sell-side	Accelerate/enhance	Slow/stop
ERP	Inside	Maintain	Maintain
eLearning	Inside	Maintain	Accelerate/enhance
Legacy HR	Inside	Slow/stop	Slow/stop
Benefit Portal	Inside	Maintain	Accelerate/enhance
Legacy Data Integration	Inside	Maintain	Maintain
Regulation Compliance	Inside	Maintain	Maintain
Supplier Rationalization	Buy-side	Maintain	Accelerate/enhance

of the projects are affected similarly by both scenarios. Why? Because projects with an *accelerate/enhance* or *maintain* impact across all scenarios are very likely to increase the stability of the portfolio. Projects with *slow* or *stop* impacts in all scenarios, conversely, may need to come under closer scrutiny. As Anderson and her colleagues test their portfolio of projects against the selected scenarios, they gain insights into the maximum and minimum possible impact each scenario would have on individual projects and on the portfolio as a whole.

For example, seven projects (Sales Force Automation, Supplier Rationalization, ERP, eLearning, Benefit Portal, Legacy Data Integration, and Regulation Compliance) make a contribution in both scenarios. This is welcome evidence that these projects will perform well regardless of the direction the wind blows—which is about the best you can hope for with frontier living! Of course, Fairland will want to confirm this finding over time, turning up the dial and building more sophistication into its scenarios.

On the other hand, the Legacy HR is slow/stop in both scenarios, which underscores Fairland's need to think more deeply about why it is doing the project. (As you can see, testing projects against future realities provides another indication of whether a company is currently investing its project resources in the best ways.)

The Fairland leadership team also notes that, for the Market Research and Retail Promotion projects, there is an extreme variance in responses between the two scenarios. Both projects are accelerated in one scenario and slowed in the other. One way to interpret this finding is that these projects present a greater risk to the organization because they are more dependent on a favorable business context. On the other hand, these projects provide contingent value by preparing Fairland to respond to an alternative future.

Furthermore, because Fairland's managers are looking for the freedom to move in different directions as the future unfolds, it strikes them that both of these projects are strong candidates for Chunking, since Chunking creates more decision points. Figure 6-4 illustrates What-if Planning and Project Chunking working together to create flexibility in the portfolio.

Looking more closely at the Sales Force Automation project, they notice that it is unique, scoring accelerate/enhance for both scenarios.

Figure 6-4: Scenario Impact on Fairland Retail Promotion Project

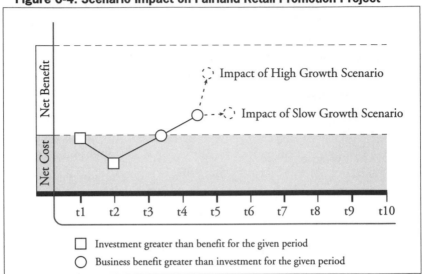

In the low/no-growth scenario, Anderson and Burkley figure they can use the increased productivity to reduce the sales force head count. In the high-growth scenario, by contrast, they decide they can use the increased productivity to help achieve their ambitious growth targets.

Not surprisingly, this observation gets Anderson and Burkley to thinking (again) about what they should do with this project. The results of their What-if Planning analysis suggest that they speed it up. But when they review their Right Brain insight—that the sales force is already overloaded with change—accelerating the Sales Force Automation project does not make sense right now. They place a note in the mental tickler file though: *Look for the opportunity to push on this one as soon as the constituents are ready for it.*

As the members of the leadership team reflect on their What-if Planning experience, they are pleased with the durability that the portfolio shows in both scenarios. They feel that they've gained insight into areas where the portfolio's flexibility could be improved. But more than the specific actions they decide on, the leadership team shares the sense that their collective mind-set has shifted. As they have thought through the future scenarios, the team has become less focused on a single target destination for the portfolio and more focused on being ready for a variety of possible futures.

Turning up the Dial on What-if Planning

While two scenarios built around a single driver are a good starting point for companies that are new to What-if Planning, additional and more in-depth scenarios can increase the usefulness of the tool. If your organization has already developed scenarios for strategic planning or other uses, use those scenarios to test the portfolio.

Although increasing the number of scenarios can better prepare the portfolio to respond to the future, it also adds complexity. Only you can determine if the increased complexity and time associated with adding scenarios are worth the value that the further insights and perspectives will bring.

Another way to turn up the dial is to more fully assess the response of the portfolio to each scenario and use this assessment to develop more-specific contingency plans. For example, in the high-growth scenario, Fairland's leadership team may be concerned about whether they could fully meet the growth in demand, given the fact that in several areas of the world, their distribution network is already at capacity.

For the moment, Fairland doesn't want to launch a major new project to prepare for a future that may not come to pass. As a result of their work, they believe that Fairland is now achieving better alignment of portfolio projects to present-day objectives, and the leadership team does not want to disrupt this improved alignment.

At the same time, Fairland wants to be ready to act, should either of the scenarios studied occur. One response is to develop *contingent* projects—initiatives that can be added without distorting alignment—to better position the organization for the future. For example, to support the high-growth scenario, an analysis of options for expanding the distribution network could be designed now, and informal relationship building with several possible distribution partners could begin.

Fairland also believes that collaborative product design may accelerate the time to market for new products. Although Fairland isn't ready to commit resources to such an effort now, it can start to get smarter about this trend so the company will be ready to launch this type of initiative when it is needed.

Summary of Tools That Provide Options

It's time to say goodbye to Ellie Anderson, Brendan Burkley, and their colleagues at Fairland Products. But as we do, we'll summarize each of the tools we covered in this chapter (see table 6-4), just as we did with the diagnostic tools in chapter 5.

Table 6-4: Summary of Fairland's Insights from Options Tools

Tool	Summary of Observations
Common Threads	• A common user interface for retailers could be leveraged by Market Research, Retail Promotion, and ERP projects. • eLearning could be leveraged for retailer training. • ERP project could consolidate data standard setting.
Project Chunking	• Chunking the Benefits Portal project realizes incremental benefits sooner, allows the second chunk to take advantage of first chunk learnings about user interface design (which becomes a Common Thread), and lets Fairland more easily accommodate a project delay related to executive turnover.
What-if Planning	• Seven projects (Sales Force Automation, Supplier Rationalization, ERP, eLearning, Benefit Portal, Legacy Data Integration, and Regulation Compliance) have value in both of Fairland's scenarios. • Legacy HR Migration is slow/stop in both scenarios, raising another flag about the project's contribution, this time as it relates to changing conditions. • Market Research and Retail Promotion projects provide contingent value, making Fairland more prepared for possible changes in the environment. Their contingent nature makes them candidates for Project Chunking.

In our experience, no one company has done it all, and in our opinion, no one company needs to do it all at once. It's better to test, evaluate, and find tools that work in your specific context, while keeping an open mind for the next set of tools you may want to put into practice. Having said that, we'd also like to reiterate that these tools *work,* and can deliver real value to your company and its shareholders.

In our next and final chapter, we restate our central premise, test this premise in a complicated real-world context—the auto industry—and close by describing techniques for monitoring your progress as you adapt to our changing world.

7

the elephant in the hallway

An ounce of action is worth a ton of theory.

FREDERICK ENGELS (1820–1895), GERMAN SOCIAL PHILOSOPHER

In 1793, an English canal surveyor named William Smith made an observation that was part inspiration and part heresy. He had come to the conclusion that the ground underneath England could be mapped the same way the features above ground could be charted—an idea that was as profound as it was simple. Today, Smith is considered by many to be the father of modern geology. His initial map, produced in 1815, still resides at Burlington House, a museum on the north side of London's Piccadilly.

Let's look a little more closely at Smith's inspiration. Since Roman times, people had been mucking around in the bowels of the English countryside. As the Industrial Revolution took off in England, thousands labored beneath the earth's surface to supply factories with the tin, lead, and coal necessary to fuel a rapidly growing economy. Meanwhile, additional workers dug their way across the surface of the landscape, creating a network of barge canals to bring these commodities to market. So by the time Smith came along, the English were quite accomplished at digging across and through the ground. Although thousands saw the cross-sections of sediment rock, no one had made the leap of logic that Smith had, while at work in the Somerset Coal Canal.

Smith theorized that the layers of rock beneath England were distinct and could be identified by the fossils they contained. If that were true, these layers could be identified and mapped across England. To test his theory, he crisscrossed the nation, from the north of England to its southern shores, taking thousands of samples along the way. Twenty-two years later, he finished his heretical map.

Why "heretical"? Because it went against all orthodoxies. In 1658, an Irish prelate had calculated the creation of the Earth to have occurred precisely at 9:00 A.M. on Monday, October 23, 4004 B.C. Until Smith came along, few challenged this accepted wisdom. Contradictory evidence of the Earth's age was explained away as either God's curious work or the result of secretions from inside the Earth. Smith challenged these foundations of both theology and science.

Smith's pioneering journey is helpful for understanding our own reality. Through a measure of genius and some hard work, Smith opened a new way of thinking. He certainly didn't invent mining, but he did *transform* the way people and companies understood their world. He made the process of finding value—in this case, minerals—easier, more systematic, and more predictable. And those companies that moved more quickly to exploit his insights enjoyed greater gains.[1]

On today's frontier, lots of people are playing roles similar to Smith's. They are articulating new ways of finding value. From Harrah's customer loyalty to Li & Fung's supplier relationships to Carlson Hospitality's project chunking, value creation is occurring inside and across organizational boundaries.

This book is undertaken in that spirit. Just as English landowners used Smith's map to make better choices about where to find value, our alignment approach is designed to help organizations make better choices about allocating resources and directing their project portfolios to accelerate their settlements of the information frontier.

HOW FAST IS INNOVATION AND
PRODUCT PROLIFERATION OCCURRING?

The number of new consumer products has *doubled* between 1991 and 2001, to approximately 32,025 new product launches in 2001.[2]

But our mapmaking metaphor has limitations. Unlike coal seams, which are sedentary until they are mined, the frontier offers little constancy. The world keeps rushing forward in an increasingly unpredictable and volatile manner. And, as the art of the possible evolves at an ever-faster rate, the shelf life of innovations is shrinking. The best our map can do, therefore, is to guide organizations to be more adaptive and responsive by embracing the broader characteristics of the frontier.

Increasingly, companies are realizing that the advantage goes to those who learn to embrace the new reality. This is a fundamental shift in mind-set, and its importance can't be overemphasized. Since the dawn of the Industrial Age, organizations have made a *virtue of predictability,* and a *vice of variance.* But the increase in volatility associated with the frontier and other global affairs means that getting your predictions right is much more difficult. So organizations are looking for new ways to reorient themselves.

Where does opportunity lie in this strange new environment? We believe that it resides in the relationships among entities and, in particular, in the ability to shape these relationships to create value at market speed. The recent convergence of technology innovations allows organizations and constituencies to play multiple roles, reducing friction in existing relationships and integration points and creating completely new relationships and communication channels. The ability to transcend boundaries—making it easier to integrate and collaborate—is reshaping both organizations and business ecosystems.

Settlers used to rely on almanacs, which laid out the times to sow and harvest based on centuries of observation. This book provides guidelines for frontier living, which involves sowing and harvesting in unpredictable conditions. Instead of matching your actions to the seasons, our guidebook focuses on aligning *your actions* (projects) with *what you want to achieve* (intentions).

Alignment is never perfect or complete. (Even "perfect" alignment today would soon turn into misalignment, given the constant rate of change.) Protecting alignment is all about monitoring, assessing, and making changes based on those assessments. Later in this chapter, we provide some insights into the challenge of maintaining alignment.

First, though, let's try an experiment. Let's put an entire industry under a microscope and see whether the recent experience of that industry substantiates both our analysis and our prescription. Wherever possible, we'll use our traits language to interpret the evidence.

Shifting Gears: Back to the Auto Industry

Let's return to the automotive frontier, described in chapter 2. In a relatively brief period of time, an entire industry was born, an extensive infrastructure was built, and people's mind-sets were changed in extraordinary ways. Then, gradually, the automotive frontier receded; it became part of everyday life, and new fields of opportunity emerged.

In the decades since its opening, the domestic U.S. automobile industry has been viewed as a bellweather for U.S. industrial strength, and has been perceived as everything from the preeminent example of an industrial colossus to the proverbial "canary in the coal mine," symbolizing a relative decline of the U.S. manufacturing sector. And no, over the past fifty years or so, no one has thought of the auto industry as a center for frontier thinking. But from the power of globalization and new production techniques to the impact of economic booms and busts, the automobile industry has served consistently as a barometer of the present as well as a harbinger of what the future might hold.

And as it turns out, this industry is deeply involved in coming to terms with the information frontier. What's going on, and how is it going? What will this industry look like in the future? How is it transitioning for the new frontier? How does the trait prescription pertain? By looking at the changes under way in the auto industry, we find indications of the phenomenon also taking place within the global economy.

First, some scene setting: We are in Detroit, Michigan, the fabled Motor City. The choice is arbitrary; we could just as well be in Wolfsburg, Germany (the sprawling home of the Volkswagen empire), Turin, Italy (Fiat), or Toyota City, Japan.

Outside this window sits a vast complex of aging factories. Geared to achieve economies of scale for mass markets, this factory in its heyday produced every conceivable part needed for an automobile. In one end went the raw materials of coal, iron ore, and rubber, and out the other end—at the far end of one of the world's most complicated assembly lines—emerged an endless string of more or less identical cars.

This particular factory has survived two world wars, the challenges of foreign competition, the fuel crisis of the 1970s, and many economic booms and busts. Today, however, it is largely abandoned—the victim of changing times and changing economics.

But this depressing landscape is a misleading symbol for the larger industry. Although this factory and others like it have been much reduced from their former glories, the automobile industry still employs an estimated one in six members of the global workforce. In 2001, the industry sold some 57 million vehicles worldwide, generating hundreds of billions of dollars in sales.[3]

And although the factory outside our window is not what it once was, it is still part of a dynamic and complex industry. From overcapacity and labor force changes to fuel-cell research and environmental regulation, there are literally thousands of forces, including many relatively new ones, impacting the players in this industry. Today, we're aware that the shapes, sizes, and functions of cars are changing; we're less aware, though, that the entire industry is being reshaped.

This frontier is a global phenomenon, and—from the design studios of Germany to the factory floors of Japan—it is being addressed on a global basis. In light of such extensive change, let's narrow our analysis a bit, focusing on three trends: (1) the manufacturer's changing relationship with its customers, (2) new partnerships with suppliers, and (3) the reinvention of the factory floor. We pick these trends in part because they are fundamental, in part because they are exciting, and in part because they represent a convergence of progressive thinking from major players around the globe. So with this background, let's turn to the details.

Getting behind the Wheel: Big Changes in Customer Relationships

Perhaps the biggest change in the industry is something that is unseen by the general public, yet is emerging as the greatest potential asset of the traditional automobile manufacturer. This is the industry's *relationship with its customers.* For decades, there really hasn't been a relationship between the manufacturer and the customer. The automaker designed and produced the car, and the customer bought it through a third party, the local dealer.

Henry Ford took this to the extreme, as he is quoted as saying: "You can have any color you want, as long as it's black." Alfred Sloan's General Motors made the astounding decision to *give customers choices.* Sloan's upstart announced annual model changes and introduced different models for different price ranges. Ford's market share went into decline and didn't recover until the company adopted GM's product proliferation strategy methods.[4]

And although *some* choice was better than no choice, for the better part of seven decades, planned obsolescence and a two- or three-tier pricing structure remained the extent of customer choice. People chose from the menu that the global manufacturers put in front of them.

Where are we today? The bad news is that some of this "company-centric" thinking is still with us. To a large extent—at least among laggard automakers—customers are still treated generically. Some manufacturers persist in producing vehicles, setting prices, and providing service to customers in a one-size-fits-all manner, with the result that they underserve highly valuable customers and overserve less valuable customers.[5] Automakers, in these cases, are out of touch with their customer base.

The result is a vicious circle. Since manufacturers don't know what cars people actually want, they tend to speculatively produce (and overproduce) cars. (Current estimates of overproduction in North America and Western Europe are 25 percent and 30 percent, respectively.) These unwanted cars are pushed through to the dealers and are eventually sold through generous incentives that facilitate a customer's compromise. Necessarily, this translates into reduced margins. But manufacturers also miss an opportunity to leverage their knowledge of existing customers to build consumer loyalty, which results in a second "hit," this time to future margins.[6]

This creates a significant problem. Currently, the average customer defection rate for U.S. automakers is between 55 and 60 percent, meaning that *more than half* of today's U.S. customers will defect to a different manufacturer for their next purchase.[7]

That's the bad news. The good news is that—among manufacturers that are embracing an Outside-In stance—customers are starting to feel more empowered. Two words capture the essence of this customer-centric approach—*customization* and *personalization.*

Increasingly, customers are being given the opportunity to customize their purchases, including everything from the exterior shape to the interior features. In addition, as manufacturers and dealers build stronger relationships with their customers and better understand their needs, they can personalize their interactions with customers—treating them as individuals rather than part of a mass market. The key to achieving customer loyalty is to personalize customer interactions when it matters most—at the point of vehicle sale and servicing.

For manufacturers this is a great leap forward, and not one easily accomplished. To be effective, manufacturers are beginning to track all their interactions with the customer. But these interactions generally take place at the dealership, entities where many manufacturers have strained relationships. The manufacturers and dealers that redefine their relationship and find innovative ways to collaborate to personalize the customer's experience stand the greatest chance of unlocking the hidden value of customer relationships.

For both the manufacturer and the dealer, this opportunity is substantial. By better understanding the customer's needs and preferences, they also begin to understand which customers create the most value for them. Collectively, the automobile industry is one of the world's largest mass-marketing spenders. By better understanding customer needs and more precisely targeting their most profitable customers, manufacturers and dealers can focus spending on retaining and growing relationships with their most valued customers.

To switch to our frontier language, the buying experience is increasingly predicated on an Outside-In relationship, in which the entire value network—the automaker, its suppliers, the dealer, and the customer—are collaborating to build each customer his or her own "perfect car." "Behind all this," says BMW chairman Dr. Joachim Milberg, "is a principle: the customer's desires and specifications for the individual car drive the process, not the vehicle BMW has planned."[8]

Building an Outside-In relationship puts the customer at the center of the production process. This, in turn, requires automakers to get their collective *houses in order*. If all BMW models were customized in every theoretically possible way, there would be 10^{17} (in other words, 1,000,000,000,000,000,000) potential variations. The BMW X-5 SUV alone has more than 1,000 bumper variations and 4,000 different instrument panel choices, along with 448 different types of door panels.[9]

Obviously, customers still work within a prescribed set of choices, but growing levels of precision and coordination up and down the supply

THE COST OF HOUSE *NOT* IN ORDER

The markets for trucks took off in the early 1990s, but it took General Motors until 1998 to get enough truck transmissions to meet demand. General Motors admits that this delay cost the company roughly $5 *billion* in net earnings.[10]

chain continue to expand this selection set. As Ralf Hattler, manager of BMW's logistics planning in Munich, put it:

Our logistics challenge is to let the customer change their choices right up until the production process starts. If we are successful, the right parts in the combination the customer wants arrive on the right line at the right time, and the customer never notices the logistics behind it. The key for a global production network like ours is a standardization process for the supply chain, which we develop along with our manufacturing plants and our suppliers so that the logistics process is the same wherever we operate.[11]

Customers are not only looking for customization, they also want *speed of delivery*. The interval between when an order is placed to the time the car is delivered—commonly referred to as "order to delivery"—is steadily shrinking. BMW, for example, currently requires about twelve days. In the near future, they plan to further reduce order-to-delivery time to just ten days.[12]

In a sense, the production process is shrinking. And of necessity, so is the design process, which is compelled to keep up with the velocity of consumer trends. Today, instead of taking more than four years to design a new model, manufacturers take less than eighteen months. General Motors, for example, plans to roll out one new model every twenty-seven days. The result is more car choices so customers can buy more of what they like, and therefore, increase profits.[13]

What else? Traditionally, with the exception of financing and warranties, the transaction with the customer began and ended with the purchase of the car. Today there is opportunity for a relationship that extends far beyond the car purchase. In most cases, the foundation of this relationship is car financing, but it is rapidly broadening as cars evolve into electronic appliances.

Currently, Delphi Automotive Systems estimates that 22 percent of a car is electronic content. They expect this to increase to 40 percent within ten years. In the near future, through wireless Internet connectivity, the car, its owner, and the manufacturer will be in continuous communication. In this Outside-In-driven world, the manufacturer will deliver everything from monitoring of the car's vital systems to information services through the car itself. General Motor's OnStar service today has some 2 million subscribers and executes approximately 14 million transactions a month. This kind of wireless connectivity (or "telematics," as the industry calls it) will only grow. The Japanese Ministry of Posts and Telecommunications estimates that 42 million cars in Japan will be equipped with online navigation systems by 2015—up from 5.5 million cars today.[14]

This, in turn, will shape the form and function of future cars. In almost all areas—from design and financing to maintenance—the manufacturer will move from a point transaction to a continuous Outside-In-based customer relationship. This dramatic shift is already well under way.

Getting under the Hood: Changing Supplier Relationships

Now let's turn to the supplier. In the past, especially in North America, the relationship between the automaker and its suppliers could aptly be described as, well, *adversarial*. In their relentless efforts to increase profits while holding down prices, traditional manufacturers were heavy-handed, often imposing cost reductions that cut deeply into suppliers' margins. And just to keep things at a high level of tension, car companies would often build "shadow" organizations to second-guess their suppliers and keep them on their toes. The result was low quality levels and bad supply-chain relationships.

KEEPING IN TOUCH

Subaru has launched a series of outdoor-oriented Web portals designed to provide Subaru owners with up-to-date information on a host of outdoor activities. The sites also give drivers the ability to purchase special products and services from Subaru and its partners, such as L.L. Bean.

Recently—taking a cue from their Japanese and European competitors—U.S. automakers have become more Eco-Driven. Today they are striving for better relationships with their suppliers and channel partners. In the bad old days, in part to maintain control of the design and engineering processes, Detroit relegated its suppliers to providing bins of parts. Today, instead of simply purchasing parts from suppliers, manufacturers now purchase entire subassemblies, such as doors, power trains, and electronics. "For example," reports *The Economist,* "Chrysler used to buy its seals and engine gaskets from a company called Freudenberg NOK. Then the supplier came up with the idea that it should take over responsibility for preventing lubricants and other fluids leaking from Chrysler engines. It went on to design and supply packs of parts to achieve that."[15] Here and elsewhere, traditional roles are rapidly blurring.

The desire to work with partners to outsource subassemblies is leading to a radically new infrastructure to support the design, procurement, and logistics processes of the manufacturers. Consider the case of GM, once the archetypal adversary of suppliers, which recently constructed a private Web portal called GM SupplyPower. The site is designed to deeply integrate GM with the back ends of suppliers' systems, better coordinating procurement and design. By connecting with its suppliers and sharing demand and forecasting data, GM is improving quality and responsiveness as well as reducing costs. General Motors now estimates that 68 percent of its direct materials procurement will be done over the Internet by 2004.[16]

In 2000, in a remarkable example of how far Eco-Driven can extend in an industry, the traditional "Big Three" of Detroit—along with Renault and Nissan—collaboratively launched a digital marketplace called Covisint. By building a system based on open standards, the industry is integrating and eliminating the expensive process of developing proprietary point-to-point connections. Covisint's members now

GOING MODULAR

When a leading industry consortium asked what percentage of new compact cars would be fabricated using modular assembly by the year 2004, the average supplier estimated *45.7 percent.*[17]

include representatives of the entire value network. Given its relative youth, it's not yet clear what form Covisint will ultimately take; but the venture does illustrate the Eco-Driven direction in which value networks will move to reduce friction. And the promise is notable. In 2001 alone, one year after the launch of the new system, GM auctioned approximately $100 billion through Covisint.[18]

What's going on here? As noted, the industry is becoming more Eco-Driven. Increasingly, manufacturers are focusing their time and attention on marketing, sales, and product design. As the manufacturers better understand where they can create the most unique value, they are increasingly leaving the job of production to others.

The effort to get closer to the customer, as well as the effort to recast the supplier relationship, points these same companies toward the need to get their Houses in Order. For example, as GM worked to foster higher levels of collaboration among its divisions and between the corporation and its suppliers, it realized it had a fundamental problem. There were nearly *two dozen* different and incompatible engineering systems in use across this spectrum of players. And this was only one example of the thousands of independent systems that could be found throughout the company and which stood as effective barriers to collaboration (and House in Order). In a massive effort to "digitize GM," the company has rapidly consolidated and standardized systems, investing approximately $1.7 billion in Internet-related applications. Initial reports are very positive: These projects were not only self-funding, they also contributed $2 billion in operational savings back to GM.[19]

Out on the Shop Floor: Where the Rubber Is Made Ready for the Road

Let's peer out that window in Detroit again, and look a little more closely at the industrial landscape. Emphatically, this is *not* the kind of factory that was pioneered by Henry Ford nearly a century ago. The steel foundries, glass factories, and other freestanding enterprises have long since been shut down and sold off. Today, this factory is far less a manufacturing plant than an assembly facility.

The process is called "modular assembly": Cars are now designed around common platforms, with component systems (or modules) for each major subsystem. This means that cars can be configured and assembled more quickly and efficiently. It also means that today's factory can be much smaller and, at the same time, far more productive, flexible, and faster than the factories of previous generations. For example, a study conducted by a major car manufacturer found that modular assembly could cut almost 10 percent off the cost of the vehicle cockpit.[20]

Modular assembly is more than simple outsourcing. Whereas outsourcing provides savings largely through labor costs, modular assembly achieves new levels of efficiency, reflected in materials and engineering costs, and new scale economies at the supplier level. For example, in the just-mentioned study of the vehicle cockpit, 44 percent of the savings came from reduced materials costs.[21] In the future, supplier partners will take over entire design and engineering processes, in order to further increase efficiency and quality.

In light of these increasingly close relationships with suppliers, the factory is no longer a single assembly line. Rather, it is an assembly *process* that allows multiple cars to be assembled on one line. In this new setting, manufacturers work collaboratively with suppliers to assemble cars together. Perhaps unexpectedly, the leading edge of modular assembly is found in Brazil. DaimlerChrysler, Volkswagen, Fiat and Renault, GM, and Ford all have built modular assembly operations there. And although most modular assembly still assumes an "arms-length" relationship between manufacturer and supplier, the Volkswagen plant actually has suppliers' employees on the production line.[22]

So, judging from the changes that are already under way, the automobile factory of the future will be smaller, leaner, and more market-responsive. Instead of being designed to create 750,000 more or less identical cars annually, the new factory will be designed to produce 200,000 vehicles customized to the customers' wishes. These factories will also be able to shift and change at market speed. For example, instead of taking the one to two months traditionally required to retool an automotive factory, Honda can reorganize and reprogram its entire operations *overnight* cutting production downtime to as few as three and a half days—a 56 percent decrease since 1998.[23] With the ability to literally shift gears and change production in a matter of hours, rather than weeks, companies are far better equipped to deal with an increasingly unpredictable competitive environment.

TRAITS: A MANUFACTURER'S CHECKLIST

> Eco-Driven

- Forging partnerships with suppliers.
- Joint product design and assembly on factory floor.

> Outside-In

- Becoming more customer-centric.
- Enabling buyers to customize cars.
- Building customer loyalty.

> Fighting Trim

- Modular assembly.
- Rapid factory reconfiguration.

> House in Order

- Logistics prepared for mass customization.
- New standards and unified systems.

Closing the Shade on the Auto Case Window

We took this whirlwind tour of the automobile industry to see how an entire industry is responding to the fundamental changes of the information frontier. But we could have focused on any number of industries that are going through the same wrenching changes. If the tradition-bound automobile manufacturers—with more than a century of assets and mind-sets in play—can recast themselves to be successful settlers, then many other industries will follow suit.

Fundamental changes in technology, communications, and non-business sectors keep elbowing their way into the picture, advancing the ever-changing art of the possible. Thanks to ubiquitous connections and information streams and the power of the open-source movement, the business environment is increasingly intertwined with both economic and traditionally noneconomic actors.

Change, change, and more change—and faster. This is inherently neither good nor bad. The accelerating pace of change is a threat that can be transformed into an opportunity (or vice versa). So the question really is: What's your mind-set, as *you* journey forward?

Connecting the Dots

First, we argue, it's important to understand the *context*, the nature of the changes that are under way, and then turn your attention to summarizing an intelligent response. As a street-level guidebook, we asserted in chapter 1 (and demonstrated in subsequent chapters) that companies are better served by adapting themselves for life on the frontier than by trying to predict its future boundaries. We also stated that the project portfolio is, in effect, a company's currency, and an overlooked vehicle for unlocking hidden value while the company adapts for the future.

Settlers are better off leveraging existing assets—tangible and intangible—than starting from scratch. Although organizational legacies often seem to slow the company down, these relationships and assets can also serve as a solid foundation for settling the frontier.

Prepare, rather than predict, and *play the hand you've been dealt*. Both of these principles help prepare the organization for the future and work in concert with the organization's set of intentions (short-term, long-term, and trait objectives). These principles are the complementary parts of a mind-set that—when supported by tangible capabilities—is a prerequisite for success on the information frontier. Without this mind-set, no amount of technology or process redesign will prepare the organization for the promise and the perils of the future.

We have also used the word "mind-set" in connection with our four traits. These traits—Eco-Driven, Outside-In, Fighting Trim, and House in Order—are the mental models that prosperous organizations are beginning to exhibit. We argue that, for some time to come, traits need to emerge as conscious, deliberate intentions of the organization. Traits provide constancy on our changing landscape and focus the organization where it needs to be headed. Traits also provide a guiding principle for the actions of the organization.

Many of these actions reside in the project portfolio. Our approach uses the project portfolio and looks for ways to reshape its component parts—individually and together—to better deliver on the organization's tripartite intentions. Starting with the project portfolio makes sense because it's the path of least resistance; it's where action already is taking place; its projects are already funded; and it already has managerial support and attention. In fact, we argue that the project portfolio is an underrecognized organizational change agent, and is the best indicator of where an organization is actually heading.

With a little tweaking, we apply portfolio and options theory as tools to help managers navigate the unpredictability of the business context. The foundations of this approach aren't novel or new; instead, they are extended from traditional, proven concepts borrowed from the financial realm and applied to a topical and timely area of opportunity: alignment. In our reframing, portfolio and options theory can assess and manage projects as a group. As a result, risk is diversified, efficiency is increased, and the chances of getting where you want to go—that is, fulfilling your intentions—are substantially increased.

By working more closely together—with better alignment—the organization's intentions and its project portfolio can deliver substantial benefits, including increased shareholder value and confidence, greater ROI, and the development of "good habits."

Our set of tools, introduced in chapter 1 and revisited throughout the book, is designed to help you create alignment in an adaptive way. As you have seen, this robust set of tools isn't designed for formulaic application. They are intended to be used artfully to provide insight and an approach, the interpretations of which are necessarily context-specific. Remember, there is no substitute for your good management judgment.

Monitoring: Ensuring Tomorrow's Alignment

The term "alignment" often conjures up an image of a one-time activity. But as the Greek philosopher Heraclitus observed, "It is impossible to step into the same river twice."

In an unpredictable world, the process of maintaining alignment is not a one-shot deal, or even an annual activity tied to the capital budgeting process. Instead, it is a *continuous* activity. As priorities change, as more information becomes available, and as the art of the possible continues to evolve, organizations come under increasing pressure to

REPRESENTATIVE CURRENT ALIGNMENT VIEW

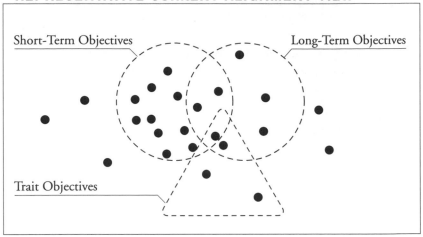

Short-Term Objectives   Long-Term Objectives

Trait Objectives

ASPIRATIONAL ALIGNMENT VIEW

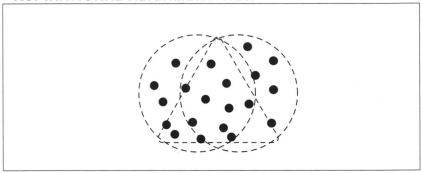

● = Project

continually reallocate the limited resources of the portfolio, recalibrate its objectives, and reevaluate its overall effectiveness. Since what gets measured in organizations is generally what gets done, maintaining alignment requires regular (and eventually, continuous) evaluation of the portfolio. After the initial adjustment of the portfolio—which may or may not be a dramatic intervention—regular monitoring seeks to build momentum for the traits and create greater levels of alignment.

Encouraging and continuously building alignment occurs through two simultaneous routes. The first is simply incorporating elements of our approach into the evaluation of proposed projects or capital expenditures. Before projects are initiated, in other words, the organization's leaders would ask a series of questions, such as:

- How does this project align to the company's intentions?

- Does the scope of this project promote trait development?

- Is the project designed to leverage the tools of Common Threads, Project Chunking, and/or What-if Planning?

This is a relatively easy and painless adjustment to the way the organization currently operates. There are no new processes or investments required—merely the inclusion of several additional evaluation criteria.

The second route is the regular measurement of the portfolio and its alignment to intentions. This creates an ongoing mechanism for monitoring and adapting the portfolio. It starts with the creation of a monitoring process. On a regular basis, the company gathers key managers to look at the project portfolio as a whole and review the organization's investments for conformity. As they employ the tools, managers and leaders are evaluating, at both a portfolio and a project level, how the portfolio can better align to intentions. They are looking for several specific factors:

- Can the resources available to the portfolio be better allocated so the portfolio has the best possible chance of meeting expected implementation goals? The common truth is that projects are often approved and started in a vacuum. By revisiting how resources are allocated and organized within the overall portfolio, companies can recraft the portfolio to operate at peak performance.

SUCCESSFUL MONITORING PROCESS CHECKLIST

1. Accurate lists of projects underway.
2. Right people in the room to make decisions and act.
3. Frequency of evaluation matches market velocity.
4. Looks backward for lessons and forward for action.

- In light of the rapidly changing environment, should basic assumptions be reviewed and altered? Assumptions such as adoption rates, technology adaptability, and people's change capacity can all be causes of persistent alignment gaps. By stepping back and challenging assumptions, these hidden risks can be found and managed.

- Have the intentions of the organization changed? As the What-if Planning tool reminds us, the environment in which the organization operates changes, sometimes dramatically. When this happens, the project portfolio needs to adopt a new strategy for achieving alignment.

At regular intervals, the organization can make midcourse corrections and rebalance the portfolio to improve alignment. Once this monitoring process is in place, the next evolution is to *optimize the value of the process*. By this, we mean several things. A good process will maintain alignment, minimize the lag time between new information and action, and continuously improve the alignment process.

The goal in this step is to improve the *quality* and the *timeliness* of the information received. By looking at the process of collecting information—from whom? how? how often?—and finding opportunities to automate or reduce the cycle time and the expense of data collection, the monitoring process can be more frequent and more effective.

The value of our approach to alignment will increase as the process grows more sophisticated and effective over time. As projects are completed, the organization builds a valuable library of reusable components for Common Threads, as well as a foundation for future projects. In the future, each project not only contributes at a project level, but at an overall portfolio level as well. Furthermore, as more projects are conceived in this context, they are guided to be more trait-centric and better embody the principles of Common Threads, Chunking, and What-if Planning.

Over time, the monitoring process is refined, becoming more streamlined and exception-based. As the portfolio is continually reviewed and as new projects consistent with the principles of alignment are added, the need to review every project in the portfolio wanes. There is less need to stop and perform a full review of the entire portfolio; instead, continuous monitoring keeps projects on track. The adaptation process becomes mutually reinforcing, further building momentum for progress and competitive success on the information frontier.

Revisiting the Elephant in the Hallway

As we conclude this book, we want to venture a look at the future of the information frontier and its implications for management. (No, this isn't crystal ball gazing; it's more in the nature of informed speculation.) When you review the record of previous technology-enabled frontiers, you find that they have been broadly defined in three phases. The first is *exploration*. This is the phase in which new ideas are found, new technologies commercialized, and optimism abounds. It's a phase of infinite promise.

The second phase of a technology-enabled frontier comes when organizations that were not the initial pioneers begin to invest. Economists call this "capital deepening"; we call it the *arrival of the settlers*. It won't surprise you to learn that despite the dot-com implosion and economic downturn, the odds are that your company still spends mightily on technology. Many different factors contribute to capital deepening and these extraordinary levels of spending. Past successes with technology projects, demonstrated productivity increases, new or greatly altered technology-based distribution channels, sustaining the base you already have, new categories of virtual products—and the art of the possible—all push technology spending higher.

The massive investments associated with this second phase significantly contribute to what we call the Elephant in the Hallway phenomenon. This particular elephant, like most others, is *big*, and it is rapidly getting bigger. Industry pioneers such as Vinod Khosla predict that over the next ten years, technology spending will rise to 10 percent of sales (up from 3.5 percent today), and that the technology industry sector will mushroom to 40 percent of GDP (up from 25 percent in the United States today).[24]

Now put those sobering numbers together with another startling fact: Today, approximately 80 percent of all companies spend more than 50 percent of their IT budgets simply to "keep the lights on"—in other words, to keep doing what they're already doing.

The rapid and large investment leads to the third phase, *business performance*, which we believe we are quickly entering. As the investment in technology continues to grow, companies look for two things: (1) greater returns on the technology spending and (2) better leveraging of the investment to benefit the business. With technology spending now accounting for more than 50 percent of capital expenditures, "technology investment performance" translates into "business performance."

Instead of scanning the horizon for the next big thing or automatically upgrading to the latest (and often allegedly the greatest) technology, companies over the next few years are more likely to continue to take their existing technologies and apply them to the business in new ways, creating additional business value by bringing latent value to the table. Figuratively speaking, management's time and attention will be focused on rearranging the factory floor—that is, taking existing assets, people, processes, and technology, and shaping them to conform to the realities and possibilities of the frontier.

We argue that there are compelling reasons to fix what's not quite right today. We also posit that shareholders will increasingly demand that companies be held accountable for delivering tangible results from their investments overall, and from their IT investments in particular. It is crucial, then, to *tame the elephant* and focus on optimizing the business, in large part by better harnessing the power of the business technology investment.

Performance has both tactical and strategic ramifications. Because technology represents such a large percentage of capital spending, the company's investment in technology is a de facto strategy of the organization. Gaining control of the elephant is not only an imperative for improving efficiency today, but for ensuring future value creation.

Some Parting Thoughts

Every day, we see evidence of organizations on the move—toward and across the information frontier. They are mastering the ability to manage in conditions of uncertainty; discovering new value by creating stronger relationships between projects, constituencies, and organizations; and intelligently redefining the art of the possible. Companies are taking control of their portfolios, forging new ways of doing business, and harnessing the power of their technology investments. From individual departments to entire industries, we see traits being embraced and alignment being increased. We take this as good evidence that any and all organizations can make similar progress.

So, this book is a call to action. But it's not a call for revolution or the implementation of dramatic new strategies. Instead, it's a call for a thorough and ongoing reorientation of the project portfolio and the corporate mind-set to bring them into alignment with your organization's specific intentions—in a manner that reflects the realities of frontier living.

We've equipped you to be a more prosperous settler by helping you transform your organization's mind-set from one that "walks to the future backward" to a forward-facing stance. The future, we believe, is a realm of great promise and manageable perils. So if you haven't done so already, we encourage you to embrace and make the most of the information frontier.

Happy trails!

notes

Preface

1. Center for Earthquake Research and Information, The University of Memphis Web site, <http://www.ceri.memphis.edu/public/myths.shtml> (accessed 20 August 2002). See also F. Hadland Davis, *Myths and Legends of Japan* (New York: Dover Publications, 1992), 244.

2. F. Warren McFarlan, "Portfolio Approach to Information Systems," *Harvard Business Review,* September–October 1981.

Chapter 1

1. James Hagberg and Steve McCole, "Energy Expenditure During Cycling," in *High-Tech Cycling,* ed. Edmund R. Burke (Colorado Springs, CO: Edmund R. Burke, 1996).

2. As reported by the New Scientist Online <http://216.239.53.100/search?q=cache:f6MeOnxf9PUC:www.newscientist.com/lastword/answers/827animals.jsp%3Ftp%3Danimals1+geese+flying+in+formation&hl=en&ie=UTF-8> (accessed 4 September 2002). See also recent research conducted by NASA <http://www.dfrc.nasa.gov/PAO/PressReleases/2001/01-61.html> (accessed 4 September 2002).

3. TechRepublic and Ted Smith, *IT Project Management Research Findings* (Louisville, KY: TechRepublic, 13 November 2000).

4. Project Management Institute, Inc., *PMI Project Management Factbook: Second Edition* (Newton Square, PA: Project Management Institute, Inc., 2001).

5. Forrester Research and Bruce D. Temkin, *TechStrategy Report, Tech Recovery Update: Coming Off the Bottom* (Cambridge, MA: Forrester Research, Inc., 19 March 2002); Morgan Stanley, Mary Meeker, and Fabrizio Cascianell, *The Technology IPO Yearbook: 8th edition, 22 Years of Tech Investing* (New York: Morgan Stanley, 18 March 2002).

6. GartnerGroup and S. Mingay, *A Project Checklist,* Gartner Research Note #TU-11-0029 (Stamford, CT: GartnerGroup, 17 May 2000); GartnerGroup, B. Rosser, and K. Potter, *IT Portfolio Management and Survey Results,* Gartner Research Note #SPA-13-5755 (Stamford, CT: GartnerGroup, 13 June 2001); TechRepublic and Smith, *IT Project Management Research Findings.*

7. Forrester Research and Temkin, *TechStrategy Report, Tech Recovery Update.*

8. Morgan Stanley, Meeker, and Cascianell, *The Technology IPO Yearbook.*

9. Quoteworld.org Web site <http://www.quoteworld.org/browse.php?thetext =advers,difficult,trial&page=4> (accessed 19 August 2002).

Chapter 2

1. David G. McCullough, *The Path Between the Seas: The Creation of the Panama Canal, 1870–1914* (New York: Simon & Schuster, 1977).

2. Time.com Web site <http://www.time.com/time/nation/article/0,8599, 320734,00.html> (accessed 26 August 2002).

3. Stephen E. Ambrose, *Undaunted Courage* (New York: Simon & Schuster, 1996), 77.

4. The Gold Rush Web site <http://www.isu.edu/~trinmich/fever.html> (accessed 26 August 2000).

5. Richard S. Tedlow, "Nineteenth Century Retailing and the Rise of the Department Store (A)," Case 9-384-022 (Boston: Harvard Business School, 1983). For an excellent summary of the evolution of the supermarket, see David B. Sicilia, "Supermarket Sweep," *Audacity* 5 (Spring 1997): 11.

6. Nick Baldwin, G. N. Georgano, Brian Laban, and Michael Sedgwick, *The World Guide to Automobile Manufacturers* (New York: Facts on File, 1987).

7. PBS online Web site, "People's Century Timeline," <http://www.pbs.org/ wgbh/peoplescentury/timeline/tindex.html#top> (accessed 28 August 2002). See also Gerald Bloomfield, *The World Automotive Industry* (North Pomfert, VT: David and Charles, Inc. 1978); James J. Flink, *The Automotive Age* (Cambridge, MA: MIT Press, 1988).

8. Donald B. Dodd, *Historical Statistics of the U.S., 1790–1970* (Tuscaloosa, AL: University of Alabama Press, 1976), 619.

9. Martin Brookes and Zaki Wahhaj, "Global Economics Paper No. 49" (New York: Goldman Sachs, 20 July 2000).

10. Thomas P. Hughes, *Networks of Power: Electrification in Western Society* (Baltimore, MD: The Johns Hopkins University Press, 1983), 201–226.

11. For a brief history of gunpowder see: <http://www.grc.nasa.gov/WWW/ K12/TRC/Rockets/history_of_rockets.html> (accessed 15 October 2001).

12. We use the term purportedly because there is some dispute as to whether Faraday actually said the quote. See <http://physicsweb.org/article/world/15/6/2> (accessed 3 September 2001).

13. Frederick Jackson Turner, *The Significance of the Frontier in American History*, edited with an introduction by Harold P. Simonson (New York: Ungar, 1963).

14. U.S. Census Bureau Web site, <http://www.census.gov/mso/www/pres_lib/app/app.ppt> (accessed 2 January 2002).

15. Alan Greenspan, "Technological Change and the Economy" (paper presented at the Annual Convention of the American Bankers Association, Boston, MA, October 1997).

16. The Economist Group, "Solving the Paradox," *The Economist*, 21 September 2000.

17. David Kirkpatrick, "Rabble-Rouser: Nowhere to Hide," *eCompany Now*, January 2001, <http://www.business2.com/articles/mag/0,1640,8984,FF.html> (accessed 26 August 2002).

18. This is a central premise of Coase's theorem. To learn more about Coase, see <http://cepa.newschool.edu/het/profiles/coase.htm> (accessed 12 December 2001).

Chapter 3

1. Adam Brandenburger, Barry Nalebuff, and Ada Brandenburger, *Co-opetition* (New York: Doubleday, 1996). See also Adam Brandenburger's and Barry Nalebuff's Web site <http://mayet.som.yale.edu/coopetition>.

2. Adam Brandenburger, "Business Strategy: Getting Beyond Competition: An Interview with Adam Brandenburger," interview by Walter Kiechel, *Harvard Management Update* (December 1996).

3. Deloitte Research, "Creating Value Networks in the e-Economy: The Impact of Transaction Costs on Markets for Intellectual Capital" (unpublished Deloitte Research, 2000).

4. Anonymous, interview with author, San Francisco, CA, 7 January 2002.

5. Rick Mullin, "Few Follow Dupont in Outsourcing," *Chemical Week*, 7 March 2002.

6. Exult Company Press Release, 6 May 2002. See also Bank Systems and Technology Web site, <http://www.banktech.com/story/techFocus/BNK20010220S0010> (accessed 10 July 2002).

7. Christine Spivey Overby with John C. McCarthy and Emily H. Boynton, "US Outsourcing Decelerates," *Forrester TechStrategy Report*, February 2002. See also Julekha Dash, "Business Process Outsourcing," *Computerworld*, 1 January 2001, <http://www.computerworld.com/managementtopics/management/story/0,10801,55557,00.html> (accessed 28 August 2002).

8. Deloitte Research, *The Relationship Portfolio: Intelligent Partnering in the New Global Economy* (New York: Deloitte Research, 2001).

9. Data Downlink Corporation, *Mergerstat* (Jersey City, NJ: Data Downlink Corporation, October 2000).

10. Catherine Curan, "Sara Lee to Exit Textile-Apparel Manufacturing: Will Divest 13 U.S. Yarn and Knit Operations," *Daily News Record,* 17 September 1997.

11. "Sara Lee Corporation De-verticalizes United States Yarn and Textile Manufacturing: First Transaction in Company's Three-Year Restructuring Program," *PR Newswire,* 5 January 1998; Sara Lee Corporation, *10-K: Annual Report,* 20 September 2000.

12. Deloitte Research, *Collaborative Commerce—Going Private to Get Results: Trends, Opportunities, and Challenges* (New York: Deloitte Research, 2001).

13. Deloitte Research, *Digital Loyalty Networks: e-Differentiated Supply Chain and Customer Management* (New York: Deloitte Research, 2000).

14. Mark Moran, "Company Care: Employers Turn to On-site Clinics," *AmNews,* 2 April 2002.

15. Henry Petroski, "The Boeing 777," *American Scientist,* 1 November 1995; Peter Fingar, Harsha Kumar, and Tarun Sharma, *Enterprise E-Commerce* (Tampa, FL: Meghan-Kiffer Press, 2000).

16. Peter Fingar, "Don't Just Transact—Collaborate," *CIO Magazine,* 1 June 2001.

17. Ibid.

18. Faith Keenan, "Opening the Spigot," *BusinessWeek,* 4 June 2001.

19. Moen Company Press Release, "Moen Incorporated Introduces Supplynet," available online at <http://www.moen.com/Consumer/Press/Article.cfm?ArticleId =127> (accessed 10 July 2002).

20. Keenan, "Opening the Spigot."

21. Peggy L. Tracy, "Supply Chain Case Studies from the PHCP Industry" (report prepared for AMD/IPD joint task force on supply chain management, 9 October 2001).

22. Keenan, "Opening the Spigot." See also Tracy, "Supply Chain Case Studies from the PHCP Industry."

23. Deloitte Research, *Myth vs. Reality in Financial Services: What Your Customers Really Want* (New York: Deloitte Research, 2000).

24. J. W. Marriot Jr., "Our Competitive Strength: Human Capital" (prepared remarks presented at the Detroit Economic Club, Detroit, MI, 2 October 2000).

25. Thomas W. Brailsford, "Building a Knowledge Community at Hallmark Cards," *Technology Management,* September/October 2001. See also Keenan, "Q&A with Hallmark's Tom Brailsford," *BusinessWeek,* 9 July 2001.

26. Brailsford, "Building a Knowledge Community at Hallmark Cards."

27. Jason Black, "Lean On Me: Companies on the Web Are Learning That Paying Attention to Users Who Call the Shots Makes Good Sense for Business," *Internet World,* 15 May 2001.

28. Keenan, "Q&A with Hallmark's Tom Brailsford." See also Brailsford, "Building a Knowledge Community at Hallmark Cards."

29. Susannah Patton, "Staying Power," *CIO Magazine,* 1 December 2001, <http://www.cio.com/archive/120101/power_content.html> (accessed 26 August 2002).

30. Kathleen Melymuka, "E-nergizing the Company," *Computerworld*, 11 October 2001, <http://www.computerworld.com/softwaretopics/software/appdev/story/0, 10801,62911,00.html> (accessed 26 August 2002).

31. Mark Gordon, "Next Day Change Guaranteed," *CIO Magazine*, 15 May 2001.

32. Ibid.

33. Sarah D. Scalat and Lafe Low, "Closing the Gap: Come Together," *CIO Magazine*, 1 January 2001.

34. Anne Stuart, "E-Business Models Clicks & Bricks," *CIO Magazine*, 15 March 2000.

35. See, for example, the work of Richard Nolan and Stephen P. Bradley, *Dot Vertigo* (New York: John Wiley & Sons, 1998). The authors make prescriptions for what they call the "permeable" corporation.

36. Theodore H. Clark and David C. Croson, "H. E. Butt Grocery Company: A Leader in ECR Implementation (A) (Abridged)," Case 9-196-061 (Boston: Harvard Business School, 1997); F. Warren McFarlan, "H. E. Butt Grocery Company: The New Digital Strategy (B)," Case N9-301-125 (Boston: Harvard Business School, 1997).

37. Ibid.

38. Miguel Helft, "Fashion Fast Forward," *Business 2.0*, May 2002; Otto Pohl, "In Spain, A Home Sewn Exception to Globalization," *Christian Science Monitor*, 26 July 2001.

39. The Economist Group, "Over the Counter E-commerce," *The Economist*, 26 May 2001.

40. Ibid.

41. Ibid.

42. Marcus Kabel, "Convenience Stores Make High-Technology Leap," *Toronto Star*, 21 June 1999.

43. Daniel Costello, "Leveraging Store Knowledge" *Food Logistics*, 1 July 2001.

44. The Economist Group, "Over the Counter E-commerce."

45. Michael Fradette and Steve Michaud, *The Power of Corporate Kinetics: Create the Self-Adapting, Self-Renewing, Instant-Action Enterprise* (New York: Simon & Schuster, 1998).

46. William Glanz, "AOL Time Warner Scrutinized," *The Washington Times*, 25 July 2002.

47. Jeffrey Schwartz, "Fidelity Pours Resources Into XML," *Internet Week*, 6 August 2001.

48. Ibid.

49. Lucas Merian, "Fidelity Makes Big XML Conversion Investment," *Computerworld*, 28 September 2001.

50. Lee Copeland, "Corporations Tackle Legacy Data Woes," *Computerworld*, 6 August 2001.

51. Textron Web site <http://www.textron.com/profile/facts.html> (accessed 3 July 2002); John Galvin, "Manufacturing the Future," *Smart Business*, 1 March 2001.

52. Galvin, "Manufacturing the Future."

53. Ibid.

54. Meredith Levinson, "Jackpot!—Harrah's Entertainment," *CIO Magazine*, 1 February, 2001, <http://www.cio.com/archive/120101/power_content.html> (accessed 26 August 2002). See also Christopher T. Heun, "Harrah's Bets on IT to Understand Its Customers," *InformationWeek*, 11 December 2000.

55. Levinson, "Jackpot!—Harrah's Entertainment."

56. Levinson, "Harrah's Knows What You Did Last Night," *Darwin Magazine*, May 2001.

57. David Rocks, "Web Smart for a Changed World," *BusinessWeek*, 29 October 2001.

58. Jennifer Maselli, "Businesses Find CRM Value in Assortment of Apps," *Information Week*, 22 April 2002. See also Maselli, "Customer Focus Is Strong, But CRM Vendors' Sales Slip," *Information Week*, 28 January 2002.

59. Anonymous, CIO of disguised company, interview with author, San Francisco, CA, 11 January 2002.

60. Fred Young and F. Warren McFarlan, "Li & Fung," Case 9-301-009 (Boston: Harvard Business School, 2000). See also Li & Fung's Web site, <http://www.lifung.com> (accessed 5 July 2002).

61. Young and McFarlan, "Li & Fung."

62. Ibid.

63. Ibid.

64. Ibid.

65. Ibid.

66. Joanne Lee-Young and Megan Barnett, "Furiously Fast Fashions," *Industry Standard*, 11 June 2001, <http://www.thestandard.com/article/0,1902,26769,00.html> (accessed 26 August 2002).

67. Young and McFarlan, "Li & Fung." See also Li & Fung's Web site <http://www.lifung.com> (accessed 5 July 2002).

68. Young and McFarlan, "Li & Fung."

69. Ibid.

70. Ibid.

71. Ibid.

72. Ibid.

73. Robert I. Sutton, *Weird Ideas That Work: 11 Practices for Promoting, Managing, and Sustaining Innovation* (New York: The Free Press, 2002).

Chapter 4

1. Harry Markowitz, *Portfolio Selection: Efficient Diversification of Investments* (New Haven, CT: Yale University Press, 1959).

2. John L. Maginn and Donald L. Tuttle, eds., *Managing Investment Portfolios* (Boston: Warren Gorham & Lamont, 1990); <http://www.contingencyanalysis.com>; <http://www.investorwords.com> (accessed 8 January 2002).

3. F. Warren McFarlan, "Portfolio Approach to Information Systems," *Harvard Business Review,* September–October 1981, 142–150.

4. Gartner Group, B. Rosser, and K. Potter, *IT Portfolio Management and Survey Results,* Gartner Research Note #SPA-13-5755 (Stamford, CT: Gartner Group, 13 June 2001).

5. Scott Berinato, "Do the Math—IT Value," *CIO Magazine,* 1 October 2001 <http://www.cio.com/archive/100101/math.html> (accessed 26 August 2002).

6. Anonymous, client project, New York, NY, 2001; company Web site (accessed 13 March 2002).

7. Anonymous, client interview by author, San Francisco, CA, August 2001.

8. Andy Grove, "Grove's Law," (presentation at Riffing with the Masters: A Conference on What Works, San Francisco, CA, November 2000).

9. TechRepublic and Ted Smith, *IT Project Management Research Findings* (Louisville, KY: TechRepublic, 13 November 2000).

10. Amazon.com Web site <http://www.amazon.com/exec/obidsos/search-handle-form/104-1298527-9267105> (accessed 12 June 2002).

11. Paul A. Strassmann, "General Electric's B2B Retreat," *Computerworld,* 2 July 2001.

12. Anonymous, site visit with client by author, Lodi, CA, January 1998.

13. Ibid.

14. Thomas W. Brailsford, "Building a Knowledge Community at Hallmark Cards," *Technology Management,* September/October 2001.

15. Carliss Y. Baldwin and Kim B. Clark, "Managing in an Age of Modularity," *Harvard Business Review,* September–October 1997.

16. Anonymous, Deloitte client case, San Francisco, CA, 2001.

17. Ibid.

18. Ibid.

19. John Lamb, "Moving Inside the Virtual Classroom," *Financial Times,* 21 March 2002.

20. Gary Flood, "Dow Saves $34 Million with Web Studies," *IT Training,* October 2001. This article was found online at <http://www.train-net.co.uk/news/news_story.asp?NewsID=486> (accessed 3 July 2002).

21. Stephanie Overby, "The World's Biggest Classroom," *CIO Magazine,* 1 February 2002. This article was found online at <http://www.cio-asia.com/pcio.nsf/unidlookup/51461ADAA35AD00648256BE500103E89?OpenDocument> (accessed 26 August 2002).

22. Ibid.

23. Overby, "Quick Change Artists: Seven Secrets to Make Change in a Hurry," *CIO Magazine,* 15 August 2001.

24. Mitch Wagner, "Steps Toward Java Reuse: IT Managers Say Relationships Important Between Developers, Units," *InternetWeek,* 18 June 2001.

25. The Standish Group International, Inc., *Chaos: A Recipe for Success* (West Yarmouth, MA: The Standish Group International, Inc., 1999).

26. Anonymous, client has requested anonymity in this context, telephone interview by author, 11 January 2002.

27. Sarah D. Scalet, "Stage Managers," *CIO Magazine,* 15 July 2000 <http://www.cio.com/archive/071500_stage.html> (accessed 26 August 2002).

28. To understand in detail the chunking stages see: Jon Udell, "Carlson Hospitality keeps its eyes on the prize," *FTP Online,* 1 February 1999, <http://www.fawcette.com/archives/listissue.asp?pubID=5&MagIssueId=171#> (accessed 4 September 2002).

29. Scalet, "Stage Managers."

30. Ibid.

31. Information on this award available at <http://www.hospitalitynet.org/news/4010532.html> (accessed 4 September 2002).

32. Scalet, "Stage Managers."

33. Doug McCracken, company memo, New York, NY, April 2001.

34. Marty Chuck, interview by author, Palo Alto, CA, 11 June 2002.

35. David Pringle, "How the U.S. Took the Wireless Lead Away from Europe," *The Wall Street Journal Europe,* 20 February 2002 <http://www.network365.com/news.jsp?id=145> (accessed 26 August 2002).

36. Ibid.

37. Ibid.

Chapter 5

1. D. A. Leonard and Jeffrey Rayport, "Spark Innovation Through Empathic Design," *Harvard Business Review,* November–December 1997, 102–113 and working paper 97-606, Harvard Business School, Boston, 1997.

2. Kathleen Melymuka, "E-nergizing the Company," *Computerworld,* 11 October 2001.

3. Dina ElBoghdady, "Naked Truth Meets Market Research; Perfecting a New Shower Head? Try Watching People Shower," *Washington Post,* 24 February 2002.

4. Ibid.

5. Moen Company Press Release, "Extensive Research by Moen Provides What Consumers Want in a Great Shower Experience," 7 July 2001. This release was found online at <http://www.moen.com/revolution/pressRoom.cfm> (accessed 3 July 2002).

6. Ibid.

Chapter 6

1. Stephanie Overby, "The World's Biggest Classroom," *CIO Magazine*, 1 February 2002.

2. Matt Hicks, "Sign of the Times: Digital Sigs," *eWeek*, 24 July 2001.

3. Ibid.

4. Overby, "Quick Change Artists: Seven Secrets to Make Change in a Hurry," *CIO Magazine*, 15 August 2001, <http://www.cio.com/archive/081501/quick_content.html> (accessed 26 August 2002).

5. Sarah D. Scalet, "Stage Managers," CIO Magazine, 15 July 2000, <http://www.cio.com/archive/071500_stage.html> (accessed 26 August 2002).

6. Scalet, "Stage Managers."

7. Overby, "Quick Change Artists."

8. The Standish Group International, Inc., "Chaos: A Recipe for Success," (West Yarmouth, MA: The Standish Group International, Inc., 1999).

9. Eric Berkman, "A Project Win," *CIO Magazine*, 1 September 2001, <http://www.cio.com/archive/090101/win.html> (accessed 26 August 2002).

10. David Pringle, "How the U.S. Took the Wireless Lead Away from Europe," *The Wall Street Journal Europe*, 20 February 2002.

Chapter 7

1. This section on William Smith is heavily indebted to the book by Simon Winchester, *The Map That Changed the World* (New York: HarperCollins Press, 2001).

2. Marketing Intelligence Service, *"Build a Better Mousetrap" 2001 New Product Innovations of the Year* (Naples, NY: 21 December 2001), <http://www.productscan.com/mouse01.pdf> (accessed 9 September 2002).

3. Deloitte Research, *Automobile Digital Loyalty Networks: Driving Shareholder Value Through Customer Loyalty and Network Efficiency* (New York: Deloitte Research, 2001); J. D. Power-LMC, *J.D. Power and Associates Reports: January Global Light-Vehicle Sales Drop Slightly* (Agoura Hills, CA and Oxford, U.K.: J.D. Power-LMC, 11 February 2002).

4. James J. Flink, *The Automobile Age* (Cambridge, MA: MIT Press, 1998).

5. Deloitte Research, *Automobile Digital Loyalty Networks.*

6. Deloitte Research and Stanford University Research, "General Motors: Integrating Demand and Supply Chains—Building a Digital Loyalty Network," unpublished research (New York, NY and Palo Alto, CA: Deloitte Research and Stanford University Research, 2002); Deloitte Research, *Automobile Digital Loyalty Networks;* The Economist Group, "Incredible Shrinking Plants," *The Economist*, 21 February 2002.

7. Deloitte Research, *Automobile Digital Loyalty Networks.* Original research from R. L. Polk & Co., the automobile industry's oldest source of statistics.

8. John Parker, "Delivering Drivers' Dreams," *Traffic World Magazine,* 8 October 2001, <http://nl3.newsbank.com/nl-search/we/Archives?p_action=doc&p_docid=0EF3C51865282C0F&p_docnum=1&s_username=ellee> (accessed 26 August 2002).

9. Ibid.

10. Alex Taylor, "Finally GM Is Looking Good," *Fortune,* 1 April 2002, <http://www.fortune.com/indexw.jhtml?doc_id=206909&channel=artcol.jhtml> (accessed 26 August 2002).

11. Parker, "Delivering Drivers' Dreams."

12. Ibid.

13. Steve Konicki, "Time Trials," *Information Week,* 3 June 2002; Scott Miller, "BMW Focuses on Top Line to Boost Profit: Car Maker Banks on Success of Its Redesigned 7-Series," *The Asian Wall Street Journal,* 21 March 2002.

14. Deloitte Research, *Automobile Digital Loyalty Networks;* Gregory White, "Onstar Renewal Rate is 56%, GM's Financial Chief Says," *The Wall Street Journal,* 19 March 2002; Don Butler, "On the Road" (paper presented at the CTIA Wireless Conference, Las Vegas, NV, 2002).

15. The Economist Group, "Incredible Shrinking Plants."

16. Deloitte Research and Stanford University Research, "General Motors."

17. Sean P. McAlinden, Brett C. Smith, and Bernard F. Swiecki, "Michigan Automotive Partnership, Research Memorandum No. 1. The Future of Modular Automotive Systems: Where Are the Economic Efficiencies in the Modular Assembly Concept?" (Ann Arbor, MI: University of Michigan Transportation Research Institute, November 1999).

18. Derek Slater, "GM Proves E-Business Matters," *CIO Magazine,* 1 April 2002.

19. Deloitte Research and Stanford University Research, "General Motors: Integrating Demand and Supply Chains—Building a Digital Loyalty Network."

20. McAlinden, Smith, and Swiecki, "Michigan Automotive Partnership, Research Memorandum No. 1."

21. Ibid.

22. Ibid.

23. The Economist Group, "Incredible Shrinking Plants." See also, Alex Taylor III, "Honda Goes its Own Way," *Fortune,* 22 July 2002.

24. Anthony B. Perkins, "The Angler: Seeing the Future in Real Time," *Red Herring,* 1 July 2001.

lexicon

Alignment

Responding to today's uncertain environment, alignment better connects what an organization is *doing*—reflected in its project portfolio—with what it intends to *achieve*—its corporate objectives.

Common Threads

An options-oriented tool designed to find reusable and shareable project components to increase portfolio efficiency and flexibility while reducing portfolio and project risk.

Constituencies

Groups that influence and impact an organization's value network. Constituencies include customers, employees, suppliers, business partners, competitors, regulatory agencies, and investors.

Diagnostic Tools

Analytic tools including Trait Meters, Intentions, Sides, and Right Brain designed to assess the current level of and uncover opportunities for greater alignment.

Eco-Driven

The trait, or mindset, that supports effective collaboration and focuses on converting interenterprise relationships, such as suppliers and customers, into corporate assets.

Fighting Trim

The trait that represents the agility, coordination, and options-orientation required to timely respond to opportunity and external change resulting in a more adaptive organization.

House in Order

The trait that provides the foundation for an efficient, connected, collaborative, intraenterprise operation that enables the other traits and facilitates efficient, cross-enterprise cooperation.

Information Frontier

A metaphor to describe the evolving nature and patterns of today's unpredictable environment. The characteristics of the information frontier include organizational transparency, increased velocity, opportunity for reduced friction, and role blurring.

Intentions

The term used to describe an organization's collective set of objectives—short-term, long-term, and traits. The intentions framework identifies and illustrates the relationship between these three objectives.

Intentions Tool

A diagnostic lens designed to focus the direction and increase the efficiency of the portfolio by assessing the alignment of the portfolio to the organization's intentions (set of short-term, long-term, and trait objectives).

Options Tools

A set of tools—Common Threads, Chunking, and What-if Planning—that support the organization in reducing risk and building flexibility into its portfolio by creating more alternatives and decision points.

Outside-In

The trait that instills the mindset of looking at the organization from the constituency's point of view to uncover opportunities for building stronger relationships and loyalty.

Project

The term *project* represents plans, programs, initiatives, activities, and similar organizational efforts.

Project Chunking

An options-oriented tool that reduces portfolio risk and increases portfolio flexibility by structuring projects in a manner that better ties investment to return, using scope and timeframes as primary levers.

Right Brain

A diagnostic tool that reduces risk by identifying and assessing portfolio level change capacity issues.

Sides

A diagnostic tool that sorts projects into main business activities (sell-side, inside, and buy-side) to focus the direction and increase the efficiency of the portfolio by removing inherent organizational bias and finding synergies.

Tools

Set of seven diagnostic and options-oriented analytic tools, including Trait Meters, Intentions, Sides, Right Brain, Common Threads, Project Chunking, and What-if Planning, designed to improve the alignment of the project portfolio with organizational intentions.

Trait Meters

A diagnostic tool that translates the principles of each trait to help assess, plan, measure, and track trait development.

Traits

Traits represent the mind-sets, or mental models, necessary to prosper in our changing business landscape. The four traits are Eco-Driven, Outside-In, Fighting Trim, and House in Order.

What-if Planning

A forward-looking options tool that decreases portfolio risk and increases portfolio flexibility by considering responses to possible future scenarios.

index

about the authors

Cathleen Benko is the Global e-Business Leader of Deloitte Consulting, the world's largest privately held consultancy. Her primary focus is advising Fortune 500 clients on the convergence of business strategy and technology execution. As a member of Deloitte Consulting's leadership team, she understands first hand the challenges of meeting today's objectives while preparing for the future. Prior to joining Deloitte Consulting, Cathy was vice president of business systems for Shearson Lehman.

A respected and accomplished advisor, Cathy has been recognized as one of the 25 Most Influential Consultants and a Frontline Leader by *Consulting Magazine*. She has also been recognized by the *San Francisco Business Times* as one of the most influential women in the Bay Area and has been the subject of several articles and media productions on business transformation and women in the global business arena.

Cathy earned her M.B.A. from Harvard Business School (HBS) and Bachelor of Science degree with majors in both M.I.S. and operations management from Ramapo College. She lives in northern California with her husband, George, and their two children, Brendan and Elyssa.

F. Warren McFarlan, the Albert E. Gordon Professor of Business Administration for Harvard Business School, has been a pioneer in information systems management since the first course on the subject was offered at HBS in 1962. He is a longtime educator and has held positions as Chairman of Executive Education, Senior Associate Dean of External Relations, and Senior Associate Dean, Division of Research. He is currently the Senior Associate Dean and Director of HBS's Asia-Pacific Initiative.

Professor McFarlan's work has been published extensively in the *Harvard Business Review*. He is the author of several books, including (as co-author) *Creating Business Advantage in the Information Age* and *Corporate Information Strategy Management: Text and Cases*. In addition, he is the editor of *Information Systems Research Challenge* and former senior editor of the *MIS Quarterly*. He is a member of several corporate and nonprofit boards.

Professor McFarlan earned his A.B. from Harvard University and his M.B.A. and D.B.A. from Harvard Business School. He currently lives in Wellesley, Massachusetts with his wife, Karen, and has three grown children.